ADMIRAL HALSEY'S STORY

A Da Capo Press Reprint Series

THE POLITICS AND STRATEGY OF WORLD WAR II

General Editor: Manfred Jonas

Union College

ADMIRAL HALSEY'S STORY

☆ ☆ ☆ ☆ ☆ ☆ ☆ ☆ ☆ ☆ ☆ ☆ ☆ ☆

FLEET ADMIRAL

William F. Halsey, USN

AND

LIEUTENANT COMMANDER

J. Bryan III, USNR

☆ ☆ ☆ ☆ ☆ ☆ ☆ ☆ ☆ ☆ ☆ ☆ ☆ ☆

DA CAPO PRESS • NEW YORK • 1976

Library of Congress Cataloging in Publication Data

Halsey, William Frederick, 1882-1959.
  Admiral Halsey's story.

  (The Politics and strategy of World War II)
  Reprint of the ed. published by Whittlesey House,
New York.
  1. Halsey, William Frederick, 1882-1959.
2. World War, 1939-1945—Personal narratives,
American. 3. World War, 1939-1945—Naval operations,
American. 4. World War, 1939-1945—Pacific Ocean.
I. Bryan, Joseph, 1904-   joint author.
E746.H3A3 1976   940.54'26'0924 [B]
ISBN 0-306-70770-5   76-13462

This Da Capo Press Edition of *Admiral Halsey's Story* is an
unabridged republication of the first edition
published in New York in 1947.

Published by Da Capo Press, Inc.
A Subsidiary of Plenum Publishing Corporation
227 West 17th Street, New York, N. Y. 10011

ADMIRAL HALSEY'S STORY

ADMIRAL HALSEY'S STORY

☆ ☆ ☆ ☆ ☆ ☆ ☆ ☆ ☆ ☆ ☆ ☆ ☆ ☆

FLEET ADMIRAL

William F. Halsey, USN

AND

LIEUTENANT COMMANDER

J. Bryan III, USNR

☆ ☆ ☆ ☆ ☆ ☆ ☆ ☆ ☆ ☆ ☆ ☆ ☆ ☆

Whittlesey House

McGRAW-HILL BOOK COMPANY, INC.

NEW YORK : LONDON

ADMIRAL HALSEY'S STORY

The quality of the materials used in the manufacture
of this book is governed by continued postwar shortages.

PUBLISHED BY WHITTLESEY HOUSE

A DIVISION OF THE MCGRAW-HILL BOOK COMPANY, INC.

PRINTED IN THE UNITED STATES OF AMERICA

To
the officers and men of the
United States Navy and Naval Reserve,
with respect, affection,
and gratitude

Foreword

It would require an extra chapter for me to list all the men who have helped me prepare this book. Certain of them, however, have been outstandingly prodigal of their efforts to make it complete and accurate. They have reminded me of important events I had forgotten and have sharpened my account of events dimly remembered; they have supplied names and dates, dispatches and other documents; they have saved me from countless sins of omission and commission; and if, here and there, I have still fallen into pits of ignorance and tactlessness, it is largely because I overrode their advice. These special benefactors include the following former members of my incomparable staffs: Vice Adm. Robert B. Carney, USN, my Chief of Staff in the South Pacific and the Third Fleet; Capt. H. Raymond Thurber, USN, my Operations officer in the South Pacific; Capt. Ralph E. Wilson, USN, my assistant Operations, then Operations, officer in the South Pacific, and my Operations officer in the Third Fleet; Col. Julian P. Brown, USMC, my Intelligence officer on the *Enterprise* and in the South Pacific; and Comdr. William J. Kitchell, USNR, my flag lieutenant for more than three years during the war.

Other members of my staffs for whose help I am greatly indebted include Capt. Leonard J. Dow, USN, my Communications officer from the outbreak of the war until July, 1945; Capt. H. Douglas Moulton, USNR, my flag secretary from six months before the outbreak until August, 1943, and my Air Operations officer from then until November, 1945; Capt. Harold E. Stassen, USNR, my flag secretary from August, 1943, until the termination of the war, with the exception of the time when he was a delegate to the United Nations Conference at San Francisco; and Lt. Herbert C. Carroll, USN, who served on my staff longer than anyone else, from June, 1940, until November, 1945.

I am also indebted to Lt. Comdr. Frederick L. Gwynn, USNR, for his diligence in research; to Mr. Louis H. Bolander, the librarian of the United States Naval Academy, for furnishing me with many details pertinent to my early days in the Navy; to the Public Relations Section of the Navy Department, for supplying many of the photographs and for scrutinizing the manuscript for security; to the undeservedly anonymous authors of "Combat Narratives" (issued by the Office of Naval Intelligence), for details of our early raids and of the South Pacific campaign; to Ship's Clerk John W. Brintzenhoff, USN; Chief Yeoman James W. Sands, USN; Yeoman First Class Albert C. Cedarstrom, USNR; and Yeoman First Class Joseph Bandrofchek, USNR, for preparing the typescript; to Capt. Gene Tunney, USNR, and Mrs. Tunney, for graciously lending me their house at Hobe Sound, Florida, in which delightful atmosphere most of my preliminary work was done; and to *The Saturday Evening Post*, for kindly permitting me to reprint here such of my story as first appeared in its pages.

And lastly, I have been particularly fortunate in having Lt. Comdr. Joseph Bryan III, USNR, as my collaborator. He is well known as a writer for *The Saturday Evening Post*, *Collier's*, *The Reader's Digest*, and other national magazines, and as the coauthor, with Philip Reed, of *Mission beyond Darkness*, one of the most gripping books to come out of the war. The public knows less of his splendid war record. As an Air Combat Information officer, he first saw action in the New Guinea campaign. Following a tour of duty on the *Massachusetts*, he was at New Georgia and Bougainville. Still later, he took part in the Marianas campaign on the *Lexington* and in the Iwo Jima and Okinawa campaigns on the *Yorktown*. He has been subjected to countless attacks, both bombing and *kamikaze*, and he has flown a number of combat missions over enemy territory, from shore bases and from fleet carriers. His well-rounded naval career coupled with his writing ability have made his assistance invaluable to me.

One final note: I assume full responsibility for all opinions I have expressed in this book and for the accuracy of all statements.

WILLIAM F. HALSEY,
Fleet Admiral, USN

Introduction

Fleet Admiral Halsey was attending a reception in 1946 when a woman broke through the crowd around him, grasped his hand, and cried, "I feel as if I were touching the hand of God!"

On the day that Pearl Harbor was attacked, William Frederick Halsey, Jr., was a vice admiral with the signal number 41, which means that he ranked forty-first among the officers of the United States Navy. He had won the Navy Cross in World War I and also held the Mexican Service Medal and the Victory Medal with Destroyer Clasp. In addition, Greece had given him the Order of the Redeemer, and Chile, the Al Merito, Primera Classe. His vice admiral's stripes and his long years of diversified service had made him well known in the Navy, but although he was listed in "Who's Who," as are all naval officers above captains, few civilians had heard his name.

By the time of the reception, five years later, he had become not only the most famous man in the United States Navy but the most famous living naval man in the world. He had jumped from the obscure pages of the "Navy Register" to the front pages of the world's newspapers, and from there into the pages of history.

He had been promoted two grades, his signal number was 7, and his five decorations had increased to twenty-four. He had been awarded the Navy's Distinguished Service Medal with three Gold Stars, the Army's Distinguished Service Medal, the Presidential Unit Citation with star, the American Defense Service Medal with Fleet Clasp, the Asiatic-Pacific Area Campaign Medal with twelve combat stars, the Philippine Liberation Campaign ribbon with two stars, the American Area Campaign Medal, and the World War II Victory Medal. Great Britain had made him an Honorary Knight Commander of the British Empire, and Guatemala, a Supreme Chief in the Order of the Quetzal. Chile had raised him to the Grand Cross of the Legion of Merit. Colombia had given him the Grand

Cross of Boyaca; Cuba, the Order of Naval Merit; Ecuador, the Abdon Calderón; Panama, the Grand Cross of Balboa; Peru, the Order of Ayacucho; and Venezuela, the Order of the Liberator.

Neither his renown nor its trappings impress him at all. His pleasure in the array of ribbons on his chest is a candid pleasure in something gaudy. He speaks of them as "my neon sign" and pretends to forget what some of them represent; others he dismisses with, "I got that one for having lunch with the Grand Vizier, or whatever he was." He considers them tributes not to himself but to the men he has commanded. Nor is he dazzled by the gold stripes that run from his cuff to his elbow. He says, "It's a blessing they can't promote me again; one more stripe, and I couldn't bend my arm to take a drink."

The public's refusal to accept him at his own value always bewilders and frequently irritates him. When the ecstatic woman at the reception had tottered away, he turned to his flag lieutenant: "Did you hear that idiot? For sixty-three years I've been plain Bill Halsey and now I'm suddenly God! It'll take some getting used to."

So far he has failed even to make the attempt. He stubbornly continues to regard himself as a simple mortal who has been projected into eminence partly by his ability, partly by luck, and mostly by the courage and resource of the United States Navy.

The Navy itself, however, has attributed to him at least one aspect of divinity; as early as his cadet days, forty years ago, his classmates noted that "he looks like a figurehead of Neptune." His head is appropriately heroic; his caps have to be specially made, and although he can wear a $7\frac{3}{4}$, he feels "easier" in a $7\frac{7}{8}$. A committee of illustrators recently announced that his head was "one of the six most startling and exciting in the world"; the others were the heads of Ernest Hemingway, Ernest Bevin, Walter Reuther, Tyrone Power, and J. Edgar Hoover. He has a heavy jaw which seems to pull him forward, so that his blue eyes peer up through his thick eyebrows, but his expression is never as Olympian as the comparison with Neptune implies. He has dignity when the occasion demands it, but he grins more readily than he scowls. Most of the photographs that show him scowling were taken at his desk. They libel his natural disposition; the scowl usually means only that he has forgotten his glasses and is reading without them.

He has been tattooed and he has owned a parrot, but otherwise he resembles the popular conception of a "briny shellback" no more profoundly than he resembles Neptune. He stands close to 6 feet, but far from toting a quarterdeck paunch, he weighs only 165 pounds, 10 less than when he was a cadet. His weight is in his chest; his belly is flat, and his legs are slender. Exercise keeps him trim; he played football at the Naval Academy and rowed on the crew, and he is still an excellent swimmer and a fair golfer. In recent years he played deck tennis daily when he was at sea, weather and combat permitting; ashore he takes long walks. His gait is not rolling, but a stiff march, with no swing to his square shoulders. His companions have observed that he invariably changes his step to match theirs. Walking out of step is lubberly; it makes him uncomfortable.

Mrs. Halsey accuses him of clumsiness. She once told him, "If a man has a nervous wife he wants to get rid of, all he has to do is send for you. Five minutes after you've come in, bumping into sofas and knocking over chairs, she'll be dead of heart failure."

His family and his staff tease him continually—about the raucous neckties he wears with civilian clothes, his helplessness in the grip of bores, the terror he inspires when he takes the controls of a plane, the junk he collects and lugs around with him. Any present, no matter how trivial, he treasures forever. In his right trouser pocket he carries a pouch of kangaroo hide, containing a New Zealand coin given him by the Governor General, and a silver dollar. In his wallet is a four-leaf clover mounted in isinglass, from "Clover Charlie"; a ten-yen note with the inscription, "Recovered from the paymaster's safe of the Jap cruiser *Nachi*, sunk 5 Nov. 1944"; and a dozen membership cards for officers' clubs long since dissolved. His pet keepsake is a tiny strip of white linen on a straw staff, a Hawaiian symbol of good luck; he mislaid it once on his flagship and had flag country turned upside down until it was found.

His rooms are cluttered with Japanese swords and mess knives; souvenir ash trays, such as one made from the case of the first 5-inch shell fired against Marcus Island on October 9, 1944; the flags that he flew from various ships and stations; a Swiss music box and a cloisonné urn that formerly belonged to the Japanese vice admiral commanding the Yokosuka Naval Base; and a large assortment of other trophies. Souvenir hunters level the balance by pilfering his caps, buttons, pins, and even his toilet gear. At Leyte, one of them made off with his class ring, which he had removed before going swimming; his staff presented him with a new one. Besides the ring and his gold identification bracelet, he wore a New Zealand tiki bracelet of greenstone until someone suggested that he was beginning to look like Carmen Miranda; he blushed and never wore it again.

Despite his talismans and luck pieces, he denies that he is superstitious. It is true that his old mistrust of Friday the thirteenth has cooled, but he still knocks wood after an optimistic statement, and he still tries to avoid flying in the same plane with Fleet Admiral Nimitz, whose pilots are notorious for the poor luck that dogs them.

"That's not superstition," he says. "It's common sense. Chester is bad joss in the air."

When his son and daughter were children—both now have children of their own—and Mrs. Halsey caught them leaving towels in the basin or clothes on the floor, she used to remind them, "You never see your father doing that!" His neatness is almost an obsession. No member of his staff ever discovered how he spends the two hours between getting up and breakfast, but they suspect that he is a bathroom dawdler, that he clips and cleans his nails, shaves, bathes, dusts himself with powder, and brushes his hair, then goes through the whole routine again, and possibly a third time. When he eventually appears, he is immaculate enough to preside at an operating table instead of a breakfast table. He is never overdue on a haircut; his shoes are always polished, his buttons bright, his uniform crisp.

There is ample precedent for high-ranking officers to shade the regulations about uniforms—General MacArthur and General Patton, for example—but Admiral Halsey avails himself of the privilege only to the extent of wearing miniature wings below the Navy pin on his garrison cap; pilots have been forbidden to flaunt them there since 1943.

His neatness stops well short of dandyism or stiffness. If formality conflicts with his ease, whether in costume or conduct, formality never takes precedence. His staff always stood up when he came in to breakfast, and he always ordered them, "Sit down, goddamit! How many times do I have to tell you?" He meant it, but they still stood up.

Few flag messes were freer than his. Junior officers were encouraged to speak as frankly as the Chief of Staff. Admiral Halsey provoked the discussions and arbitrated them but withheld his own opinion until the time for decision. The value of these square-table conferences was demonstrated repeatedly. The radical strategy of his spectacular raid on the Marshall Islands in February, 1942, was suggested with the soup and approved by the dessert.

He eats lightly, whatever is set before him. Like most Navy men, he drinks coffee and smokes cigarettes all day long. Occasionally he takes a beer or a Martini, but his staple drink is Scotch whisky and plain water. He has said, "There are exceptions, of course, but as a general rule, I never trust a fighting man who doesn't smoke or drink." His favorite toast is

> I've drunk your health in company;
> I've drunk your health alone;
> I've drunk your health so many times,
> I've damned near ruined my own.

He enjoys parties, especially dances where young people predominate. He has survived most of his contemporaries, and most of the rest are too sedate for his taste when he "hits the beach." Even his flag lieutenants were hard put to keep up his party pace. It is nothing for him to turn in at four o'clock on three mornings in a row and still get up at six. At breakfast after a party, he shakes his head and says, "It seemed like a good idea last night, but—" His son Bill, then an ensign, spent New Year's Eve of 1942 with him at his headquarters in Nouméa. Next morning, when the Admiral turned him out at six as usual, Bill protested, "Most people are going to bed at this time today, Dad, and here we are getting up!"

His talk is not "salty" to the extent of "shiver my timbers" or "avast and belay," but he would never be mistaken for other than a seagoing man. He tells his barber, "Cut off about 6 fathoms of my hair." The rear seat of an automobile is its "stern sheets." His baggage is his "gear." A farewell party is a *"despedida"*—a souvenir word from the Philippines. He says that one of his greatest

xiii

regrets is his ignorance of foreign languages, but he can stumble through a conversation in French or German, and during his tour of Central and South America in the summer of 1946, he delighted his hosts by his fluency in Spanish.

Two mysterious idiosyncrasies bob up in his speech: he accents "opponent" on the first syllable, and when he mentions a date, he says, "That was in nineteen and twenty-six," or, "We've been friends since eighteen and ninety-four." A few names seem to elude him. Empress Augusta Bay, in Bougainville, he calls "Emperor Augustus Bay," and the former Assistant Secretary of the Navy for Air, "Di" Gates, he refers to as "Guy" Gates. "Diary" also gives him trouble. He will say, "It's in my war dairy—damn it, *diary!*" His staff could always tell when he had been chatting with Britishers; he would bring back a broad A which took an hour or so to evaporate.

Before Pearl Harbor, his brother officers knew him professionally as an able commander, not brilliant, but solid, with a conspicuous gift for handling men. Socially they knew him as a good companion who recognized no inferiority in fewer stripes or stars. Their wives held him up as a model of courtesy, an ideal guest, prompt, pleasant, and appreciative. Some of these old friends who have not seen him since Pearl Harbor and have followed his career only through the newspapers have expressed fears about the battle change he seems to have suffered. They gather that he is no longer the mild-spoken Bill Halsey of a few years back, but a fire-breathing swashbuckler, whose every other word is a blasphemy.

Their apprehension is understandable, but it has no base. He is still mild-spoken. His man-to-man conversation is sprinkled with "hell" and "damn," but no more thickly than before; in mixed company, he sometimes looses a "heck"; never, under any circumstances, is he obscene. His heaviest broadside, detonated only by extreme stress, is "Jesus Christ and General Jackson!" He has not changed. He is merely a victim of the press's conviction that the American public requires its military heroes to be picturesque. Until he became Commander of the South Pacific in October, 1942, he had never been interviewed, and when the correspondents made clear their disappointment at his failure to fit their "gruff sea dog" mold—which is standard for senior naval officers—

he obligingly rolled out the appropriate curses. (A member of his staff has said, "The Old Man can put on a good show when he wants to. He's a seagoing Hamlet.") In subsequent interviews, the correspondents noticed that the reek of brimstone was far fainter, but they had already cut the stencil of his public personality, and they never modified it.

Although he may color his phrases to suit circumstances, the opinions that they express are a fixed black or white. A friend of his once warned a toastmaster, "If you don't want to know what Bill Halsey thinks, don't call on him, or he'll certainly tell you." He speaks his mind bluntly, heedless of diplomacy and tact. Secretary Forrestal jocularly dubbed him "the Henry Wallace of the Navy." Unlike many public figures, however, he confines his opinions to his own province. This is not so much because of discretion as because the Navy absorbs him to the neglect of all other interests. He reads, but at random; he has no hobbies, no diversions. A casual acquaintance would think he had no life ashore, and even his staff officers have never heard him mention a personal problem. One of them said, "I don't know whether he shucks them off or buries them deep, but I know he doesn't wear them around his neck."

He has often declared that when he retires, he hopes to live within sight of the sea, but for all his devotion to the Navy, he has no special feeling for any of his many ships, except the *Enterprise* and, to a lesser degree, the *Saratoga*. Such indifference is strange in one so sentimental and emotional. An occasion that might bring a small lump to the throat of another man will move Admiral Halsey to tears. He speaks contemptuously of "my nut mail," yet the rare letters that accused him of callousness toward human life— every top combat officer has received them—made him mope for days afterwards. His staff lost him at Guadalcanal and discovered that he had slipped off to locate the grave of an acquaintance's son and have it photographed. When he had to order a dangerous mission, he would tell his staff—half defiantly, half apologetically— "You can't make omelettes without breaking eggs!" And until the mission was completed, he paced up and down, twiddling a cigarette, taking out his lighter, putting it back, twiddling the cigarette again.

His conception of the Navy is the same as Nelson's: "a band of brothers." Driving near Pensacola one night, he came upon a wrecked motorcycle and a badly injured sailor. A Navy ambulance had already been sent for. Soon after it arrived a Navy doctor drove up. He loaded the sailor into the ambulance and signaled it to start back.

Admiral Halsey asked, "Aren't you going to ride with him?"

"No, sir. I've got my own car."

"Damn your car! Get into that ambulance!"

Sailors know that their welfare is his vital concern, so his "loyalty down," in the Navy phrase, is met more than halfway by their "loyalty up." Before he hauled down his flag for the last time, their respect and affection for him were evident whenever one of his men met a shipmate from a former command. To the Navy's immemorial greeting, "What ship you on now, sailor?", a Halsey man returned not the name of his ship, but a proud, "I'm with Halsey!"

His own loyalty goes up as well as down. Not even in private conversation with intimate friends has he ever been heard to disparage higher authority. His staff often tried to entice him into comment on certain national policies which he was believed to disapprove, but because these policies stemmed from the President, his Commander in Chief, he kept silent. In the early days of the war, General MacArthur's theatricals were a favorite topic among Navy men and Marines in the South Pacific. Criticism by Marines was especially acid, since MacArthur, as Chief of Staff, had attempted to abolish their Corps. But when Admiral Halsey was invited to endorse their opinion, he would say firmly, "You must be mistaken. The General is a good soldier."

Any summary of personality should include qualities of both the mind and the spirit. Admiral Halsey's mind is the Navy mind—well-trained within professional limits. But his spirit is the historic spirit of leadership. Here his courtesy and, by extension, his modesty count for little; they are merely bonuses. His loyalty counts for more. But his paramount quality, the stuff that men follow as an oriflamme, is his courage. He is a fighter, a combat man, blooded and proven. When he commanded the Third Fleet, he did not send men into battle; he led them in. It is morale that wins wars, and what personal leadership does for morale is nowhere better stated than by Sir Thomas Malory, who describes a battle of King Arthur's, and then observes,

"All men of worship said it was merry to be under such a chieftain, that would put his person in adventure as other poor knights did."

Admiral Halsey is such a chieftain.

J. BRYAN III,
Lt. Comdr., USNR

ADMIRAL HALSEY'S
STORY

1

M Y LIFE reached its climax on August 29, 1945. I can fix even the minute, 9:25 A.M., because my log for the forenoon watch that day contains this entry: "Steaming into Tokyo Bay, COMTHIRDFLEET in *Missouri*. Anchored at 0925 in berth F71." For forty-five years my career in the United States Navy had been building toward that moment. Now those years were fulfilled and justified.

Still, I don't want to be remembered as "Bull" Halsey, who was going to ride the White Horse. "Bull" is a tag the newspapers tied to me. I was named for my father, so I started out as "Young Bill"; then I became plain "Bill"; and more recently I suppose it is inevitable for my juniors to think of me, a fleet admiral and five times a grandfather, as "Old Bill." Now that I am sitting down to my autobiography, it is Bill Halsey whom I want to get on paper, not the fake, flamboyant "Bull."

Correction: This will not be an autobiography, but a report. Reports are the only things I know how to write, since half my time in the Navy has gone to preparing them. Although I intend for this once to throw in as many stories as I like, rattle some skeletons, and offer some apologies and second guesses—amusements which official reports discourage—I don't intend to discard the official form completely. This report will be as clear and true as I can make it; it will contain all the pertinent facts I can remember, whether they're to my credit or not; it will avoid fields like philosophy and politics, where I am easily lost; and it will be consecutive, beginning with my ancestors and ending with my retirement from active duty.

When I filter the old Halseys whose records or traditions survive, I find that most of them were seafarers and adventurers, big, violent men, impatient of the law, and prone to strong drink and strong language. The most famous sailorman among us was Capt. John Halsey, whom the Governor of Massachusetts commissioned as a privateer in 1704. Captain John's interpretation of his commission is implicit in the title of a book which describes his exploits, "A History of the Robberies and Murders of the Most Notorious Pirates." I enjoy reading how his little brigantine once took on four ships together and captured two of them, with $250,000 in booty; but the most moving passage tells how he died of a fever on Madagascar in 1716 and how he was buried there. Part of it is worth quoting:

The prayers of the Church of England were read over him, colours were flying, and his sword and pistol laid on his coffin, which was covered with a ship's jack; as many minute guns fired as he was years old, viz: 46, and three English volley and one French volley of small arms. He was brave in his person, courteous to all his prisoners, lived beloved and died regretted by his own people. His grave was made in a garden of water melons, and fenced in with pallisades to prevent his being rooted up by wild hogs, of which there are plenty in those parts.

The seafaring strain in the Halseys now ran underground for a century, then emerged for good. In 1815, Capt. Eliphalet Halsey, sailing out of Sag Harbor, took the first Long Island whaler around the Horn. In the next forty or fifty years, a dozen other Halsey whaling masters sailed in his course. Following them, my father went into the Navy; I followed him, and my son followed me.

My father entered the Naval Academy in 1869, with the class of 1873. He pitched on the baseball team—underhand, in those days—and had the reputation of being nimble with his fists. One of his classmates told me that just before they graduated, he and my father "Frenched out" (went into town without permission) and were spotted by a master-at-arms as they were returning. Both were up to the limit in demerits and knew they would be dismissed if they were reported. So my father took a big chance; he rushed the "jimmylegs" and knocked him out before he could recognize them.

2

Father and Mother were married in 1880. She was Anne Masters Brewster, one of fourteen children of James Drew Brewster, of New York City, and Deborah Grant Smith, of Philadelphia. I was born in my grandfather Brewster's house in Elizabeth, New Jersey, at 134 West Jersey Street, on October 30, 1882, and there I spent my early childhood. (The house is now a tearoom, "Polly's Elizabeth Inn.")

Dad had been ordered to sea shortly after his marriage, and when he finally returned ashore, to duty at the Hydrographic Office in New York, I was two and a half years old. His first sight of me must have given him a shock. To my joy, and to Mother's anguish, he hustled me down to a barber and had my long yellow curls chopped off. He was shrewd enough to preserve them, though, and whenever I misbehaved, he could always bring me to heel with a threat to paste them on again.

My young sister Deborah and I had the usual childhoods of "Navy juniors." We lived in six cities before I reached my teens. In the fall of 1895 I went to Swarthmore Grammar School, near Philadelphia. At the end of my second year there—the first time I had spent two consecutive years at the same school—Dad returned to the Naval Academy, as an instructor in physics and chemistry. I had always intended going into the Navy and I was now approaching fifteen, the lowest age for a naval cadet, so we began looking about for an appointment. We wrote to every politician we knew and to many we didn't know. I had already written even to President McKinley.

EDITOR'S NOTE:
Admiral Halsey's letter was recently discovered in the National Archives at Washington:

SWARTHMORE GRAMMAR SCHOOL
SWARTHMORE, PA.
Jan. 26, '97

Major William McKinley.
Dear Sir:—
I do not suppose you remember the note some of the boys of school sent you. If you do I wish to say that my note is not of the same character. It may not be as nice to you as theirs was; although I hope sincerely it

will be. I want to ask you, if you have not already promised all your appointments to the Naval Academy that you will give me one. My father is a Naval officer, and is at present navigator on the U.S.S. Montgomery. As you know as a general rule Naval officers have not much influence, and the presidents are generally willing to give their appointments to a naval officer's son if he has not promised all of his appointments. I know people do not like to give important positions such as this is away without knowing the person they are giving them to. But then you know that a naval officer would not keep his position long if he were not the right kind of a man. I know plenty of respectable people who would testify to my good character. My father was appointed by Secretary Robinson [Robeson] of the Navy, who had been law partner of my grandfather. I have been with my father on shore and on ship board a great deal, and have always wanted to enter the Navy. My parents encouraged me in this desire and gave me their consent to enter if I could get the appointment. I do not know any congressman, and the appointment from the district where I live which is Elizabeth, N.J. is at present filled. I have lived three years at the Naval Academy where my father was instructor in English. I am at present a border of this school and am in the class that graduates in 1898. I was fourteen last October, the thirtieth. My father is now senior lieutenant about 95 on the list for promotion. It is almost needless to congratulate you on your grand victory which every good American sees is for the best. It has been told you so many times by men it is hardly worth while for us boys to say it.   Yours respectively,

                                                    W. F. Halsey, Jr.

I received no answer, but we were so confident of an eventual appointment that Dad entered me at Professor Wilmer's prep school for the Academy. A year passed, and still the appointment didn't come through. When the second year failed us, I decided that if I couldn't get into the Navy as a cadet, I could as a doctor, and Dad agreed to let me study medicine at the University of Virginia.

I picked Virginia because my closest friend, Karl Osterhaus, was going there. I didn't learn much, but I joined Delta Psi—I still wear its emblem on my watch chain—and I had a wonderful time. My natural disinclination to study was abetted by my growing passion for football. I wasn't good enough to make the varsity, but I was occasionally allowed to play on the scrubs, at left end. In our last practice before the important Georgetown game, a play came toward me, and when it was untangled, the star quarterback had a broken leg. I was in the same fix as many a military man in many a campaign—they didn't know whether to give me a Medal of Honor or a court-martial. The student body would have been happy to hang me, but the coach took me to Washington with the team. Most stories like this end with the despised scrub redeeming himself by the winning touchdown. My story is an exception. I didn't even get into the game.

The following spring, Congress authorized five additional presidential appointments to the Academy, and Mother camped in McKinley's office until he promised her one for me. I had to cram like the devil to pass the entrance examinations, but I managed it and was sworn in on July 7, 1900.

The class of 1904 has several distinctions: we were the last to enter the Academy with less than 100 men, the last to be designated "naval cadets" instead of "midshipmen," and the last that never lived in Bancroft Hall, the present dormitory. On the other hand, we were the first whose senior cadet officer was a five-striper. My first year at the Academy—my plebe, or fourth-class year—the cadet body totaled only 238, or enough for a battalion, which was commanded by a four-striper; but by my first-class year we totaled more than 600, enough for a regiment, and the cadet commander sprouted another stripe. I was not he. I never had more than the two stripes that went with my duties as adjutant of the second battalion.

The Annapolis-West Point system of marks is unique, as far as I know: 4.0 is perfect, and 2.5 is barely passing. If you average 3.4 or better, you are entitled to wear a star behind the anchor on your collar. Although I broke into the top half of the class my final year, my average was usually closer to "bilging" than to a star. In fact, at the end of my first month of theoretical mechanics, I had a 2.28, and Dad strongly advised my dropping football. When I told him I had rather bilge, he was furious. Fortunately for me, a good many other men were rated unsatisfactory in the same subject, so we arranged for the bright members of the class to tutor us for the next examination and to dope out the questions for us.

When the exam was over, I went to Dad's quarters for lunch. He met me at the door and asked if the marks had been posted.

5

"Yes, sir."

"What did you make?"

"I got 3.98, sir."

Dad stared at me for a full minute. "Sir," he finally asked, "have you been drinking?"

My football was confined to the scrubs, the "Hustlers," for the first two years, but just before the opening game of the 1902 season, the regular fullback was badly injured and I was put in. I kept the job that season and the next, my last. Here is as good a place as any to state that those two teams were probably the poorest that the Academy ever produced, but poor as they were, they were no poorer than their fullback.

More than forty years later, General of the Army Eisenhower, whom I had never met before, came up to me in Fleet Admiral King's office in Washington. His first remark was not, "I'm glad to meet you," or, "How are you?" but, "Admiral, they tell me you claim to be the worst fullback that ever went to the Naval Academy."

I wasn't sure what this was leading to, so my answer was a bit truculent. "Yes. That's true. What about it?"

Eisenhower laughed and stuck out his hand. "I want you to meet the worst halfback that ever went to the Military Academy!"

Army beat us 22 to 8 in 1902 and 40 to 5 in 1903, the stiffest beating in our rivalry. As one of the two men who played the entire game, I was thoroughly beaten myself. Each of those aches and bruises came back to me one day in 1943, when I was Commander of the South Pacific, and Maj. Gen. Charles F. Thompson flew over from Fiji for a conference. I told him, "General, the last time I saw you, you were rubbing my nose all over Franklin Field."

"Big Charlie" grinned. "How did I know you were going to become COMSOPAC?"

So much for the bitterness supposed to grow from inter-Academy sports!

EDITOR'S NOTE:

Following is an extract from *The Philadelphia Public Ledger* for November 29, 1903:

6

"Early in the second half little Halsey electrified the Navy contingent by making the longest run of the game. Catching the ball from a kick off on his 4 yard mark he sprinted straight up the field, dodging and eluding half a dozen West Point tackles until he reached the 43 yard line, where he was brought to earth."

Next to studies and football, my strongest recollections from my Academy days are of parades and summer cruises. Parades were our bane, but hardly a moment of our three cruises was less than a delight. This opinion was not held, of course, by the poor wretches who had a tendency toward seasickness. I am lucky. I have never been seasick in my life. (Many of my shipmates on the old *Kansas* were made even queasier, during a North Atlantic gale, by watching me guzzle a large Camembert cheese.) I have been slightly deaf since youth, but if I had to choose between deafness and a delicate stomach, I would keep the status quo.

Our transition from salty-talking landlubbers to real sailormen began on these cruises. Half of each we spent on a steamship, such as the old battleship *Indiana*, and half on a windjammer, usually the *Chesapeake*, a steel square-rigger. I was a royal yardman on my third-class cruise on the *Chesapeake*. Two years later, I had worked up to port captain of the maintop, the second most responsible job in our class. I was doubly pleased with my promotion; Dad had been navigator of the cruiser *Newark* during the Spanish-American War and was now not only head of the Department of Seamanship but captain of the *Chesapeake*, and I wanted to show him that I might become the fine all-around sailorman that he was. The folly of my ambition was impressed on me when the Academy's chief master-at-arms told me at graduation, "I wish you all the luck in the world, Mr. Halsey, but"—he shook his head sadly—"you'll never be as good a naval officer as your father!"

When we were on the *Indiana* our third-class year, several of us decided to get tattooed, as a certificate of sea-dogginess. Some artist among us drew the design—a foul anchor in blue, with its chain forming an "04," and a red "USNA" on the crown—and a coal passer who was in the brig for drunkenness engraved it on our shoulders. It was hard to tell which was filthier, he or his instruments, and Lord knows why we all didn't die of blood poisoning. However, the risk passed, but the tattoo remains, to my frequent embarrassment. Dad had been tattooed four times and had advised me against such foolishness, but as usual I was too headstrong to listen.

The Navy underwent a great expansion during Theodore Roosevelt's presidency. In order to furnish officers for the new ships, the Academy course was slightly shortened, and the class of 1904 was graduated on February 2 instead of in June. Sixty-two survived from the original ninety-three. My final standing was only forty-third, but that didn't matter; what mattered was that I was now Passed Midshipman Halsey.

EDITOR'S NOTE:

Every year the first-classmen at the Naval Academy publish a classbook called *The Lucky Bag*. The 1904 *Lucky Bag* had this to say about Admiral Halsey:

"Willie," "Pudge." *Lucky Bag* Staff. Class Supper Committee (2). Class Crest Committee (4). Christmas Card Committee (4). Hustlers (4). Football team (2,1). Graduation Ball Committee (2). President Athletic Association (2,1). Class German Committee (1).

"It's my opinion there's nothing 'e don't know. All the wickedness in the world is print to him." —DICKENS.

The only man in the class who can compete with General [a classmate, Arthur Gill Caffee] in the number of offices he has held. Started out in life to become a doctor and gained in the process several useful hints. . . . A real old salt. Looks like a figurehead of Neptune. Strong sympathizer with the YMCA movement. Everybody's friend and Brad's [his roomate, Bradford Barnette] devoted better half.

The Lucky Bag neglects to mention that he also was the winner of the Thompson Trophy Cup, awarded annually to the first-classman "who has done most during the year for the promotion of athletics at the Naval Academy."

All this was long ago. Nearly two-thirds of my classmates are dead, and not one of us is left on active duty. But there might be one if a close friend of mine received his justice. I refer, and will refer again, to Husband E. Kimmel.

New graduates of the Naval Academy were usually granted one month's leave. I wasn't. I had requested duty on the battleship

8

Missouri, and when my orders came through, I found that I had only five days before she sailed for Guantánamo, for winter training. It is a curious coincidence that my seagoing career began on one *Missouri*, the "Mizzy," and ended on another, the "Mighty Mo." Although each, at the time, was the most modern battleship in the Navy, the forty years between them brought some interesting changes:

	MIZZY	MIGHTY MO
Main battery	four 12-inch	nine 16-inch
Tonnage	12,500	45,000
Speed	18 knots	32.5 knots
Over-all length	388 feet	887 feet
Beam	72 feet	108 feet
Complement	652	2,640

From Guantánamo we moved up to Pensacola for the fleet's annual target practice. I was watching it from our bridge one morning when I heard a heavy blast and saw a geyser of flame spout 400 feet from the top hatch of our after 12-inch turret. Almost immediately there was a second, sharper blast. Four 90-pound bags of powder had caught fire in the turret, and sparks had spattered down into the handling room, igniting a dozen more bags. Twenty-six enlisted men and five officers were roasted alive. The date of the disaster, April 13, 1904, still looms monstrous in my memory. Indeed, it has cast a shadow over the rest of my life. I dread the thirteenth of every month, and if it falls on Friday, my apprehension almost paralyzes me.

That autumn I was detached from the *Missouri* for temporary duty at the Academy as assistant backfield coach under Paul Dashiell, who had been given the job in the hope that he would pull our teams out of the slough where professional coaches had left them. Although Army beat us 11 to 0 that year, we tied them in 1905, when I was assigned to the same duty; and in 1906 we licked them, for the first time in seven years.

Shortly after the 1905 season, I left the *Missouri* for good, with orders to the *Don Juan de Austria*, a former Spanish gunboat which had been salvaged from the bottom of Manila Bay and was now about to be commissioned. Someone said that she had been designed as a yacht for the Dowager Queen of Spain, when Alfonso XIII was in the offing; certainly our quarters, which occupied the after third of the ship, were as luxurious as a liner's.

We took the *Don Juan* to the Caribbean and began a tour of duty that was stupefying in its monotony. Our job was helping to police Santo Domingo and backing up the customs collectors in a couple of ports. For six solid months we never moved out of Samana Bay. Our only amusement was the comic-opera revolutions, and our only excitement the weekly mail steamer from the States.

No, I had one other excitement. On February 2, 1906, exactly two years after my graduation, I received my first commission in the Navy, that of ensign. A passed midshipman was not a commissioned officer but an appointed officer, and an appointed officer received no retirement benefits for a disability incurred in line of duty. Now I had not only this protection, but a substantial increase in my base pay, and a refulgent gold stripe on my cuff. Lord, how proud I was of that stripe! When I became a five-star fleet admiral, my broad stripe and four single ones cost more than the rest of the uniform. Our three Admirals of the Navy, Farragut, Porter, and Dewey, must have had independent incomes to dress up to the demands of their rank.

In March, 1907, I reported aboard our newest battleship, the *Kansas*, which was being rushed to completion for President Roosevelt's Round-the-World Cruise. Sailormen believe that a ship should have a bottle of the finest vintage champagne broken across her prow when she slides down the ways; there is an old superstition that christening one with water is as unlucky as drinking a toast in water. We knew that Kansas was a dry state, but we were enraged to discover that our ship had been christened with a bottle of Château Kansas River. When the official party visited us to present a silver service, we retaliated by offering them only lemonade.

Roosevelt's big-Navy policy made it hard to find crews for all the new ships. However, we filled our complement eventually, and late in the fall we sailed from Hampton Roads—sixteen battleships and five destroyers, under Rear Adm. Robley D. Evans, Commander in Chief of the Atlantic Fleet.

We spent Christmas in Port of Spain, Trinidad, then ran down to Rio de Janeiro and on to Punta Arenas, Chile; continued through the Straits of Magellan and stood north toward Valparaiso; then on to Callao, Magdalena Bay, and San Diego. Here we paraded, and Ensign Halsey, strutting at the head of his company, saw an urchin point at him and heard a yell, "Hey, pipe the guy with a face like a bulldog!"

Something happened in San Francisco that I would have given a month's pay to see. The *Kansas'* skipper, Capt. Charles E. Vreeland, had gone east on a short leave. The train that brought him back also brought half a dozen passed midshipmen, freshly graduated and coming out to join the fleet. Captain Vreeland was in mufti, so they sized him up as a credulous civilian and proceeded on that basis. They described the hazards of Navy life, the importance of their duties, the high esteem in which Admiral Evans held them. They loaded their conversation with Navy jargon, much of it spurious. And with winks and nudges, they explained the functions of the "mail buoy," the "water-cooled sextant," and other imaginary devices.

Captain Vreeland listened to it all, outwardly grave, inwardly rejoicing. When the train reached San Francisco, he thanked them for their company and expressed the hope that he would have the pleasure soon again. He had it in less than an hour, at the fleet landing. The youngsters couldn't imagine what business would bring a civilian there and were even more surprised when he asked if he could be of service.

They laughed, "Not unless you can take us out to our ships."

"Delighted," the "civilian" said, "My gig here is at your disposal."

It must have been a glum ride for the young devils, particularly for the one who was reporting aboard the *Kansas.* . . .

San Francisco was a strenuous round of parties and parades. So were Honolulu, Auckland, and Sydney. We needed the stretches at sea to rest from the hospitality ashore. Melbourne was as gay as the others, but I remember it chiefly because of an incident when I was officer of the deck. Our liberty boat came alongside, and as the party swarmed aboard, I noticed a package left on the floor boards and called down to the last man, "Lad, bring that package up with you!"

His reply took me full aback—a breezy "Right you are, sir!"

He seemed sober, so when he made the deck, I questioned him and found that he was an Australian whom a bluejacket had persuaded to swap clothes and countries. We took the uniform away and turned him over to the police, but we never caught his accomplice. In fact, the fleet left a large number of stragglers in Melbourne. I have heard that some of them became prominent citizens.

Our course from Melbourne to Manila lay through Lombok Strait and the Straits of Makassar, then through the Celebes Sea into the Sulu Sea. By now the fleet had attained such efficiency that a cherished wish of mine was fulfilled: between the time I relieved the watch one morning and the time I was relieved, four hours later, I kept the *Kansas* in perfect station without once speeding up or slowing down—the only time in my naval career that I have been able to do so.

From Manila we stood up to Yokohama. Despite the entertainments and the tuneless singing of "The Star-Spangled Banner" and the shouts of *Banzai!* (May you live ten thousand years!), I felt that the Japs meant none of their welcome, that they actually disliked us. Nor was I any more convinced of their sincerity when they presented us with medals confirming the "good will" existing between the two governments. I don't know what became of my medal, but a number of cruisemates sent me theirs after Pearl Harbor, with a request that I return them to Japan at my earliest opportunity. When I took Task Force 16 toward Tokyo in April, 1942, I deputized Jimmy Doolittle to complete delivery for me. He did it with a bang.

Of the many parties we attended in both Yokohama and Tokyo, one stands out with special vividness—a party on the battleship *Mikasa*, the flagship of Adm. Count Heihachiro Togo, who had commanded the Japanese fleet at the Battle of Tsushima Straits, where the Russian fleet was almost annihilated. Before war had been declared, Togo had made a treacherous torpedo attack on the Russians in Port Arthur; and before that, in 1894, as captain of the cruiser *Nariwa*, he had sunk without warning the Chinese troopship *Kowshing*, thus precipitating war with China. Yet when this national characteristic of deceit was redisplayed at Pearl Harbor, some Americans were naïve enough to be shocked!

Many dignitaries were present on the *Mikasa*, including our

12

ambassador, Thomas J. O'Brien. When the party reached its climax, our hosts insisted on paying their highest compliment to Mr. O'Brien and Rear Adm. Charles S. Sperry, who had relieved "Fighting Bob" Evans. We were alarmed when the Japs laid hands on them, as both men were tall, thin, and delicate, but all they got was three gentle tosses accompanied by *banzais*. Naturally, we had to return the compliment to Admiral Togo. We were big, and he was a shrimp, so instead of tossing him gently, we gave him three real heaves. If we had known what the future held, we wouldn't have caught him after the third one.

The next time I stepped on board the *Mikasa*, history had made some radical changes: she was no longer afloat, but was reverently preserved in concrete at the Yokosuka Naval Base, near Tokyo; and I, I was the commander of a conquering fleet. Although thirty-seven years had passed, I easily identified the spot where we missed our chance that evening.

Christmas, 1908, found us steaming up the Red Sea, toward liberty in Cairo. All hands had dreamed about it and all had been promised it: half to go from Suez, at the Red Sea end of the canal, and the other half, including me, from Port Said, at the Mediterranean end. The first half came back with such wonderful tales that we squared away to make the transit in record time. Alas, just as we started through, we received word that an earthquake had razed Messina, and that we were to rush there at best possible speed. Cairo is still on my rubberneck list.

We could do little for Messina beyond leaving it the *Connecticut*, with all the fleet's medical personnel. The rest of our ships scattered to various French and North African ports and reassembled at Gibraltar, where we found a number of British warships and a few Russians, some of which were survivors of Tsushima. Each British ship took an American and a Russian under her wing. Our sponsor, the cruiser *Devonshire*, we shared with the battleship *Sevastopol*. At the *Devonshire's* opening dinner, the chief engineer of the *Sevastopol* was seated between our chief, Lt. Edward C. Kalbfus, and his assistant, a Lieutenant Vincent. "Dutch" Kalbfus fancied himself a linguist, and wishing to bring the silent Vincent into the conversation, pointed toward him and explained to the Russian, "*Mon premier assistant.*"

Vincent bowed and made his only remark of the meal, "*Oui, Monsieur.* What's more, *je suis le plus bel premier assistant dans le whole goddam United States Navy!*"

Gibraltar to Hampton Roads was the last leg of the cruise. We ploughed through a North Atlantic gale and arrived home on Washington's Birthday, 1909, to pass in review before President Roosevelt on the *Mayflower.* I have another reason for remembering this review: the *Kansas'* newest sister ship, the *New Hampshire,* took part, painted gray instead of the usual white. I recall how startled I was by her low visibility and how I speculated on its advantages in a battleship duel. I should have saved my wits. Now that radar has been invented, it makes little difference if a ship is painted like a circus poster.

The Round-the-World Cruise, in my opinion—the opinion of a young and inexperienced officer—was a success by every standard. Navally, it brought the fleet to the peak of perfection. Nationally, it increased the prestige of the United States in every country where we showed our flag. And diplomatically, it is not inconceivable that our appearance in Japanese waters at this time prevented a war, or at least postponed it. Japan was fuming over our intervention between her and Russia and was looking for an excuse for trouble. The cruise was one of President Roosevelt's "big sticks." He brandished it in Yokohama and Tokyo, and the Japs piped down.

☆
☆ 2 ☆
☆ ☆

THE FLEET split up after the Round-the-World Cruise, and I was ordered to Washington to be examined for promotion. The subjects included marine and electrical engineering, international law, ordnance and gunnery, navigation and seamanship, communications, Navy regulations, and courts and boards. I was not much of a scholar, and the cruise had given me little chance to study. My knees still shake when I think of the ordeal of those exams—six days of questions and answers, eight hours a day! Seven of us ensigns took them, and I was one of four who passed. Normally we would have spent the next two years or more as lieutenants junior grade. Actually we spent about two minutes. There were vacancies in the grade of senior lieutenant, so we were sworn in as j.g.'s, then promoted immediately afterward.

My new orders sent me to the Charleston Navy Yard, to take command of a torpedo boat, one of a motley assemblage of old buckets that had been laid up for years. Still, no subsequent command is ever as important or as thrilling as your first, and I was a proud man when we hoisted the colors and the commissioning pennant on the *Dupont*. Right there I began a career in torpedo boats and destroyers that lasted for twenty-three years. From this date until June, 1932, except for one year as executive officer of the *Wyoming*, I spent all my sea duty in destroyers.

That fall, after maneuvers with the fleet off Provincetown, we steamed down to Jacksonville, where I was detached and granted a month's leave. I was going to get married. Three years before, the *Don Juan* had stopped at the Norfolk Navy Yard for some of the

15

repairs she was continually requiring, and I was drilling a squad on her well deck one afternoon when something hit my cap and knocked it off. It was a muff, obviously thrown by a pretty girl standing near by with the wife of our exec.

I learned later that the girl had asked, "Who's that young officer over there—the one who takes himself so seriously?"

The exec's wife told her. Then came the muff.

I dismissed the men, who were laughing, and recovered the muff. The girl tried to get it back, but I refused until she told me her name. She was Frances Cooke Grandy, from Norfolk, a first cousin of Wiley Grandy, Charlie Hunter, and Armistead Dobie, all of whom had been close friends of mine at the University of Virginia. Despite the boys' sponsorship, the elder members of Fan's family were something less than enthusiastic toward the aspirations of a Yankee Navy officer. One of Fan's uncles had been chief engineer of the *Merrimac* in her historic battle with the *Monitor*, which had taken place almost within sight of the Grandy house, and I found myself branded with partial responsibility not only for the *Merrimac's* defeat, but for Gettysburg, the burning of Richmond, and the surrender at Appomattox as well. However, I persevered. Whenever I was given leave, I spent as much of it with Fan as her family would allow; I bombarded her with souvenirs and ardent letters from every port on the World Cruise; and when we returned, my double jump in promotion and pay gave me courage to propose. She accepted me, and our wedding was set for December 1, 1909.

While I was packing my gear at Jacksonville, Lt. Harold R. Stark came in and inquired precisely how and when I was going to the railroad station. His abnormal solicitude should have aroused my suspicions, but it didn't. Flooded with rapture and benevolence as I was, I assumed that something of my mood had infused my friends too. I foolishly gave "Betty" the information, and he saw to it that I was escorted the whole way by a brass band blaring "The Wedding March."

Fan and I were married in old Christ Church, at Norfolk. My best man was Dave Bagley, and my ushers were Tommy Hart, Husband Kimmel, and Karl Ohnesorg, all of the Navy. A few days before, my scabbard had tripped on the step of a Jacob's ladder and upended, and my sword had been given the deep six,

16

so Fan had to cut the cake with a borrowed sword. Ever afterward, when I was required to board or leave a ship, I passed the upper sling of the belt between the grip and the guard, so that the sword could not fall out.

In April, 1910, after three months as exec of the destroyer *Lamson*, I was ordered to the *Franklin*, the receiving ship at the Norfolk Navy Yard, for duty in charge of the training camp. Now I became the prey of a specter that haunts most naval officers at least once in their careers; I contemplated retiring to civilian life. Fan had told me some news that cast a dazzling light over the prospect of years, not hours, with my family; of swift advancement in a business of my own choice; of an office that would be dry and steady; and of a permanent home. (Everyone has noticed how many old sailormen christen their houses "Dunroamin," "Snug Harbor," and the like.) I was interested in marine engineering and in personnel work, and believing that I could handle a job in either field or possibly both, I applied to a friend who had considerable weight in two large engineering firms. His advice was, "Stick to the Navy!" I stuck, but on many a sleepless night during the Guadalcanal campaign, nights when men were dying because my orders kept them there, I wondered whether the advice had been sound or whether I had been a fool to follow it. . . .

My quarters in Norfolk were a comfortable house on the Berkley side of the river, and here our daughter was born, on the tenth day of the tenth month of 1910; she didn't make her appearance at 10 o'clock, however, but around dawn. The band had the word by 8, when morning muster was held; they started the parade with "I Love My Wife, But Oh, You Kid!" We named her "Margaret" for two of her mother's relations, and "Bradford" for Brad Barnette, my roommate at the Academy.

My shore duty ended in August, 1912, when I was ordered to command the destroyer *Flusser*. I had hardly settled myself aboard when, to my chagrin, the division was placed in reserve at Charleston, owing to the shortage of personnel. We stayed there all winter, but early the next summer I received permission to bring two ships to Newport to exercise with the fleet, which was simulating war conditions by attacking various Army posts. The young destroyer skippers played for keeps. One of them secured to the Army dock

17

at Fishers Island, led a landing force ashore, and arrested the commander of the Army garrison.

Presently I was directed to take the *Flusser* to Campobello Island, Canada, and report to the Assistant Secretary of the Navy, Franklin D. Roosevelt, who wished to survey the naval installations in Frenchman Bay, Maine. Now began a friendship that endured until Mr. Roosevelt's death. Unlike most Assistant Secretaries of the Navy (and Secretaries, for that matter), he was almost a professional sailorman. I did not know this then. All I had been told was that he had had some experience in small boats, so when he asked me to transit the strait between Campobello and the mainland, and offered to pilot us himself, I gave him the conn (steering control) but stood close by. The fact that a white-flanneled yachtsman can sail a catboat out to a buoy and back is no guarantee that he can handle a high-speed destroyer in narrow waters. A destroyer's bow may point directly down the channel, yet she is not necessarily on a safe course. She pivots around a point near her bridge structure, which means that two-thirds of her length is aft of the pivot, and that her stern will swing in twice the arc of her bow. As Mr. Roosevelt made his first turn, I saw him look aft and check the swing of our stern. My worries were over; he knew his business.

Ships of mine had the privilege of flying his flag twice again. Soon after the armistice in 1918, while I was commanding the destroyer *Yarnall*, I was ordered to take him from Dover across to Ostend. The coast of Belgium had been heavily mined, and although channels had been swept, they were poorly buoyed. A strong tide was running in our channel, and such a thick fog set in that we had to reduce speed. When we nearly passed on the wrong side of a buoy, I said, "The hell with it!", dropped my anchor, and sent Mr. Roosevelt the rest of the way in our motor launch. I might have risked him and the *Yarnall* separately, but not together.

The last time I had him on board was in San Francisco harbor, during the Democratic convention of 1920. A few days later I met him on Powell Street. "Bill," he said, "I've just had a fight."

He was a powerful man then, so it was natural for me to ask, "What hospital is he in, Mr. Secretary?"

He was referring to his scuffle for the Tammany banner, when

18

its delegation refused to join the demonstration for President Wilson. It was at this convention, of course, that Mr. Roosevelt was nominated for Vice President.

In August, 1913, I took command of the *Jarvis*, a brand-new oil-burning destroyer. Those who have never served on a coal burner can't realize the bliss of an oil burner; with the exception of my one year on the *Wyoming*, I never again had to go through the nuisance and filth of coaling. We had target practice off the Virginia Capes during the fall, and in January we sailed for Guantánamo and the regular winter maneuvers—war games, ship's drills, and target practice with guns, torpedoes, and small arms.

The Commander of the Atlantic Destroyer Flotilla was Capt. William S. Sims who, as a young lieutenant, had made such a cogent case against the fleet's poor gunnery that President Theodore Roosevelt appointed him inspector of target practice. Sims did an excellent job, and Roosevelt shoved him along, to the extent that he was only a commander when he was made skipper of the battleship *Minnesota*—the first and only time a commander has been permanent captain of a battleship in the Battle Fleet. This did not increase his popularity with his seniors, although his juniors loved him. I doubt if he was aware of either opinion; he cared no more for popularity than he cared for convention. He seemed to exult in affronting authority. When he was our naval attaché in Paris during the Spanish-American War, he sent back an expense account on which some bureaucrat disallowed a number of petty items, such as cab fares, on the ground that they were not accompanied by signed receipts. Sims replied that he could obtain an abundance of signatures in exchange for a loaf of bread, and if his country had reached a stage where evidence of that sort was preferred to the word of a naval officer, he would resign his commission.

In 1910, he made a speech at London in which he stated, "Speaking for myself, I believe that if the time ever comes when the British Empire is menaced by an external enemy, you may count upon every man, every drop of blood, every ship, and every dollar of your kindred across the seas."

The severe reprimand that President Taft sent him for his tactlessness, Sims framed and hung in his cabin. And when Secretary Daniels offered him a Distinguished Service Medal for his work

19

in World War I, he refused to accept it; he said that it had been cheapened by indiscriminate award.

I remember him as tall and vigorous, a crisp, decisive talker, and a great believer in conferences. In Guantánamo, he liked to hold them at the officers' club, and frequently attended in tennis clothes. If he became bored or if the discussion got out of hand, he would break it up by heaving a tennis ball at the speaker.

From Guantánamo we proceeded to Pensacola. Conditions in Mexico had an ugly look, so we arranged that when the ships in the harbor blew a certain number of blasts, all personnel ashore would return aboard at once. The whistles blew on the morning of April 9—the Tampico incident had occurred—and the entire flotilla put to sea at best possible speed. On the way down we were told to prepare landing forces. This was an unusual assignment for destroyers; we didn't have the khaki uniforms which a landing force requires, and all we could do was approximate the color, by boiling our whites in coffee. My whole ship smelled like a Greasy Spoon.

American refugees poured out from Tampico in two American yachts, one flying the German naval flag and the other the British ensign, since both these countries were neutral. It was humiliating for us to lie outside a foreign port and see our nationals protected by other flags, but we had strict orders not to provoke further incidents. The refugees were put on board the *Dixie*, which departed for Galveston, and right there trouble began. It began for the refugees, because there was no extradition treaty between Mexico and the United States; when they arrived in Galveston, a platoon of sheriffs was waiting on the dock. It began for the *Dixie*, because the refugees refused to leave her, and she couldn't return to Tampico with them aboard. And it began for us because the *Dixie* was our only tender; we ran out of fresh provisions and ice and could get no more until she returned. Ever since that week of canned salmon three times a day, I have never been able to look the stuff in the face.

Eventually the *Jarvis* was ordered to Veracruz. Bad luck had made me acquainted with a number of boisterous Marine officers on duty there, but plain stupidity was responsible for my accepting their invitation to join them on a horseback ride. I knew nothing about horses, and you may be sure my hosts took no pains to pick me a quiet one. I had hardly gotten aboard when he wheeled, hurdled a pile of trash, and started making 40 knots down the highway. There I was in the stern sheets with no steering or engine control, and if someone hadn't had mercy on me and overhauled us, he might be running yet.

I was still raw from this experience when a worse one befell me. The destroyers were taking turns at the mail run to Galveston. The afternoon before the *Jarvis'* turn, a fireman reported aboard. He must have thought we were a tourist liner, because he jumped ship two hours later, returned that night roaring drunk, and when the master-at-arms went to put him under arrest, plunged over the side. Those are shark waters. We combed them with searchlights and small boats, only to discover that he had climbed aboard and hidden himself under the after torpedo tubes. He was hauled out and locked up, and next morning at mast I gave him a summary court-martial and made him a prisoner at large awaiting trial.

By then we were under way for Galveston. We touched there, picked up our mail, and had barely headed back to Veracruz when the master-at-arms reported that our fireman had jumped ship again, and again had returned drunk and obstreperous. I had him brought before me and told him, "If you want to be treated like a man, act like a man. If you want to be treated like a mad dog, act like one, and by God, I'll chain you up!"

The man said meekly, "Aye, aye, sir. I'll behave myself."

Within an hour he was raising hell again. He was still crazy drunk, so—as much for his own protection as for his shipmates'— I gave orders for his arms and legs to be chained around a stanchion in the storeroom. Unluckily, his hands were left enough play to reach a file on a shelf near by; he cut his fetters, and hell broke loose for the third time. I had a bellyful of this brawler by now. I ordered him spread-eagled for the rest of the night, his hands chained to one stanchion and his feet to another.

When we released him after breakfast, sober at last, I learned for the first time that the only two stanchions that permitted spread-eagling had a low hatch-coaming between them. I was sorry our drunk had spent such an uncomfortable eight hours, but God knows I wasn't sorry when we reached Veracruz, and I was

21

able to transfer him to a battleship's brig, since we had none. This sort of conduct bordered on mutiny, so I preferred charges and requested a trial by general court-martial. (The commanding officer of a ship could not order a general court; the only person then so empowered was the Secretary of the Navy.) My recommendation was approved, and the man was tried and convicted.

I hoped that this would end the incident, but some weeks later I received an official letter from the Navy Department enclosing a letter from the man's parents, who accused me of cruel and inhuman treatment in chaining their son, and additional inhumanity in endangering him by blundering around the congested waters of the Gulf of Mexico with no lights showing, and at a speed perfectly impossible to attain with my ship! Not only that, but with the letter came a personal note from a friend at court, warning me to reply with the utmost care, as Secretary Daniels had hinted that he was going to make an example of me!

At that moment my naval career was in its most serious jeopardy. Conscience and common sense told me that the steps I had taken were proper, but I doubted my ability to convey this to the Secretary. I sweated over a dozen drafts of my reply, then had it checked and edited by friends. The final version called attention to the inaccuracies in the parents' letter and pointed out that I had fully explained and acknowledged the restraining measures in my sample charges and specifications—in short, that the Secretary had been in possession of all the facts when he ordered the court.

I sent my letter and held my breath. Mr. Daniels never answered.

The destroyers proceeded north to Norfolk at the end of spring, and I was reunited with my family. At Haiti I had acquired a small, bold, vicious parrot who developed such an inordinate appetite for alcohol, and became so vulgar and irresponsible under its effects, that I was reluctant to take him home. However, my chief engineer enjoyed the company of this depraved bird and induced me to swap him for one of his own, a handsome Brazilian named Pedro. My wife's welcome to Pedro was cool, but young Margaret adored him. He had only two tricks: he would wail like a spanked child—suggesting to the neighbors that we were brutalizing Margaret—or he would laugh like a madman. Between tricks, he applied his criminal wits to escaping from his cage and perpetrating new deviltries.

I noticed he was unusually quiet one day, and when I investigated, I found him happily scissoring the crown from my only civilian hat. It is hard for me to find a hat to fit my large head; I am ashamed to say that I slapped Pedro across the floor. He had no use for me from then on and tried to nip me whenever I approached. He also hated our Negro maid. I have seen him back her into a corner and nip at her feet until she screamed.

That year, 1914, was the year that Secretary Daniels issued his famous Order 99, directing that all alcoholic beverages be removed from Navy ships before July 1. On the night of June 30, the *Jarvis* gave a party on her fo'c'sle to mourn the demise of the drinking Navy. It was a melancholy occasion for the officers, but the enlisted men took it in their stride. Although they had never been allowed to have liquor aboard, many of them habitually smuggled it in, and when it ran out, drank even alcohol from the torpedoes. The authorities had tried to make "torpedo juice" unpalatable by adding croton oil and other adulterants, but the thirstier bluejackets simply bought a loaf of stale bread, sliced off its heels, poured in their "torp," and squeezed out pure alcohol.

I have never been convinced of the wisdom of Order 99. True, it stopped midday drinking and thereby ensured a full afternoon's work; but to a man who has just had a tense, hazardous flight or a cold, wet watch, there is no substitute for a tot of spirits, as the Royal Navy well knows. Soon after Pearl Harbor, I took the law into my own hands. As Commander Aircraft Battle Force, I directed my representative ashore, Rear Adm. Aubrey W. Fitch, to requisition 100 gallons of bourbon for our flight surgeons to issue to our pilots. This eventually became standard practice. I don't remember if it was ever officially approved, but I do remember that "Jake" Fitch accused me of inaugurating highly unorthodox procedure and leaving him to hold the bag.

However, we had little time for griping about Order 99. World War I broke out in August, and the *Jarvis* was assigned to patrol off New York Harbor. Part of our job was to keep an eye on the *Winchester*, a yacht so fast that one of the belligerents was expected to buy her and try to take her abroad, in violation of our neutrality

23

as it was then interpreted. A British patrol—a cruiser or a battle-ship—also watched the *Winchester*. Early in the fall, our destroyers began a series of maneuvers which were to end off Sandy Hook Lightship. The weather shut in, and the *Jarvis* was unable to get a single celestial fix during the whole of a 600-mile run on various courses at various speeds. One morning, with only the vaguest idea of our position, we popped out of the thick weather, and there, dead ahead, was a strange warship. It proved to be the Britisher, but both vessels had a miserable few minutes, each expecting the other trigger-happy crew to open fire.

We popped back into the weather and into fresh danger. I didn't see it; I didn't even know what it was; I simply knew it was there—a hunch too strong to be ignored. I ordered, "Full speed astern!" and when our way was off, I hailed a fisherman close aboard and asked for my position.

He yelled back, "If you keep going for half a mile, you'll be right in the middle of the Fire Island Life Saving Station!"

What caused me to back my engines was probably a feeling of drag from the shoaling water, or the sudden appearance of large swells off the stern. I don't know; but something told me I had to act and act fast.

In 1915 I was assigned duty at the Naval Academy, in the Discipline Department. Excepting the plebes and a few upper-classmen, the midshipmen were on leave when I reported. The night they returned, I had another hunch—I knew that the first man I would have to put on report would be the son of a friend of mine. Sure enough, my routine inspection after supper took me into a room filled with contraband tobacco smoke. I asked, "Who's in charge of this room?"

A fine-looking lad said, "I am, sir."

"Your name?"

· "Midshipman Macklin, sir."

"Are you a son of General Macklin?"

"Yes, sir."

I cried, "My God, I knew it!"

I immediately started a one-man campaign to have the smoking regulation changed. A regulation that can't be enforced is a poor regulation, and my own experience as a cadet had convinced me that this was one of them. The Commandant of Midshipmen warned me that the medical officers would fight, and they did. But the regulation was eventually changed, and I hope that my efforts contributed.

By now I had eleven years' experience in handling enlisted men, and I saw no reason why midshipmen should not be handled the same way. I would punish trivial offenders with no more than a bawling out—a jacking up—but major offenders would have the book thrown at them. My theory was solid, but it ignored one factor which I should have kept in mind: midshipmen regard discipline as a game, with the duty officer their opponent and an unpunished infraction their goal.

For instance, there was a genius in the class of 1916 who rigged a smoke consumer in his shower. The smoke simply vanished; I have no idea how. Another genius in a later class established supernatural control over all the bells, buzzers, lights, and even elevators in Bancroft Hall, and operated them at his whim. My Chief of Staff in the South Pacific and in the Third Fleet, Rear Adm. Robert B. Carney, was a member of 1916. There is a persistent fable that I caught him in enough infractions to make his first-class year miserable, but this is utterly untrue. "Mick" Carney himself admits that he was far too smart for me ever to catch him. (I have heard, however, that his last night at the Academy was spent on the *Reina Mercedes*, the prison ship.)

The midshipmen had a special adjective for these devil-may-care lads who lived outside the regulations; they were "touge." Nonregulation clothing, such as trousers with side pockets, was considered the acme of tougeness; so was Frenching into town. As a plebe, I had been strongly impressed by a certain first-classman who not only was the cadet four-striper but stood at the top of his class scholastically; none the less, he Frenched regularly after supper and was never apprehended. He was a real touge cadet then; today he is a fleet admiral—Ernest J. King.

In the summer of 1916, Congress passed a bill to enlarge the Navy, and I became eligible for the rank of lieutenant commander. I wanted the promotion for many reasons, but chiefly because it carried a raise of about $100 a month, and I now had a son, William Frederick Halsey III, born September 8, 1915. First I had to hurdle another set of examinations. I boned for them night and day and managed to pass, but they left me exhausted.

The next year was a stale repetition of the one before. I was becoming bored with nursing midshipmen. Part of my sourness came from the fact that we weren't in the war. Back in May, 1915, I was reading the bulletin that announced the torpedoing of the *Lusitania*, and a workman beside me declared, "By God, if we don't fight now, we ought to take a licking!" It is probably just as well that we didn't fight then; our national sympathies were too diffuse. By the winter of 1916–1917, however, they had crystallized in favor of the Allies, and when it became clear that our participation was inevitable, we unfortunate officers ashore began itching to join our brothers at sea.

The declaration of war, in April, made my hopes soar. Every time the phone rang, I expected to be told to pack my gear. It was all laid out, but the days passed, and the weeks, and the months. I was relieved of my disciplinary duties and was made director of athletics. I was also assigned to drill a class of Reserve officers. They were the highest type of young Americans, all graduates of our leading colleges, and it was a privilege to work with them, but September came, and October, and I was still ashore. Then, in November, a friend of mine discovered that Admiral Sims, commanding our naval forces in Europe, had sent the Department a list of officers he desired, and my name was on this list! Thus armed, I approached the Commandant of Midshipmen, who told me that if the Superintendent agreed, and if proper relief were secured, I could go.

On December 26, 1917, I was detached from the Naval Academy with orders to proceed to Queenstown, Ireland, for duty with destroyers.

3

MY SHIP wasn't shoving off until January 7, so I had a few days in New York with Fan. I was waiting for her outside a big store one morning when an imperious woman ordered me, "Call my car!"

Within the next few minutes, eight more persons accosted me and asked directions to various departments of the store. It made me mad for citizens of a country at war to know so little about their Navy that they could mistake an officer for a doorman. I told each of them, "Go to the top floor, walk to the opposite side of the store, then turn right and go as far as you can. There's your department."

I arrived in Queenstown on January 18, 1918, and reported to Capt. Joel R. P. Pringle, who had his pennant on the destroyer *Melville*, with additional duty as American Chief of Staff to Adm. Sir Louis Bayly, of the Royal Navy. Captain Pringle assigned me to the destroyer *Duncan* for a month as a "makee-learn" under Comdr. Roger Williams. Our principal duty was with convoys; we would pick up an outgoer off some Irish, English, or French port, escort it 500 miles westward, and exchange it for an incomer. Occasionally we did rescue work or had a submarine hunt. Our routine was five days at sea and three days in Queenstown, with five days for cleaning boilers after every fifth trip. The "break" ashore was always gay, thanks largely to the hospitality of the Royal Cork Yacht Club. We dubbed it the "Royal Uncork Yacht Club" and devised a special decoration, the F.I.R., for officers who had difficulty returning to their ships after an evening there. "F.I.R." stood for "Fell in River."

On February 7, I was promoted to the temporary rank of commander, and on the nineteenth, Captain Pringle gave me a destroyer of my own, the *Benham*.

She was an excellent ship, with a fine crew which included one of the most famous chief boatswain's mates in the Navy—a superb sailorman but a periodic rummy, with the added disadvantage that you could never tell from his appearance whether he was drunk or sober. They were getting under way at Newport News once, with this chief supervising hoisting the anchor and reporting to the bridge , "Anchor at short stay, sir . . . anchor up and down . . . anchor's aweigh . . . anchor's in sight, sir!" This last report should be followed by, "Clear anchor" or, "Foul anchor," but what the bridge heard was, "Jesus Christ, it's got an automobile on it!"

Naturally, they assumed that he was drunk again, so an officer went forward to investigate. An automobile *was* hanging from the anchor!

Which reminds me of a story about another fine sailorman with the same failing. His captain told him, "You're one of the best men on this ship when you're not drinking, and there's no limit to the rate you could hold. Why can't you behave yourself? Why don't you drink like an officer?"

The man said, "God Almighty, Captain, my constitution couldn't stand it!"

I kept a personal log during my tour of duty at Queenstown, and as I look through it now, nearly thirty years later, I find a few passages which may be of interest:

FEBRUARY 22nd. Hurrah for George! . . . At 9:40 A.M. picked up a convoy consisting of the *Von Steuben*, *President Lincoln*, *Finland*, and, appropriate to the date, the *Martha Washington*.

FEBRUARY 23rd. At sea escorting troop convoy. . . . Can see the *Antigone*, our nearest ship, is crowded with soldiers. Keep them on deck as much as possible while in submarine zone. Suppose other transports are equally crowded. You look at them and pity them having to go in the trenches. Suppose they look at us and wonder why anyone is damn fool enough to roll and jump around on a destroyer. Anyway we are all here for the same purpose, to get the Kaiser, and may that time be soon!

FEBRUARY 24th. Held target practice. Put over a raft made of barrels with a flag and staff. Men painted the Hun flag on target bunting and the

28

motto "Kill the Kaiser." Fired four rounds from each 4-inch and played with the machine guns.

MARCH 7th. Was yanked up to the Admiralty today to have tea with Admiral Jellicoe. He is very charming and perfectly natural. Most easy for a naval officer to talk to. Had been prepared by Admiral Sims's talk as to his appearance. His nose is certainly prominent! Small of stature, but very active and young-appearing.

Adm. Sir John Jellicoe had been, of course, Commander in Chief of the British Grand Fleet at the Battle of Jutland.

MARCH 9th. About 11:00 P.M. passed between two steamers on opposite courses about 500 yards apart. Inky black and drizzling and no lights. It sure is a hell of a sensation! You see nothing until they are right on top of you, and then only a black hump, with no possibility of telling which way they are heading. It is a case of pray you will go between. This is by far the greatest danger in these ship-infested waters, Hun subs and mines notwithstanding. It is what makes the wildcat wild. . . . Just before leaving, we took on board as a passenger a so-called British Admiralty pilot of Liverpool. Think him altogether too wise for a mere pilot and suspect he also belongs to Intelligence.

My suspicion was never confirmed, but it was encouraged by the fact that although he told me he had been a pilot for a great many years and had never been seasick, for the next four days he was the most seasick man I ever saw in my life. He was aboard, incidentally, because we were going out to meet the *Leviathan*, which was so large and vulnerable that they did not wish her to stop and transfer a pilot off the Mersey River, as incoming ships usually did.

MARCH 15th. At 4:30 A.M. two lookouts reported large wake crossing starboard bow. The water was phosphorescent, and this wake made for the bow, then apparently stopped and spread. Thought I surely had a Fritz! My first impression was that we had surprised him, and he had been forced to dive immediately under our bow. Was just about to drop a depth charge when I looked over the side again and saw the wake jumping in all directions. A large school of fish!

Fish, particularly porpoises, sent my heart into my boots time after time during these patrols. At night, in phosphorescent water, a porpoise has a strong resemblance to a torpedo. You'll see one heading for your ship; you have no time to maneuver; you hold your

29

breath; and when the wake reaches the side, you brace yourself for the explosion. Then it appears on the opposite side, and your heart begins to beat again.

MARCH 21st. The [destroyer] *Manley* came in. My youngsters went on board and say she is a horrible wreck.

The *Manley*, delivering dispatches to a British vessel, had collided with her in a heavy seaway. Some depth charges on the Britisher jarred overboard and detonated, in turn detonating the *Manley's* charges, which blew off her stern. The casualty list might have been longer but for the peculiar properties of TNT. The *Manley's* after torpedo tubes, loaded, overhung the stump of her stern and therefore caught the full heat of a blazing fuel tank abaft the engine room, but although the war heads became white hot, they did not explode.

MARCH 22nd. Passed several barrels and other wreckage, including a spar sticking about 18 feet out of water. Maybe it was Fritzi's trick periscope with a mine below. Anyway, we did not tackle it.

The Germans were known to use dummy periscopes with mines attached, so we were on the lookout for them. The Nips used the same lure off Pearl Harbor in the early days of World War II. Their dummy periscopes that I saw were not mined, however.

MARCH 30th. The Admiral was very chatty this morning, the first time I have seen him so.

Admiral Bayly was a splendid officer and gentleman. The Royal Navy in general considered him a martinet, but those who had the privilege of serving directly under him loved and respected him to a man. His extreme reserve is emphasized by the fact that when it relaxed, as on that day, I was surprised enough to note it in my log. He addressed us juniors not by our own names, but by our ships'. Thus his greeting to me, reporting in after a cruise, would be, "Good morning, Benham," and almost before I had time to respond, he would invariably follow with, "What is the condition of your ship?"

Whatever its condition, you answered—if you were wise—"Quite all right, sir," because Admiral Bayly held unpreparedness a crime more heinous than treason or mutiny. Similarly, to his next question, "When will you be ready to go to sea?" the wise skipper answered, "As soon as I can complete with fuel, sir."

One young skipper was not that wise; he rattled off a list of defects as long as his arm. The Admiral heard him out, then said courteously, "Quite right! Quite right! If you are not prepared to get under way at 3 o'clock, no doubt you can find a tug to take you in tow, and you can complete repairs on the way to Kinsale Head."

APRIL 7th. "Fly-fly" Peyton took lunch with us. . . .

Fly-fly was one of our early naval aviators. I quote this entry only to prove that the nickname is not new for World War II pilots.

APRIL 9th. Off Kinsale, [destroyer] *O'Brien* made submarine signal and steamed ahead. Went to general quarters and followed her. She dropped a depth charge. Did not see anything, but dropped one in same vicinity on general principles. First egg I have laid.

A destroyer skipper's first depth charge is like a girl's first kiss. My log notes that I "did not feel it much."

APRIL 19th. Two months ago today I took over command of this hooker. To my way of thinking, she is a different ship. Anyway, I am happy.

Here is the typical, egotistic "new broom" for you! He's not happy until he has changed things around, but after that, everything is quite all right.

APRIL 26th. The dockyard people put a line through our stern chock and made it fast under the depth-charge rack without telling anyone. Got underweigh with this line and had a hell of a time! Threw me into the [sloop] *Colleen*, and I just averted a bump by ringing emergency full speed ahead. Then I was thrown into the [destroyer] *Shaw* and again narrowly averted a bump. Finally discovered the trouble.

A lovely piece of work on my part and my officers'! It is inconceivable and inexcusable for a line to be secured on a ship, and the ship to prepare to get underweigh without its being discovered. "Everything is quite all right," eh?

MAY 17th. While standing down river, an aeroplane did some wonderful stunts. Would head right for us, and when it looked as if he could not miss our bridge, would gracefully skim just over the masts. Got about 200 feet above us and looped the loop, the first time I had seen it done.

How time and experience change one's point of view! Here I was fascinated by what I later recognized all too well as "flat-hatting." The most dangerous time in a pilot's career is when he first begins to feel confidence in his flying ability: he has the world by the tail; no maneuver is too difficult for him to perform. The casualties caused by his exuberance of youth, or—to give it its proper name—criminal foolishness, run into the thousands. "There are old pilots and bold pilots, but there are no old bold pilots." If I had ever caught one of my South Pacific or Third Fleet pilots "gracefully skimming just over the masts," I would have grounded him for life.

MAY 18th. Came into outer harbor and anchored at 3:15 A.M. This was my last trip as CO. Called the crew to quarters and read our orders. Was quite a wrench, as I have grown fond of the crowd on board.

I was being assigned to command the *Shaw*. She too was a good destroyer, but she had one structural defect that caused me special anguish; some bright designer had decided he would save weight by installing only one main condenser. His theory was excellent, because weight is vital on a destroyer, but he lacked practical experience. With two condensers, a leak can develop in one, yet the ship can be kept going on the other. With only one, you either proceed and salt up your boilers, or you stop and effect repairs, and there were not many places in those waters where you could stop in safety long.

MAY 27th. The fun popped at 1:30 A.M. The O.O.D. [officer of the deck] reported a green star fired on starboard bow—submarine signal. Jumped on bridge as the first ash can went off, then a fusillade of them. Next thing I knew, the [destroyer] *Cushing* came beating it around the rear of convoy, laying a barrage. In the meantime the [destroyer] *Sterett*, who had started all the row, was continuing her bombing astern. Both she and one of the transports had sighted this sub on the surface, and the *Sterett* proceeded to let him have seventeen ash cans. If she didn't get him, she gave him an awful headache.

About 8 A.M. passed through a regiment of empty champagne bottles, evidently from one of the transports. Guess the soldiers were pretty well shaken up last night and had a liquid breakfast.

32

The *Sterett's* CO was Comdr. Alan S. Farquhar. At dinner one night "Fuzzy" Farquhar and I began to brag about our prowess as Hun-hunters, and the bragging ended in a bet of £5 for the first of us to bag a German sub. I still can't honestly say that I ever even saw one, though I often thought I did; but almost from the day that Fuzzy took command of the *Sterett*, he ran into them continually, and the foregoing entry represented one of many occasions when I was afraid I was watching my £5 go glimmering.

JUNE 7th. At 3:45 A.M. got a radio from the P-68 [a British patrol ship] that she had just bombed a sub that had sunk a ship 8 miles from Trevose Head. Headed over at 25 knots to join the party. Fritzi had done a good job. Busted the ship wide open. Nothing left but kindling wood and a huge amount of oil. Quite an inter-Allied event—one blimp, two aeroplanes, two P-boats, two trawlers, and the *Shaw*. One trawler picked up a boat containing four men, one dead. Exchanged signals with the blimp and hustled oil wakes for 2½ hours but could see nothing definite. Finally had to return to station for escort duty. About 10:30 A.M. was taking a nap in the chart house when the O.O.D. reported, "Submarine on surface dead ahead!" Best thrill I have had since my arrival in the war zone! Made the bridge in two jumps and found the for'd gun manned and pointed at sub, with the pointer's finger itching on the trigger and not giving a damn what kind of a sub she was. About to give the order to fire when the quartermaster, who was watching her thru a long glass, reported he could see her letters and that she was a U.S. sub. Made the challenge to him, but he did not reply. By that time could see her letters with the naked eye: AL 10. Finally she fired the recognition signal. In the meantime we had been following her close, ready to open up and ram in case she made a false move. Needless to say, we were very much let down.

Salted up again on entering harbor. Another split tube. Damn that condenser!

The quartermaster who saved the sub was a full-blooded Indian, which may explain his wonderful eyesight. This was a time when I thought I saw the £5 headed toward me.

JUNE 18th. Found by virtue of seniority that I was king of the Irish Sea today. Under me had USS *Beale* [a destroyer] and HMS *Kestral* and *Zephyr* [sloops]. Had the time of my life bossing them around.

My first experience in multiple command in the war zone. I was as proud as a dog with two tails.

July 1st. At 10:30 P.M. received SOS from USS *Covington*, saying torpedoed and giving position about 150 miles south and west of Brest. Immediately headed for her at 20 knots and reported my action to C-in-C.

July 2nd. Found *Covington* about 8:30 A.M. in tow of three tugs, the [destroyers] *Reid* and *Wadsworth* standing by. She was towing easily, making about 5 knots, listed about 10° to port, and slightly down by the stern. . . . Everything went swimmingly until 2:30 P.M., when one of the tugs made signal to get all men off immediately. All hands were clear by 3:00 P.M. The *Covington* was listing further and further and rolling heavily, righting a little bit less each time. It was a pathetic sight. Reminded you of some huge animal, mortally wounded, yet struggling on. You hoped against hope that she would not go down, yet you knew she must. Finally the new, large American flag dipped in the water. Shortly after this there was an expulsion of air from aft, and the stern commenced to settle. She righted, and her bow rose majestically, almost perpendicular, with about 200 feet of the hull sticking clear. . . . As she started down, there was a black cloud given forth, probably due to the rush of air through furnaces and smokestacks. When her bow disappeared there was a bubbling on the water, as if from a depth charge. A surprisingly small amount of debris and wreckage came to the surface.

The *Covington* had already been towed about 50 miles, a third of the distance we needed to make port, and I'd had every hope of getting her there, with the help of the perfect weather and the smooth sea. This was a real heartbreak!

My message to Admiral Bayly, simply informing him that I was proceeding to assist her, may sound presumptuous, but it would have been silly to request instructions. The Admiral himself always pointed out that the man on the spot had so much better information than the man at headquarters, it was impossible for HQ to give proper instructions. This is a lesson that has stood by me all through my naval career.

July 4th. All American ships and personnel in the Queenstown area received the following signal today from Admiral Bayly: "The Commander in Chief congratulates the United States officers and men on the day and wishes them all success."

Such courtesy was typical of him.

July 8th. About 1:50 P.M., when 5 miles SSE of Coningbeg Lightship, the *Shaw* struck a submerged object. Saw a disturbance on the water,

Father, as a naval cadet, 1873

ther, my sister Deborah, and I, 1888

At school, 1894

Official USN photo

As a plebe, 1900

o *U.S.S. Missouri*'s. *Top:* "*Mizzy*," where I had my first sea-duty, 1904; the arrow points he turret which blew up on April 13. *Bottom:* "*Mighty Mo*," my flagship at end of the War

U.S.S. Don Juan de Austria, 1906

My first command, *U.S.S. Dupont* (foreground) 1909

t to right: Assistant Secretary of the Navy Franklin D. Roosevelt, unidentified com-
nder, Rear Admiral Charles J. Badger, Secretary of the Navy Daniels, Secretary of
nmerce Redfield, Secretary of War Garrison, in 1913, when I first had Mr. Roosevelt aboard

U.S.S. Benham, 1918

Skipper of the *U.S.S. Shaw*, 1918

Official USN photo

A T4M circling to come aboard the *U.S.S. Saratoga*, 1935

Official USN photo

At Pensacola, 1935

running at right angles to our wake and being circled by sea gulls. Dropped a can and brought up oil. Dropped two more cans on oil spot and brought up more oil, also keg marked "S.S. *Reserve*, c/o N.S.O., Aberdeen." This keg was slung in Manila line which extended under water for about 20 fathoms and was in turn spliced into $\frac{1}{4}$-inch wire line which was made fast to something on bottom. Lowered whaleboat and examined keg but could not hoist line into boat. Reported facts by radio to C-in-C, and two drifters with hydrophones and two trawlers were ordered out. About 9:00 P.M. secured box 8 by 2 feet and filled with cork to buoy as additional marker. While picking up whaleboat, the buoy got directly in rays of setting sun. Altho we repeatedly passed over the spot where buoy was, we never saw it again.

I thought that a radical zigzag of mine had surprised a submarine at periscope depth, and that we had hit her before she could complete her dive. As for the disappearing buoy, we figured that our depth charge had torn it loose from the sub's outer hull structure, and that her crew had later been able to retract it into some kind of watertight opening. I still don't know what really happened, but I know I came in for a lot of ragging from all hands. They dubbed me "the Duke of Aberdeen" and "the Count of Coningbeg." Somebody even whipped up a song:

> Last night over by Aberdeen,
> I saw a German submarine.
> The funniest sight I ever seen
> Was old Bill Halsey's submarine.

JULY 16th. At 10:00 last night went on the bridge. Came off at 9:30 this morning, a dead dog. Crossed convoy twice, discovered I had passed through a northbound convoy, and had lights and whistles on all sides of us all night. Fog lifted a bit at 5:00 A.M. and saw I was close to five of the ships, including the biggest and best, the *Carpathia*. Shut in again and did not finally lift till 9:30. By this time I was absolutely dead-ho. Laid down on the transom and died until 3:00 P.M.

JULY 17th. On my arrival, heard of the sinking of the *Carpathia*, bumped off three hours after we left her. A shame, as she was a fine big ship, and being 15 knots or better, should never have been in a $9\frac{1}{2}$-knot convoy.

This was the same *Carpathia* that had rescued so many people when the *Titanic* sank.

AUGUST 5th. At noon went over to meet the members of the Naval Affairs Committee from the House of Representatives. Walked down the hill with one inquisitive soul who was much interested to know whether our men drank much, even poking his head into a bar.

God, he made me mad! A friend of his who, he said, was a paid employee of the Red Cross in London (passing out doughnuts and occasionally a kind word to the troops), had told him that drunken American bluejackets caused more trouble than any other armed force. I asked his friend's age; he was young enough for combat service, so I suggested that he might do better work in the trenches than by vilifying fighting men. When this Congressman rejoined me after inspecting the barroom, he asked if it always had as many bluejacket customers as then. I said, "You've got the advantage on me. I've never been in there."

AUGUST 19th. Returned to Queenstown and found my detachment orders. When I left, the officers pulled me ashore.

AUGUST 21st. Sailed from Liverpool on HMS *Aquitania*. My old ship, the *Shaw*, escorted us out.

The administration and operation of the American destroyers working out of Queenstown was so superb that it became a pattern for our Navy at outlying Pacific bases in World War II. When we put to sea, we had excellent intelligence reports, including the general positions of the U-boats. The two American repair ships in Queenstown, the *Dixie* and the *Melville*, shared our maintenance. No matter at what hour we returned to port, an officer would come on board and request a list of necessary repairs, which he would generally O.K. The combined repair gangs were divided into three shifts of 8 hours a day, and they worked 7 days a week. This system had two conspicuous results: first, our destroyer crews were able to rest in port and recuperate from their five strenuous days at sea; second, our ships were kept in such excellent shape that they were always able to respond to a call.

The relations between the British and the Americans, from Admiral Bayly and Captain Pringle on down, were most cordial; we were not only comrades in arms, but close friends. Many years later, when Admiral Bayly presented the Naval Academy with a tablet in memory of his late Chief of Staff, he paid him the most glowing and most heartfelt tribute I have ever heard.

EDITOR'S NOTE:

For his services as destroyer commander during World War I, Admiral Halsey was awarded a Navy Cross with the following citation:

"For distinguished service in the line of his profession as Commanding Officer of the U.S.S. *Benham* and the U.S.S. *Shaw*, engaged in the important, exacting, and hazardous duty of patrolling the waters infested with enemy submarines and mines, in escorting and protecting vitally important convoys of troops and supplies through these waters, and in offensive and defensive action, vigorously and unremittingly prosecuted against all forms of enemy naval activity."

His comment is, "There was a very wide distribution of the Navy Cross to commanding officers of naval vessels during World War I. It did not have the prestige that attaches to the award in World War II."

On my arrival in the United States, I took my wife and two children to Atlantic City for three weeks, then reported to Cramp's shipyard, in Philadelphia, for duty as prospective commanding officer of the destroyer *Yarnall*, a 1,200-tonner, 200 tons larger than the *Shaw*, and the last thing in destroyer design. The armistice was signed while we were waiting to commission her, but President Wilson announced soon afterwards that he was sailing for France, and it occurred to me that escorting his flagship would give us a short, interesting shakedown cruise. I requested the duty, and my request was granted. The cruise was interesting, but far from short. I was kept in Europe for six weary months.

We delivered the President at Brest on December 13. When he stepped ashore, with him went the *Yarnall's* prestige. She was now assigned to ignominious messenger service, chiefly between Brest and Plymouth—a run so rough that it was known as "the Seasick Circuit."

Our passengers often included nucleus American crews for German merchantmen which their own crews had surrendered and brought down to Cowes. The first time I ferried a nucleus crew, the tide called for a full-speed landing alongside the German. We made our approach, but when we threw our heaving lines on board, the Huns refused to take them. I had no time to tell them

37

what I thought; I had to make a full-speed getaway to avoid being carried down on their ship; but as we drew out, I told my officers to fetch their pistols and hold them at the ready, and I posted four men who spoke German in a position where they could make themselves heard. On our second approach, we brandished our pistols and yelled a warning that unless the lines were handled, we would shoot. The lines were handled briskly.

Next I had to take an Allied commission on an inspection tour of German air stations and submarine bases. Also aboard were a German officer, representing his government, and a German merchant pilot. We were polite to them, but we had no intercourse beyond official business. We did not even let them eat in the wardroom until we had finished our own meals. Our one mess attendant, a Negro named Hasty, had a devilish sense of humor. Somewhere he obtained a recording of "The Marseillaise," and as soon as the Germans started to eat, Hasty started playing his record and played it throughout their meal.

—Which reminds me of another piece of malicious mischief it gave me pleasure to countenance. Whenever I went on an inspection trip ashore I was accompanied—at his own request—by one of my chief petty officers, who spoke German. He knew the stiffness of the German officer caste and was well aware that his leggings and belt marked him as an enlisted man, so he took special delight, which I shared, in forcing these officers into familiar conversation. Such presumption fairly frosted their monocles, but there was nothing they could do to stop it.

One inspection trip, to Warnemünde, on the Baltic, showed me a sight I shall never forget. We were being escorted through a building where a number of German sailors were painting overhead. They watched us, the conquerors, pass below. And nothing happened.

If conditions were reversed, I thought to myself, *and if those paintbrushes were in the hands of American bluejackets, some German officers would have to buy new uniforms!*

In January we made a run to Portugal. The night we shoved off from Lisbon was black, with a long, rolling swell. While we were dropping down the Tagus River, we had to keep one of our bow anchors ready for letting go, but as soon as we cleared the mouth, I ordered it secured. The working party consisted of four men: three bluejackets and Lt. Lewis G. Smith, a Reserve from Philadelphia, who was beloved by us all. Just as they reached the fo'c'sle, the *Yarnall* dipped her nose into an exceptionally heavy sea, and three of the men, including Smith, were swept overboard. The fourth was saved because the thick sole of his boot jammed between a fire-main riser and the hatch beside it. When we reached him, every rag of his clothing had been peeled off by the sea, and the sole of the jammed boot was hanging by a thread.

We circled the area but never found a trace of the other men. Such a mass of water had struck us that the steel door in the forward bulkhead was badly bent, so it is probable that they were either stunned or killed outright. These were the first and only accidental deaths that ever occurred on a ship under my command.

I had some leave coming when I got back to Brest, so I decided to make a trip to Paris with Halsey Powell, commanding the destroyer *Tarbell*. The trip would be strictly instructive, we agreed; we even drew up a rigid itinerary of historic spots. Our first port of call was the famous Panthéon de la Guerre. We went in and were minding our own business when we heard, "Stand by to repel boarders!" and there we saw a couple of Marine friends who shall be nameless. (Both are generals now.) That ended the instruction.

Somewhere in the course of the next few days, a lieutenant joined the party. I remember him chiefly because of a protest he filed with one of the Marines. "Look here," he said. "These two commanders we've got with us—I notice you call one of them 'Bill' and the other one 'Halsey,' and the next minute you call the first one 'Halsey' and the second one 'Powell.' Are you crazy, or am I drunk?"

At the end of a week, Halsey and I had to borrow the train fare back to Brest. An American chaplain in our compartment joined in the conversation. Somehow we fell to discussing a report that people at home were criticizing the armed forces for swearing too much. The chaplain had put in a good deal of time in the front lines. His comment was, "The trouble with those goddam fools, they don't know what swearing is!"

I thought of that statement twenty-odd years later, when I was told about another fighting chaplain. A Marine was escorting him through the New Georgia jungle when they came on a wounded

Japanese. The Marine drew a quick bead, then looked to the chaplain for permission. At the beginning of the Solomons campaign, we had scrupulously respected the enemy wounded, and we continued to do so until too many of our own men, leaning over to give them succor, were killed by knives and hand grenades. Then our attitude changed. This chaplain knew his business. He ordered, "Shoot the bastard!" and even as the shot was fired, he added, "May his soul go to God!"

The spring of 1919 brought us some excitement. On May 16, three Navy seaplanes took off from Trepassy, Newfoundland, in an attempt to fly to England by way of the Azores and Lisbon. The pilots were all friends of mine—Comdr. John H. Towers; Lt. Comdr. Patrick N. L. Bellinger, whose second in command was Lt. Comdr. Marc A. Mitscher; and Lt. Comdr. Albert C. Read. Pat's plane and Jack's were forced down on the first leg; Pat was picked up by a merchantman, and Jack managed to taxi into the Azores. But "Putty" Read flew the whole way—the first plane to cross the Atlantic from west to east. When he left Lisbon, on the thirty-first, the *Yarnall* was stationed along his route to watch for him. I remember how proud we were to see his NC-4 buzz overhead, and how his radioman kept calling us in a code we didn't have, and how peeved he was when we didn't answer.

The peace conference ended in June. President Wilson embarked on the *George Washington* again, and again we were part of his destroyer escort. I had a few days' leave with my family, then took the *Yarnall* to Hampton Roads to join the new Pacific Fleet which was being formed under Admiral Hugh Rodman. Just before we sailed for the Panama Canal, I was given additional duty as a division commander (there were then six destroyers in a division), and I continued as one until I was detached from destroyers two years later.

☆
☆ 4 ☆
☆ ☆

THE NEW fleet's first port of call on the West Coast was San Diego. Here Secretary Daniels came aboard. Because of his presence, and because 1919 was an election year, and because we were being displayed up and down the coast, this was dubbed the "Get-out-the-Votes-for-the-Democrats Cruise."

Now the fleet began to suffer from the discharge of officers and men who had joined up "for the duration." Priority was being given those wishing to resume studies in special courses, so a questionnaire was distributed to find their preferences. When Hasty's came back—Hasty was my Negro mess attendant—I was surprised to read that he wished to resume his studies in chemistry. I sent for him and asked what his chemical experience had been.

"Ah used to work in a drug sto', suh," he said.

"Doing what?"

"Carryin' soda to the tables."

Hasty went (but not to college), my chief engineer went, and so did too many more of our best men. Our crews shrank until we had barely enough hands to keep operating. When we didn't have even that many, the ships had to be placed in reserve.

The new COMDESPAC (Commander Destroyers Pacific Fleet) was Rear Adm. Henry A. Wiley. If ever an officer made bricks without straw, it was he. When he took command, the destroyers were well-organized and administered, but that was about all; they were as short on morale as on men. Admiral Wiley's leadership, his discipline, and his insistence on smartness made them the proudest ships in the fleet. I'm not saying this just because destroyers were my favorites. By the time Admiral Wiley was relieved by Capt. William V. Pratt, you could tell a destroyer man by the way he cocked his cap and walked down the street.

Captain Pratt, who had been Chief of Staff to Admiral Sims when Sims was COMDESLANT, was Admiral Wiley's perfect complement. Wiley put muscle into our morale, and Pratt put it into our efficiency. The divisions and squadrons began to work as teams. After two years together, the skippers in my own division could almost read one another's minds, and almost before the flagship hoisted its signals, we division commanders knew the intentions of our squadron commander. This was Capt. Frank Taylor Evans, the son of "Fighting Bob." Taylor Evans was a wonderful ship handler and knew more marlinespike seamanship than any other officer I ever met. His years of duty in destroyers had given him advanced ideas about their employment and tactics. For instance, he devised a series of formations which not only were radical but were executed by the unprecedented method of whistle signals. When a squadron of nineteen destroyers maneuvers by whistles—at night, blacked out, at 25 knots—it's no place for ribbon clerks.

In January, 1920, a number of destroyers, the *Yarnall* among them, were ordered to the China Station in command of officers just beginning their tours of sea duty. As I had been at sea for two years already, I was transferred to the *Chauncey*, which was being retained at San Diego.

Almost since the days of the *Dupont*, I had had a black dog on my shoulders, one that now began to grow heavier by the month. It was this: I knew my luck at sea was due to run out. In the eleven years that I had commanded ships, I had never suffered a really bad smash. The *Benham* had been in a collision shortly before I took over, and the *Shaw* lost 90 feet of her bow to the *Aquitania* shortly after I shoved off. But the worst that had happened to a ship actually under my command was when the *Yarnall* bumped a British destroyer at Copenhagen, and then you could have repaired the damage with adhesive tape. No doubt about it, my turn was coming. The question was: When?

The answer was, in May, on a squadron cruise to Pearl Harbor. The trouble started in the engineering department, the *Chauncey's* weak spot. This day the water in her boilers suddenly fell so low that they had to be secured on the double. The first I knew of it was when the telegraph rang up "Stop." The breakdown flag, which warns other ships that yours is not under control, was ready at the foremast, but the wind was from astern, and when we broke the flag, it fouled in the rigging. Simultaneously, we tried to blow emergency blasts on our whistle, but we had no more steam than a peanut roaster. Our only hope was that the destroyer immediately astern of us—the *Aaron Ward*, whose skipper was Raymond Spruance—would see our plight and keep clear. Unhappily, the inexperienced ensign on watch failed to call Ray; he merely slowed to one-third speed and kept advancing. We had no power, no steering control, nothing. We could only sit there and wait. The *Chauncey* barely had way on, and the *Aaron Ward* was moving at about 5 knots, when she hit us just abaft the starboard propeller guard.

Destroyers are called "tin cans" because their plates are too thin to turn even a rifle bullet. (Jap infantry put a lot of .25-caliber holes into the *Buchanan* at Tulagi.) The *Aaron Ward's* bow sliced 8 feet into our steering-engine room, flooding it immediately; disabled the starboard engine; and severed the starboard wire to the tiller. No matter; in this, my only serious collision, we didn't sustain a single casualty.

We sweated the *Chauncey* into Pearl, but I wasn't through with cripples yet; gout swelled my left foot until I had to hobble around on a cane, with a flapping slipper. It was awkward, but it led to a laugh. HMS *Renown* was also in port at the time, with the Prince of Wales aboard and Adm. Sir Lionel Halsey, my distant cousin. I had met Sir Lionel before, so when he came into the Moana Hotel, where I was sitting with some friends one night, I limped over to speak to him. He was wearing a smart white mess jacket and blue trousers with gold stripes, the kind our Navy knows as "railroad trousers"; I was in whites, but I had on one white shoe and one dingy brown slipper. We chatted a few moments, then he beckoned to the Prince and introduced me. Such a cooing and buzzing as went up from the lobby! I thought, *Surely they must be used to seeing the Prince by now!* But it wasn't for him, I learned. My slipper and cane, and the fact that the Prince came over to meet me, had tabbed me as a wounded war hero.

We left Pearl after three weeks with the *Chauncey* completely repaired, we thought. But two of her boilers burned out on the trip across, sending us to the Mare Island Navy Yard; a third burned out on the way there; and as we secured to the dock, the fourth and last one went. She was a bad-luck ship, and I wasn't sorry to shift to the *John F. Burns,* in July. The *Burns* was sturdy, but she too had her faults, one of them being an inordinate thirst for fuel oil. Nineteen-twenty was a thin year for naval appropriations; only a limited amount of oil was available, and only the most economical ships were kept in the active force, the rest being placed in the reserve. The *Burns* went there in October, and I went to the *Wickes,* which was as cheap to run as the *Burns* was expensive.

Meanwhile, one afternoon in June, I had returned from maneuvers and found a telegram from Mother in Washington: Dad was dead of a heart attack. He is buried in Arlington National Cemetery. He had retired as a captain in 1907 but had returned to active duty during the war, in charge of the Equipment Desk in the Bureau of Construction and Repair. One of our last arguments had been over the patent anchor with pivoting arms; he maintained to his death that it would never work on a destroyer.

I look somewhat like Dad—his nickname was "Ugly"—but I inherited almost none of his qualities and talents. Mother now eighty-eight, lives with my sister Deborah (Mrs. Reynolds Wilson) in Wilmington, Delaware.* Every time I visit them, I realize that I am cut more from Mother's pattern than from Dad's. She and I see problems only in black and white, without intermediate tones. We are both forthright to the point of tactlessness. Whenever I exhibit the "affinity between my foot and my mouth," as a war correspondent once described it, my wife attributes it to "that old Brewster blood." Mother will forgive me for saying that I inherited this from her; I hope that I inherited her staunchness and backbone as well.

In the early spring of 1921, our squadron was ordered to simulate a torpedo attack on four battleships. I had been the senior division commander for some time, so when our squadron commander was taken ill shortly before the exercise, I was given

---

* Editor's note: Admiral Halsey's mother died in May, 1947, as this book went to press.

44

temporary command. Ray Spruance succeeded to my division, Willy Wilcox had the second, and Johnny Ferguson the third. Three divisions of six destroyers each, plus an independent flagship: it was the biggest command I had ever held.

My own division was well-trained in quick anchorings. I had no time to train the other two, but I explained our method and warned Willy and Johnny to be alert. They laughed at me—it wouldn't work, they said.

"No? You'd better be on your toes all the same."

The night before the attack, we proceeded to Long Beach at 15 knots. As we approached the anchorage, I lowered my speed cone to two-thirds and hoisted "prepare to anchor." We were still making 10 knots when we reached the "hole," but I signaled "anchor," let go, and backed full speed. My division executed it smoothly, but some of the ships in the other two ran their chains out to the bitter ends.

As I expected, Willy and Johnny came boiling aboard, shaking their fists. All I said was, "Maybe you'll believe me next time!"

(Perhaps I should explain that although this maneuver sounds show-offish, it is actually the best means of getting light ships, such as destroyers, properly placed at their anchorages. They straggle at slower speeds and don't handle properly.)

Next morning my only instructions were to proceed to a position about 30,000 yards from the battleships and stand by for a signal to begin my attack. I put two divisions in parallel columns 1,000 yards apart and ordered the third to trail them, ready to take an intercepting course if the "enemy" tried to avoid. When the signal came, I took up a speed of 25 knots and headed for the battleship column on what I hoped was an intercepting course. As we closed them, I saw that my course was good and ordered the squadron to make smoke.

Captain Pratt, COMDESPAC, was on my bridge as an observer. He asked, "What do you intend to do?"

I asked, "What's the limit?"

"The sky."

I said, "If the battleships maintain their course and speed, I intend to put them between my two columns and fire at them from both sides."

45

I held on until I reached the firing point, roughly 3,000 yards from the leading ship, then ducked back into our smoke. My flagship did not fire; there weren't enough torpedoes to go around. But as each other destroyer reached the same point, it fired twice, for a total of thirty-six torpedoes. And out of those thirty-six we scored twenty-two hits.

Our torpedoes had practice heads, of course, with soft metal noses to absorb the impact, so that neither they nor the target ship would be damaged. But there was one factor we hadn't considered: by the time the last ships fired, the range had closed to 700 yards, a distance which torpedoes could cover at almost no expense of compressed air. As a result, they arrived with their air flasks nearly and, as it proved, dangerously full.

Of the four battleships, only the *Idaho* got off free. The *New Mexico*, the flagship of the vice admiral commanding, took a hit that ruptured her plating and flooded her paint locker. Two torpedoes exploded among the *Mississippi's* propellers and sent her to the yard. Another smashed into the compartment below the *Texas'* steering-engine room, blew all her circuit breakers, and temporarily paralyzed most of her electrical gear. In a minute and a half, we did a million and a half dollars' worth of damage. When those battleship skippers wiped our smoke out of their eyes and saw what had happened, my God, were they mad! And it didn't smooth their feathers any, when they got back to their base at Long Beach, to read this headline:

DESTROYERS DECISIVELY
DEFEAT BATTLESHIPS

A similar exercise was scheduled the next day, but just before we got under way, Captain Pratt and I were ordered to report on board the flagship, where we were strongly advised not to repeat our performance. Furthermore, the minimum range, we were told, would be 5,000 yards. That day the battleships got revenge; a torpedo ran wild and exploded under the stern of one of my own destroyers, twisting her rudder and screws so severely that she had to be towed in.

I made my permanent rank as commander in June, 1921, and in September I was ordered to Washington for duty in the Office of

Naval Intelligence. The day I was detached from the destroyers, two of the Navy's top trophies were awarded to ships in my division. I had the pleasure of notifying the *Zeilen* that her gunnery was the best of all the destroyers in the Navy; then I stepped over to my own ship, the *Wickes*, and announced that she was entitled to hoist the "meatball" at the fore, for general excellence in all forms of competition, including gunnery and steaming.

The *Wickes* was the best ship I ever commanded; she was also the smartest and the cleanest. You can tell how smart a ship is by the way she maneuvers, but if you want to know whether she is clean, the galley and the heads (toilets) are the key places. When I inspect a ship, those are the first compartments I look at.

My relief hadn't reported when I shoved off, so we couldn't hold the usual turnover conferences. I heard later that one of his first requests was for the division files. When they were broken out, he was aghast to see that they consisted of one folder containing one letter. I remembered it:

SUBJECT: Transportation, Lack of.
1. Further excuses that the engine of a liberty boat refuses to start will not be entertained. A white-ash breeze never fails. Moreover . . .

and so on. I was mad because a balky engine had again delayed a liberty party's return to the ship. If they couldn't start their damned engine, let them row. (Oars are a "white-ash breeze.") As long as they got back on time, I didn't care how they did it.

I have always hated paper work, so I try to substitute conferences, which have the added advantage of encouraging free discussion. This system works for me, but I hesitate to recommend its extension to the whole Navy. Sometimes, though, after hours of composing and dictating and correcting and signing, I think of a certain admiral who once suggested a regulation against bringing typewriters on shipboard.

My new duty in Washington was not only the first time I had been close to the throne; it was the first time I had ever commanded an LSD—a Large Steel Desk. The function of Naval Intelligence is to "collect, coordinate, interpret, and disseminate" all information of military significance. The most difficult step is the last. It isn't enough to get the right information to the right man at the right time; you have to make sure he doesn't let it molder in his "in" basket. I was just beginning to learn my way around when I happened in on a discussion about a suitable relief for our naval attaché in Germany, and to my astonishment, I heard my voice asking, "How about me?"

I don't know why I stuck my neck out. I had no special desire to go to Germany. But in the autumn of 1922, with a few Berlitz School lessons under my belt, and with my wife, my twelve-year-old daughter, and my seven-year-old son at my side, I sailed to take up my new duties. We disembarked in Plymouth, where I called on my old Commander in Chief, Adm. Sir Louis Bayly, and then proceeded to London, for briefing by the naval attaché. Our attaché in Paris briefed me again, so by the time I reached Berlin and paid my formal call on Ambassador Houghton, my job no longer seemed so frighteningly strange.

A naval attaché has a double duty: he is an aide and advisor to the ambassador, and he keeps his department informed on naval developments in the country to which he is accredited. This doesn't mean that he is a spy. Everything he does is perfectly aboveboard and with the consent of his hosts, and the information he obtains is what they see fit to grant.

In 1922–1923 the Germans were still attempting to retrieve what they could from the chaos of defeat. I was constantly approached by "friends of the United States" who wanted to sell us their inventions, usually with an implied threat that if we did not buy, they would sell to Japan. One invention was an excellent stereoscopic range finder. The British and ourselves were both using a coincidental (or split-image) range finder, which was greatly affected by vibration and the ship's guns. The German device was almost immune to these influences, so we tried it, secured it, and the Navy adopted it.

Supplementing this sort of thing, I made the rounds of a number of German industries in which the Navy was interested: the Zeppelin works at Friedrichshafen, where the dirigible *Los Angeles* was being built for us; the Zeiss and Goetz optical works; and the Krupp plant at Essen. I was also accredited to our legations in Denmark, Sweden, and Norway. The American minister to Denmark, Dr. Dyneky Prince, was especially hospitable. I remember him singing folk songs in at least twenty languages, ranging from Lettish to American Indian, and accompanying himself on the piano. (Incidentally, it was Dr. Prince who wrote the music for "The Road to Mandalay.")

I was relieved as naval attaché in July, 1924, and was ordered to command first the *Dale* and then the *Osborne*, two of the six destroyers we were still keeping in European waters, principally to continue showing the flag. Most of the next sixteen months I spent tourist-cruising in the Mediterranean. We were at Gibraltar on July 4, 1925, when Adm. Sir Roger Keyes's flagship, courteously full-dressed in our honor, entered the harbor. My official call was returned by the Admiral's Chief of Staff, Commo. Dudley P. R. Pound, who became the British naval representative on the Combined Chiefs of Staff in World War II. As his barge, handled by a midshipman (known in the Royal Navy as a "snotty"), came alongside the *Osborne*, it damaged our handmade teakwood gangway, the ship's pride and treasure. Commodore Pound not only insisted on having it repaired for us, but that afternoon sent the midshipman over to make personal apologies. I thought that the handsome, red-headed youngster's humiliation was unforgivably severe, and the next time I saw Pound, I told him that no flag officer in our Navy would treat a junior so. But when I tell the story to Royal Navy officers, they all have the identical reaction: "Splendid of Pound! Excellent training for the snotty!"

Malta was a special milestone on this cruise, because there I saw my first aircraft carrier, HMS *Hermes*. To an officer used to destroyers, she was an off-center, ungainly bucket, something a child had started to build and had left unfinished. In the years to come, though, when not only American carriers but British, too, were under my command, I realized that they have a grace and beauty of their own.

From Malta we cruised to Venice, where the *Osborne* had a memorable anchorage, in the Grand Canal, a scant hundred yards off my hotel. When I was ready to return to the ship in the morning, I'd step out on the balcony of my bedroom, hail the officer of the deck, and tell him to send a boat for me. It was as simple as that.

Ray Spruance relieved me in November. I collected my family from Switzerland, sailed home, and in January, 1926, reported as exec of the *Wyoming*. There is little to say about the year I served in her, except that she showed me a sight I never saw before or since. When she was sent to the Philadelphia Navy Yard for conversion to an oil burner, the workmen found in her bilges a deposit of slag too solid to be shoveled out. It had to be broken up with pickaxes, and a pickax being swung on a man-of-war was something new to me.

I was selected for the rank of captain in the spring of 1926, took my examination that summer, and in February, 1927, I sewed on my fourth stripe. By then I had been ordered to the Naval Academy as commanding officer of the *Reina Mercedes*. Like the *Don Juan de Austria*, the *Reina* was a prize from the Spanish-American War—an old cruiser that the Spaniards had sunk in an unsuccessful attempt to block the channel at Santiago. We had raised her and brought her to Annapolis, where she was turned into a receiving hulk.

Receiving ships are the only ones on which a commanding officer's family is allowed to live. We had wonderfully comfortable quarters in the after part, with a cook, steward, and boy to take care of us. Athletic and social events at the Academy furnished a pleasant background to my not too arduous duties, and if we found Annapolis dull, Washington and Baltimore were less than an hour away. I remained on this duty for three years and five months, and it was one of the most delightful tours in my career.

The *Reina* was best known as a prison ship. If a midshipman was caught Frenching, he was "sent to the ship" for four weeks, which meant that he ate there and lost all his privileges and liberty. This punishment was galling, but it carried no stigma, as many of today's top-ranking naval officers can confirm from experience. I am one—an alumnus of the *Santee*, the prison ship of my cadet days.

Being a warden was the least of my functions. All the floating equipment of the Academy—sailboats, motor boats, everything except racing shells—was in my charge, and the *Reina* furnished barracks space for the men who maintained it, as well as for the enlisted instructors in practical work and for a number of mess attendants. Presently the *Reina* had a new and unprecedented responsibility. That spring, the spring of 1927, she became the base of the Academy's first permanent aviation detail, and my whole naval career changed right there.

My first contact with naval aviation had been made in 1910, when I was in Norfolk. Ken Whiting, commanding three submarines at the Navy Yard, and "Spuds" Ellyson, supervising the commissioning of another, were dining with me.

Ken asked, "Spuds, have you thought anything about this flying game?"

"No, not especially."

"Well, I'm very much interested," Ken said. "I've been watching the Wright brothers and Curtiss, and I've put in an official application to the Department for a course of training in flying."

"That sounds good to me," Spuds said. "Send me a copy of your letter, and I'll put in one too."

He did, and to Ken's irritation, Spuds was ordered to flying—thereby becoming Naval Aviator No. 1—while Ken was ordered to take over the commissioning of Spuds's sub, and did not get his own flight training until two or three years later, when he became Naval Aviator No. 16.

Mention of Spuds and Ken brings to mind a rather curious coincidence. On June 22, 1945, when my Third Fleet was operating off Okinawa, *kamikazes* caused considerable damage to several of our ships, including the fast mine sweeper *Ellyson*, named for Spuds, and the aircraft tender *Kenneth Whiting*. Come to think of it, another aircraft tender damaged that same day was the *Curtiss!*

The aviation detail based on the *Reina* was commanded by Lt. Dewitt C. Ramsey, whose exec was Lt. Clifton A. F. Sprague. I disliked being in charge of something I did not understand, so I told "Duke" Ramsey he would have to educate me.

"Fine!" he said, "Let's go flying!"

I had flown twice before, once in 1913 and again the following year. Pat Bellinger took me on my first flight, at Annapolis. The plane was a Curtiss A-3, which was not much more than an engine, a prop, a pair of wings, and a float. My seat was no bigger than a bicycle saddle, and I had no safety belt. However, we staggered into the air, stayed there fifteen minutes, and splashed down again. When we taxied back to the ramp, a yeoman made me fill out a questionnaire which he had forgotten before the take-off: name, rank, residence, weight, religion, next of kin, and so on. I had climbed close to my peak weight about then—more than 210 pounds. When the yeoman read what I had put down, he told me, "You're the heaviest passenger we've ever carried!"

When all the records in early naval aviation are compiled, enter my name for that one!

My next flight was at Pensacola. This time Jack Towers was the pilot, and the plane was a seaplane with a real fuselage. Just before we took off, Jack told me about a particularly fine man in his detachment, a Marine sergeant, who had invented a fancy measuring stick to show the exact amount of fuel in an offset tank. We had been in the air only a short time when the engine suddenly conked. Jack made a beautiful dead-stick landing, then began to search for the trouble. Finally he discovered it: our tanks were dry. The fancy measuring stick had been a little too fancy. We had to borrow a bucket of gas from a near-by destroyer to get us home again.

Incidentally, while we were off Mexico that year, Pat Bellinger flew over the Mexican defenses and was fired at many times. I mention this only because I believe it is the first time an American naval plane—and probably a war plane of any kind—was ever brought under fire.

Now, after thirteen years, I flew again. Like most other novices, I became fascinated with it. I flew as often as Duke or "Ziggy" Sprague would give me a ride. It wasn't long before they were letting me handle the controls, and it wasn't much longer before I thought I was an ace. When I said, a while back, that the arrival of the aviation detachment changed my whole naval career, I was not exaggerating. Soon I was eating, drinking, and breathing aviation, and I continued to do so during the remainder of my duty on the *Reina*.

In the spring of 1930, the Chief of the Bureau of Navigation, Rear Adm. James O. Richardson, wrote me that he understood I was interested in aviation, and asked if I would like to take the course at Pensacola. I jumped at the chance. Shortly before this, all line officers had been required to take the full aviation physical examination, and I had passed easily. But now, for the first time in my career, I failed, on my eyes. I had never noticed anything wrong with them beyond normal age reactions, and I was confident that the disability was temporary. I let a week go by, then took the exam again; still no dice. I had to accept defeat.

That June I was detached from the *Reina* and ordered to command DESRON 14 in the Atlantic Fleet. This squadron consisted of nineteen destroyers—three divisions of six, and my flagship, thé *Hopkins*, all modern 1,200-tonners.

Lt. William F. Halsey III*:

I was working as an usher at NBC that summer. One day a public relations executive sent for me and told me he had seen in the papers that Dad's squadron was coming to New York. He said, "We'd like to extend your father the privileges of NBC, and we'd like to get a picture of the two of you together, both in your uniforms."

Me in an usher's uniform, and Dad in a Navy captain's! I didn't dare tell Dad about it until long after I'd left the job. He'd have pulled the guy's arm off and clubbed him to death with it.

Returning to sea duty was wonderful after more than three years on the beach, and I was particularly pleased to return to my favorite ships. I could also continue to indulge my love of flying. Planes had now become an integral part of the fleet; the pilots would spot our torpedo runs for us; so I began to watch half our torpedo practices from my bridge and half from the air.

However, not all the officers present were quite so raptly aware of our planes as was I. There was a day when one of the battleships flew off her scout with orders to rendezvous at a given spot. Something prevented the battleship from keeping the rendezvous, but she forgot to notify the plane. The pilot orbited as long as he dared and finally landed near the coast of Haiti, with barely enough gas to make the beach. The battleship's exec, a certain commander, was a friend of mine. I bought a doll, dressed it in a commander's uniform, chained a miniature plane to its wrist, and presented it to him as a future reminder.

---

* Editor's note: Admiral Halsey's family and many of his associates were reminded, on reading the completed typescript, of anecdotes which deserved inclusion. When such a contributor is or was an officer, the anecdote is ascribed to him under his present rank or the last rank he held before retirement to inactive duty. All other ranks and rates are as of the time of mention. Hence, for instance, Admiral Halsey's Chief of Staff's comments on the South Pacific campaign and the operations of the Third Fleet are ascribed to Vice Admiral Carney, as he is now, rather than to Rear Admiral Carney, as he was at the time.

In January, 1932, the Atlantic destroyers were ordered to the Pacific, where the major part of the fleet would be concentrated from then on. Another change in organization was made about this time: the division was reduced from six ships to four, so a squadron became a thirteen-ship command. I hardly had time to become accustomed to the difference. In June I said good-by to destroyers forever. In the twenty-three years that had passed since I took command of the *Dupont*, all my sea duty had been in destroyers, except my one year in the *Wyoming*. I had spent more time in them than had any other officer in the Navy, and my sea duty had been less diversified than any other officer's of my rank. In Proverbs' phrase, I had been "a companion of the destroyer." Now the companionship was broken; I never sailed in one again.

My new duty was student officer in the Naval War College, at Newport. Few years in a naval officer's life are more pleasant than this one. It is restful because you have no official responsibilities, and it is stimulating because of the instruction, the exchange of ideas, the chance to test your pet theories on the game board, and the opportunity to read up on professional publications.

Another story, apropos of nothing, comes crowding in here. We were dining with some War College friends, and a young Navy bride asked Fan for her dominant impression of Navy life. Fan told her flatly, "Buying and abandoning garbage cans all over the world!"

It was the Army and Navy's occasional custom to exchange a few officers between their War Colleges, and when I finished my course at Newport in 1933, I was ordered to the Army War College at Washington for further instruction. This was my first close association with the Army; here I met Maj. Omar Bradley and Lt. Col. Jonathan Wainwright, who were among my classmates. At Newport we had studied the strategy and tactics of naval campaigns, with emphasis on the problems of logistics. At Washington we studied on a larger scale—wars, not campaigns—and from the viewpoint of the top echelon, the Joint Chiefs of Staff.

Shortly before my year expired, I received a letter from Ernie King, then Chief of the Bureau of Aeronautics, offering me command of the carrier *Saratoga* if I would take the aviation observers' course at Pensacola. The world of aviation suddenly reopened to me; I was so excited that I regarded the privilege of commanding the *Sara* merely as a pleasant bonus.

I told my wife about Ernie's offer and asked her to consider it for forty-eight hours before giving me her opinion. When the time was up, she said she would consent if the Chief of the Bureau of Navigation, Adm. William D. Leahy, for whose judgment we both had enormous respect, agreed that the idea was sound. Bill Leahy not only agreed, he was enthusiastic.

I settled my family for the summer and started the long drive south to Pensacola. My last night on the road I spent at Tallahassee. Suddenly it occurred to me, "Bill, you're fifty-one years old and a grandfather, and tomorrow morning you'll begin competing with youngsters less than half your age!"

That night I took my last drink of liquor for a solid year.

I ARRIVED in Pensacola on July 1, 1934. Lt. Bromfield B. Nichol, who afterwards served on my staff for many years, was assigned as my instructor, and my training began at once. Squadron 1, the beginners' squadron, spent half its day at ground school and half in the air. At ground school we studied engines, radio, aerial navigation, gunnery, bombing, and torpedoes; in the air we practiced straightaway flying, primary tactics, and dead-stick precision landings.

After Brom had flown me around a few days, I decided I wanted my designation changed from "student observer" to "student pilot." From the standpoint of simple safety, I considered it better to be able to fly the plane myself than just to sit at the mercy of the pilot, who might get wounded or otherwise incapacitated. Besides, with a carrier command ahead of me, I wanted a clear understanding of a pilot's problems and mental processes. My eyes still could not pass the tests for a pilot, and how I managed to become classified as one, I honestly don't know yet, and I'm not going to ask. The fact remains, I began learning to fly.

CAPTAIN NICHOL:

There was one thing about his flying I'll never understand: the worse the weather, the better he flew.

A student pilot is required to solo after not less than eight hours of dual instruction, and not more than twelve. I took the limit, and when I finally soloed, it was the thrill of my life. One of Pensacola's customs is to dunk the last soloist in each class. I was the last in mine, and when I taxied my plane back to the ramp—Squadron 1 trained in seaplanes—my classmates were waiting for me. Most of them were ensigns, so they hesitated for a moment before tossing a captain into the harbor, but only for a moment. In I went.

My family was at Jamestown, Rhode Island, that summer. I had soloed more than ten hours before I mustered nerve to tell my wife that I had changed to the pilots' course. I knew she'd give me the devil.

Mrs. P. Lea Spruance, Admiral Halsey's Daughter:

Mother met me when I got off the ferry from Newport one morning. She was waving a letter from Daddy and she was as mad as a hornet. "What do you think the old fool is doing now?" she asked. "He's learning to fly! It must be that flying is the only thing left that will make him feel young again. He can't turn somersaults on the ground any more, so he's going to turn them up in the air. Did you ever hear such a thing? It's all your fault! You made him a grandfather!"

When we had completed our course in Squadron 1, the class was promoted to Squadron 2 and primary land training planes. Here we were taught three-plane formation flying and such elementary stunts as the loop, snap roll, falling leaf, and split-S. We also put in more work on precision landing. Something went wrong with an approach of mine one day; I overshot the circle and headed for a fence, rolling fast. It was a choice of hitting the fence or ground-looping, so I chose a ground loop. The plane wasn't damaged, and I wasn't hurt. In fact, the experience did me good; it took some of the cockiness out of me.

One of the final courses in Squadron 2 was cross-country flights with landings at outlying fields. We would take off from our home field in a formation of three planes, and each student would lead for one leg of the flight. The first time it was my turn to lead, I drew the homeward leg, and here my eyes got me into trouble. Although a student pilot flies a training plane from the rear cockpit, the only compass is mounted on the cowling of the front cockpit, 5 feet away, which is too far for me to read. I tried to brazen it out by the old trick of "flying the iron compass"—that is, following a railroad track—but my luck was out; the track branched, and I picked the wrong branch. (An instructor was flying

57

along with us, herding the sheep, but he deliberately let me go astray to teach me a lesson.) As a result, I was so late getting back to our home field that I caused considerable anxiety. For that matter, I had the unflattering impression that whenever I got in the air, my base was *always* anxious until I landed.

In Squadron 3 we flew service planes instead of trainers. These were OU's, the biplanes flown by our carrier scouting squadrons, and treacherous devils they were. Thanks to their free-swiveling tail wheels, they would ground-loop as soon as dammit. However, one maneuver that I executed, a front flip, was no fault of the plane's. I had touched down and was making a perfectly normal landing run when my wheels hit a soft spot and the plane went over on its back. The men in the tower recognized my number, and out dashed the crash truck and ambulance, with sirens screaming. They wanted me to lay off and take a breather, but I demanded another plane and went up immediately, to make sure that my nerve had not been shaken. It was all right.

Squadron 4 introduced us to the T4M, a single-engine patrol plane that carried a torpedo between its floats. We didn't drop the torpedoes; we flew the T4M's chiefly to get the feel of a heavy plane on the water before we moved up to the big twin-engine patrol jobs, which came next. In these we practiced flying on one engine and had our first lessons in horizontal bombing. I wasn't able to work with Squadron 4 as thoroughly as I wanted. The complete flight-instruction course required between twelve and thirteen months, but because spring was upon us, and I was scheduled to take command of the *Saratoga* early in July, the latter part of my training had to be condensed; I had to skimp Squadron 4 and hurry on to Squadron 5.

This was the most interesting and exciting part of the whole course. The "old fool" was flying fighting planes, F3B's and F4B's, so he had the illusion of being a combat pilot. Now we took up advanced stunting, and here let me emphasize the fact that stunt flying is not taught with ostentatious aerobatics as the sole end. On the contrary, it has definite and tremendous military value. Every stunt is designed to help a pilot evade an enemy or get into position for an attack. To be sure, the aerobatics frequently displayed by

58

Japanese pilots in the recent war did not seem to bear out this statement, but we learned later that they, too, had a practical end; the Japs' airborne radios were capricious, and when communication failed, the flight leader would use a certain stunt to signal a certain maneuver.

Two stunts we had never tried in Squadron 2 were the slow roll and the roll on top of a loop. When you make a slow roll, you have to reverse your controls twice, which takes both quick thinking and perfect coordination. I remember the first time I tried one. Halfway through it, I was beginning to think how easy it was, when I looked at my instruments; I had dived 2,500 feet and was making better than 200 knots. Even after long practice, I never mastered any stunt that took delicacy, but when it came to stunts where you simply kicked the plane around, I could usually get by.

"Jumping the rope" was another trick we met in Squadron 5. (I call it a trick because it wasn't really a stunt.) A rope hung with streamers was tied to the tops of two poles, about 10 feet high and 15 feet apart, set at the near end of the landing strip, and the trick was to clear the rope and land as close to it as possible, as practice for landing in a short field. Here my eyes handicapped me again. From the point where my approach should begin, I couldn't see the rope, and by the time I had picked it out, it was too late to adjust my flight.

Until now I had never worn corrective lenses, on the theory that unless I learned to fly without them, I would be almost helpless if I lost them in the air or broke them. Although I still didn't consider them essential to normal flying, I realized that an emergency might require them, so I had them fitted into my goggles and from then on my mistakes could be blamed only on my normal clumsiness.

CAPT. JOHN RABY:

I was one of the instructors in Squadron 5—a lieutenant j.g. When the Admiral came to us, I told him I would have his parachute carried out to his plane for him before every flight. He refused; he said he was no different from the other students and wanted no special privileges of any kind.

In those days we had an emblem called "the Flying Jackass"—an aluminum breastplate in the likeness of a jackass, with straps that buckled over your shoulders and around your waist. If you taxied into a boundary light, you were awarded the Jackass and had to wear it—except when you were actually flying—until the next man "won" it away from you. Pretty soon the Admiral taxied into a light and went up on his nose. Our skipper, Lt. Comdr. Matthias B. Gardner (later commander of a task group in the Third Fleet), lined up the entire squadron of students and enlisted men, read out a citation we had written for the Admiral, and buckled the Flying Jackass to his chest.

He had worn it a couple of weeks when a student in Squadron 2 hit a light, so I told the Admiral that he had served his time and asked him to turn in the Jackass for the new winner. He said, "No, I want to keep it. I won't wear it around here any more, but when I take command of the *Sara*, I'm going to put it on the bulkhead of my cabin. If anybody aboard does anything stupid, I'll take a look at the Jackass before I bawl him out, and I'll say, 'Wait a minute, Bill Halsey! You're not so damn good yourself!'"

My last month of instruction, May, 1935, was like a game of going to Jerusalem. I'd fly a fighter, then rush down to the beach and fly a patrol plane, then rush back to the fighters again. Between the first of the month and the twenty-eighth, I spent more than eighty hours in the air. But school was out eventually; I was designated "naval aviator," my wings were pinned on, and my wife and I drove across the continent to Long Beach, to my new duty as skipper of the *Saratoga*.

Fan had joined me in Pensacola the preceding December. When I had left her six months before, I weighed close to 200 pounds. When she saw me next, the heat and the strain of flying had peeled me down to 155. Still, I rather fancied my sylphlike figure, so I hinted that compliments were in order. Instead, she stood me in front of a mirror, grabbed a handful of the loose skin flapping under my jaw, and demanded, "What are these wattles? You look like a sick turkey buzzard!"

It was only temporary. I was back up to 175 when I got my wings.

A footnote to the year at Pensacola: One day some student pilots told me about a broadcast they had just heard by a certain notorious commentator. According to their account—and in justice to the blackguard, it should be borne in mind that I am setting down something I was told more than ten years ago—his thesis was that the Navy had sly little ways of circumventing congressional laws, for instance the law requiring the commanding officer of a carrier to be either a pilot or at least an aerial observer. Let us say, he continued, that an officer of the grade of captain is ordered to Pensacola to take the observers' course. The commandant is an old friend. The captain greets him by nickname and tells him why he has arrived.

"That's fine!" the commandant says. "I've got just the man for you!" He sends for a personable and politic young lieutenant and tells him, "Captain X here is going to take our observers' course, and you will be his instructor. . . . Is everything quite clear?"

"Yes, *sir*," the lieutenant says, and he starts Captain X on a series of mild, sight-seeing hops under sunny skies.

A few weeks pass. Captain X again drops in to see the commandant, again addresses him by nickname, and informs him, "I've completed the course; a delightful experience!"

"Splendid!" says the commandant. "It gives me great pleasure to award you these wings. Congratulations!"

Well, as I was the only captain of the line then at Pensacola, and the only one eligible to command a carrier, the fledgling pilots got the impression that the commentator had me in mind. In fact, they were sore as hell about it. I didn't care a hoot. All I did was write Ernie King and ask him to invite Big-Mouth to come for a ride with me. I added that I happened to be in the middle of the stunt course in Squadron 2, and I felt pretty sure that if the scoundrel had guts enough to accept, I could make him throw them up. He never answered my invitation, but—to be fair again—I don't know if Ernie ever passed it along.

The *Saratoga* was not designed to be a carrier. She and her sister, the *Lexington*, started as battle cruisers and were converted under the terms of the Washington Disarmament Conference of 1922. This made them somewhat stiffer than a carrier should be, but it also made them the largest warships in the world. They had power to match their size—185,000 hp. When Tacoma's power plant failed in 1929, the *Lex* hooked onto the cables and delivered enough juice to carry the whole city until it could take care of itself again, thirty days later.

61

Hitherto, the largest ship I had handled was a destroyer, except the single occasion when I brought the *Wyoming* into an anchorage, and I was curious to feel the difference between the *Sara* and the *Benham* or the *Yarnall*. I am not being an obvious idiot when I say that it was one of size and nothing else. She was simply an overgrown destroyer, and I handled her as such. I could even make a flying anchorage with her. At Coronado Roads once, I let go the hook when she was making 9 knots, backed her full, and had her dead in the water by the time we had paid out 75 fathoms of chain. That was an emergency, I admit, but it shows what she could do when you called on her.

I never had any combat experience on the *Sara*. If the *Enterprise* later became my favorite, it was because she was my flagship when the Japs attacked Pearl Harbor and because we afterward went through so many fights together. But there are two reasons why I will always think of the *Sara* as a queen and why she will always have a secure place in my heart. First, I loved her as a home; I commanded her for two years and flew my rear admiral's flag on her for two more, which means that I lived on board her longer than I ever lived anywhere else. Second, I loved her as a ship; she helped me make my debut in the carrier Navy, and she initiated me into the marvels of fleet aviation.

To employ this mighty arm of naval warfare and employ it properly, you have to know its limitations as well as its potentialities. I think I know something about them now, after six years of carrier experience; but I knew little enough then, and I had to learn the hard way—from others, while bearing the responsibility for their actions.

Carrier flying requires special training and special courage. I can say this objectively, because although I have been a passenger in many carrier take-offs and landings, I have never been the pilot. All combat pilots, land-based or carrier-based, must know how to fly, navigate, operate a radio, and shoot and bomb, but this is only the beginning of the demands on a carrier pilot's abilities, and it ignores the extraordinary hazards that confront him.

For instance, his engine may cut on take-off as he crosses the bow. Then his plane goes into the water, his wheels trip and throw it onto its nose or back, and he may be knocked unconscious. His safety belt or his canopy may jam, and he will drown. Or he may extricate himself only to be trampled down by his own ship. He faces all these possibilities every time he goes over the ramp.

Say that his take-off is normal. Say that an enemy does not cripple his plane over the ocean 200 or 300 miles from his ship, and that his engine does not fail. He still has to find his ship again. A land-based pilot departs from a fixed spot and returns to one. But the carrier may be 50 miles or more from where the pilot left it, and there are no landmarks on the ocean, no "iron compasses," no signposts. His radio will help him, of course, but the best radio is not infallible, and if it fades in foul weather, only split-second navigation will bring him back.

Here I mean split seconds of latitude and longitude, not of time. He needs split-second timing when he tries to come aboard. I have said that a ship usually pivots around a point about one-third aft of her bow, which means that the horizontal arc of her stern is twice that of her bow. A heavy sea may make this arc as wide as 25 feet, and it may also make the stern rise and fall the same distance. Add a gusty, shifting wind, and the difficulties of entering the narrow lane are evident. Carrier pilots have what it takes. They have to have it.

Something else they seem to have is an addiction to practical jokes. I remember a period on the *Sara* when "Country" Moore found that he was being treated as a pariah. No sooner would he take a seat in the wardroom or the ready room than his neighbors would offer some excuse and move away. One of them finally whispered an explanation, as they do in advertisements, and Country rushed to consult a dental officer, who asked him what toothpaste he was using. Country brought it down to show him. His friend "Cap" Brown, it developed, had taken a hypodermic syringe and shot the tube full of oil of garlic.

In the early fall of 1935, the *Saratoga* went to the Bremerton Navy Yard for a three-month overhaul, then to Panama on a winter cruise, then back to her base at Long Beach. The naval landing there was next to a merchant dock, and it was then, in the spring of 1936, that I first noticed something that I have had excellent cause to remember ever since: the constant presence of Japanese shipping. It was a rare day when I passed this dock without seeing a Jap freighter loading scrap iron. Every time we put to sea, we met a Jap tanker coming in for oil. (Am I wrong, or were the tankers handled Navy-fashion?) And, of course, part of the fishing fleet working out of San Pedro was manned by Japanese.

(I am *not* wrong when I state that these fishing boats frequently bobbed up in the midst of our maneuvers, with no commercial excuse. The Hawaiian fishing fleet was also Jap-manned to a large extent and also showed an unbecoming curiosity. In the summer of 1941, when Carrier Division 2 was operating off the Hawaiians, one sampan was so persistently intrusive that I ordered my destroyers to give it a dose of smoke and then search it. They did so, and found an alien Japanese not listed on the ship's rolls.)

Jack Towers relieved me in command of the *Sara* in June, 1937, and I did not return to the West Coast for two years. By then the *Panay* had been bombed, so my apprehension was increased by the spectacle of the Jap ships still loading scrap at Long Beach. My conviction—and it was general in the Navy—was that this scrap would eventually return to us in the form of shells and bombs. There was friction between Japan and the United States at too many points. We resented their closed-door policy in Manchuria, and they resented our Exclusion Act. But overshadowing all political and economic considerations was the inescapable fact that Americans did not like the Japanese and did not trust them.

Lt. (j.g.) Melvin Carr:
Before Pearl Harbor, I used to drive the Admiral around Honolulu. A lot of people out there are like wild men in automobiles, but when one of them bumped us, the Admiral always insisted it was our fault and took the whole blame—unless the other driver was a Jap. In that case, no matter whose fault it was, he gave the Jap hell.

My father and I disagreed on this; he was friendly with many of them. One of his classmates at the Naval Academy, the first Japanese to matriculate there, was Jiunzo Matsumura, who died a vice admiral in the Imperial Navy. In my early days in the Navy, many of our mess attendants were Japanese. Two of them I remember clearly: Kosu was a simple rickshaw puller, but I have always believed that Shozi, who was smart, quick, and crooked, was a naval officer in masquerade.

64

When I was relieved from the *Sara* with orders to return East, I telephoned from San Diego to my wife in Wilmington, Delaware, and told her that I had a chance to fly home in a fast two-seater, as copilot to an excellent aviator. . . .

I disobeyed her and flew anyway. Through inexperience, I kept the volume of my radio turned too high during the flight, and when we landed at Washington, I was temporarily stone-deaf. I phoned Fan again, to report my arrival, but I had hardly done so when she took charge of the conversation for $1.80 worth of time. I could gather from her tone that she was ripping off my skin, but I couldn't distinguish a single word. I have never been that lucky again.

My new orders took me back to Pensacola, as commandant. Our official residence was comfortable; we enjoyed seeing so many old friends again, and I was able not only to fly to my heart's content, but to bring myself abreast of the latest developments in aviation. I was particularly interested in the progress of instrument flying, and I monopolized so much of the instructors' time that they asked me to slack off for the benefit of their regular students.

I had been selected for rear admiral in December, 1936, but because promotion takes effect only when there are vacancies in the grade, I did not "make my number" for fifteen months, until after I reported in at Pensacola. It was gratifying to become a flag officer, but it cost me exactly $3,000. The difference in pay between a captain and a rear admiral of the lower half was only $300 a year, which barely defrayed my new gold lace and insignia. Then Congress passed a law—effective July 1, 1938—that only one officer of flag rank was entitled to draw flight pay (an additional 50 per cent of base pay), and I was not that officer. This law lasted only a year, at the end of which flight pay was restored to flag officers actually engaged in flying, but my flight pay for that year would have amounted to $3,000.

Meanwhile, in May, 1938, I was detached from Pensacola and ordered to command Carrier Division 2, which consisted of two brand-new sister ships, the *Yorktown*, Capt. Ernest D. McWhorter commanding, and the *Enterprise*, Capt. Charles A. Pownall. The *Yorktown* was on her shakedown cruise, so I hoisted my flag in the "Big E," which was in the Norfolk Navy Yard for repairs and alterations following her own shakedown. She was ready early in January, and we sailed for the Carribean, to join the Battle Fleet for spring maneuvers.

At the end of World War II, the United States Navy included about 100 aircraft carriers. In January, 1939, the Navy had five. The *Saratoga* was in the Pacific, but the others were together— my two in CARDIV 2, and the *Lexington* and *Ranger* in CARDIV 1, all four being under the command of Ernie King, as Commander Aircraft Battle Force. The *Lex*, commanded by Capt. John H. Hoover, who later became my Chief of Staff, and the *Ranger*, by Capt. John Sidney McCain, who later commanded Task Force 38 in my Third Fleet, were both veteran ships, smooth and efficient. The greenhorn *Yorktown* and *Enterprise* had a rugged time trying to match them, but we had no reason to be ashamed when the maneuvers were over and the fleet stood north to Hampton Roads.

CAPTAIN NICHOL:
During these maneuvers, an officer on the hangar deck made a mistake that delayed our launching one morning. Admiral King cracked down right away with a signal demanding to know who was responsible. Admiral Halsey replied, "COMCARDIV 2"—assuming the responsibility himself.

He's got broad shoulders. He takes it without passing it on. For my money, that's the mark of greatness in a naval officer. It's also the stuff that loyalty is built on.

From Hampton Roads, the fleet was going to New York for leave and liberty. A few afternoons before we were due to sail, I was driving through Norfolk when an excited yeoman from my staff stopped my car and told me that we had been ordered to proceed to the West Coast at once. We sailed next day, so suddenly that the officers and men who had been granted leave could not be recalled in time and had to meet us out there. No official explanation was ever given, but I have been told informally that our orders came direct from the White House, on the strength of a report that the Japanese were plotting to blow up the Panama Canal around July 1.

By the time we reached the West Coast, however, the tension had relaxed and the fleet went about its routine. But the Jap freighters were still loading scrap at Long Beach, and their tankers were still taking on oil. . . . I had plenty of opportunities to watch them this time; I was in and out of there for ten months, until the Battle Fleet cruised to the Hawaiians in April, 1940.

Meanwhile, the carrier divisions and their commanders were reshuffled, and I was appointed COMCARDIV 1, with my flag in the *Saratoga*. That year we conducted war games jointly with the Army. Their problem was to defend a section of California's coast against "invasion" by a division of troops; the Battle Fleet's problem was to convoy the division. My "air force"—one carrier—acted independently, harassing the Army's shore-based air. Of all the simulated attacks we made on their fields, one stands out. Capt. William D. Old had brought his bombers across from the East Coast and had based them at Reno. He was so certain that carrier planes could not penetrate 200 miles inland that he did not post patrols, and the first he knew of our attack was when our fighters swarmed over him. Some of them were impertinent enough to drop alarm clocks by parachute, with messages suggesting that it was time the Army woke up.

On the way to Pearl the Battle Fleet split into two forces, one commanded by Adm. Charles P. Snyder and the other by Vice Adm. William S. Pye. I was detailed to Admiral Pye's force. By now I had formed certain opinions on how naval aviation should be employed and certain ideas for increasing its efficiency. One of our problems was radio communication. At that time each ship had its own wave length, or channel, to its own planes. Obviously, the sooner the enemy's position is reported, the sooner you can take the offense; but under the radio doctrine then current, there was a dangerous waste of critical time. Say that planes from all ships—carriers, battleships, and cruisers—were scouting for the enemy, and that a cruiser plane made the first contact. Before the carrier commanders could order action, the cruiser had to receive the report, read it, and readdress it to the flagship, which had to read it and readdress it to the carriers.

My contention was that a single wave length should be shared by all scout planes, so that no matter who reported the first contact, the carriers would be alerted. I strongly recommended this to Admiral Pye, who concurred. We both knew that we would meet

67

opposition and we did. However, he overruled it, and our system, or one similar, has been in effect ever since.

I got into another fight over radio at about the same time. A good many communications officers were arguing that our ship-to-plane radiophones could be jammed, and that the only reliable transmission was by key. I disagreed for two reasons: (1) I maintained that the phones could *not* be jammed, and (2) whereas it takes only a few minutes to teach a man to use a radiophone, it takes months to teach him Morse. This was the spring of 1940, when the Navy was beginning to expand at an unprecedented rate. Our dive-bomber and observation-scout pilots were begging for rear-seat men, men who could operate the free gun as well as the radio. We could spare only so much time to train them; every hour devoted to Morse was an hour stolen from the guns; and I considered it more important for them to learn how to attack and to defend themselves than for them to become expert telegraphers.

Eventually we agreed to settle the argument by a test, as we should have done at the start. The communicators rigged three high-powered transmitters on a ship, and we sent out our planes. Despite every attempt to jam us, the ship and the planes exchanged oral reports at a distance of 150 miles. Our fight was won.

A month after we arrived at Pearl, I was detached from command of CARDIV 1 and appointed Commander Aircraft Battle Force, with additional duty as COMCARDIV 2. This made me a naval Pooh-Bah. As COMAIRBATFOR, I commanded all the carriers in the Pacific Fleet and their air groups; therefore, as COMCARDIV 2 I was directly responsible to my other self, just as later, for example, Fleet Adm. Chester W. Nimitz as CINCPAC was responsible to himself as CINCPOA (Commander in Chief Pacific Ocean Areas). On the same day, June 13, I was promoted to the temporary rank of vice admiral. This, too, had its Gilbert and Sullivan aspects. When Ernie King was relieved as COMAIRBATFOR, he reverted from temporary vice admiral to rear admiral, so I now became his senior and, in fact, remained so until he was promoted to admiral. (All this is inconsequential; I mention it only to illustrate the curious leapfrog of temporary rank.)

That summer at Pearl, the men in the Pacific Fleet had their first sight of a strange contraption. The *California* displayed it.

68

She had gone to the West Coast as a normal battleship, but when she returned after her overhaul and refit, she was a changed old lady; she looked as if she were wearing a bedspring on her bonnet. It was a new invention, top secret, and was said to be almost supernatural—radar.

I had been introduced to it the year before, when Capt. Roscoe C. MacFall, then in charge of fleet training at Washington, told me how their radar had picked up a plane over the east coast of Maryland and had tracked it into the Anacostia Naval Air Station, near Washington. The possibilities of such an instrument were too tremendous to grasp. I was told that it would be installed throughout the fleet, and I was impatient to see it on the *Yorktown*, my new flagship. Almost as soon as we received it, we had a chance to test it in a war game, and I remember how awe-struck I was when it located the opposing force, out of sight over the horizon, at a distance of 35,000 yards. A few months later, when the *Yorktown* went back to San Diego for overhaul, our radar not only picked up a destroyer squadron at 78,000 yards, thanks to a freak weather condition, but enabled us to find our anchorage despite a thick fog.

If I had to give credit to the instruments and machines that won us the war in the Pacific, I would rank them in this order: submarines first, radar second, planes third, bulldozers fourth.

The *Enterprise* completed her overhaul in December, so I shifted my flag to her and sailed back to Pearl early in January, while the *Yorktown* took her turn in the yard. Our next big excitement came on February 1 when, as part of a general shake-up of flag officers, my friend and classmate, Rear Adm. Husband E. Kimmel, was relieved of his command of the Cruiser Battle Force and was appointed Commander in Chief of the Pacific Fleet, with the rank of admiral.

There was no doubt of his qualifications, but he was a comparatively junior officer, and his promotion to a post of such responsibility astonished him as it did the rest of us. His splendid record gets most of the credit, of course, but part I attribute to the impression he had made during Secretary Knox's visit to the fleet the summer before. Mr. Knox had had the word passed that he wished every flag officer to call on him, and each was informed that he would be expected at a set time. This procedure was unusual, but

69

sound; it gave us a chance to meet the Secretary of the Navy against our own background, and it gave him a chance to size us up individually. I am convinced that when Husband Kimmel paid his call, his personality made an indelibly favorable impression, to the extent that his name leaped to Mr. Knox's mind when it was time to pick a successor to Adm. "Jo" Richardson.

I don't believe there was a flag officer in the Pacific Fleet who did not feel that Kimmel was an ideal man for the job. Unfortunately, even an ideal man can't do a job without proper tools, and Kimmel did not have them. The blame falls on the ostrich policy which the United States adopted after World War I. We refused to recognize the existence of predatory nations; therefore, they did not exist. On the theory that sweetness and light would prevail and that we would have no further need for the Navy, appropriations to maintain it were cut and cut again. Enlistments had to be restricted; for want of crews, ships were laid up; few new ships were built.

As our strength waned, the ambitions of the predators waxed. Providentially, President Roosevelt came into power in time to save our military establishment from complete collapse. He began to restore it at once, and although it was still perilously—almost fatally—weak when war broke out, he had managed to shore it up enough to survive the first assault. When I say "weak," I have especially in mind the Pacific Fleet. I quote from Kimmel's testimony before the Joint Committee on the Investigation of the Pearl Harbor Attack:

The Pacific Fleet was inferior to the Japanese Fleet in every category of fighting ship. . . . Japan, at the outbreak of hostilities, had nine aircraft carriers in commission. We had three carriers in the Pacific and those did not have their full quota of planes. Although the battleships of the fleet were all approximately the same age as the heavy ships of the Japanese Navy, our ships were particularly deficient in short-range anti-aircraft weapons . . .

And so on. We realized the disparity, but despite emphatic warnings from officers who had served in the Far East—notably from Adm. Harry E. Yarnell—many of us were inclined to underrate the Japs, chiefly their aviation. Let me confess here that I revised my opinion

70

after December 7. The Jap naval aviators who made that attack were good—very good indeed.

It is a bitter paradox that some of our worst deficiencies were caused by the program aimed to remedy them. When the Navy began to expand in 1940, trained men were needed as cadres for new organizations. Thousands were drawn from the Pacific Fleet and were replaced by raw recruits. As Kimmel has stated, more than 50 per cent of his officers were newly commissioned Reserves, and there were times where 70 per cent of the men aboard individual ships had never heard a gun fired.

The fleet's most desperate shortage was patrol planes and their crews. Proper defense of an island requires an 800-mile, 360-degree search by patrol planes, supplemented by a scouting force of submarines and fast surface vessels. Kimmel had neither sufficient planes nor an adequate scouting force. I am not exaggerating when I say that he did not have enough planes to maintain complete coverage of a 60-degree sector. As for crews, his original shortage was increased by orders to transfer twelve trained crews to the mainland every month. This situation offered him two alternatives: he could work his available planes and crews to the point where few, if any, would soon be operative; or he could reduce his search and conserve them for the outbreak of war. Kimmel chose to reduce his search, and although this was one of the factors that enabled the Japs' sneak attack to succeed, any admiral worth his stars would have made the same choice.

All our plans accepted the possibility of such an attack, but most of us believed that Japan's first strike would be southward, against the Malay Peninsula; we hoped so, because this would give us warning. However, if Pearl were struck first, we believed it would probably be by submarines, synchronized with sabotage. (The Hawaiian Islands have a Japanese population of 155,000.) Admiral Richardson, Kimmel's predecessor, had observed that our regular anchorage at Lahaina Roads, between Maui and Lanai, was dangerously exposed to submarines, and had ordered it abandoned. With the fleet thus concentrated at Pearl Harbor, Kimmel reorganized it into three task forces and scheduled their operations so that, as a general rule, only one would be in port at a time. As further protection against espionage, he forbade fleet

71

movements to be mentioned; hitherto we had been allowed to discuss them freely.

By the fall of 1940, we had known that war with Japan was inevitable. By the next spring, we knew it was impending. One of our first indications was received on April 4, when we were ordered to strip ship—to remove all inflammable or splinterable gear not needed for fighting: boats, cushions, wooden chests, canvas awnings, excess cordage, paint. We rigged splinter shields for the crews of our AA guns. We installed degaussing cables, to neutralize magnetic mines, and listening gear to detect submarines. On Kimmel's insistence, we stepped up war-training exercises of all types. The carrier air groups staged gunnery, bombing, and torpedo runs almost daily, and practised night take-offs and landings. We arranged for submarines to maneuver with the carriers, so that our pilots could learn to spot them at different depths. We experimented with our radars to determine their resources and their limits.

For instance, the *Enterprise's* radar was excellent at reporting the distance of a plane, but not its altitude. We evolved a rough solution to the problem by sending a squadron 100 miles from the ship with orders to shuttle at each 1,000-foot level, up to 20,000 feet. Tracking them, we found that they disappeared from the screen at certain intervals, then reappeared. We plotted the curve, established the nulls (blind spots), and computed the altitudes. This information we gave to the Army as well as the fleet. In the course of the test, our screen once showed that our second division of planes, then some 50 miles away, was straggling out of position. The pilots were not yet aware of radar's powers and were mystified when we called them and told them to close up.

Kimmel conferred frequently with his task-force commanders— Vice Admiral Pye, commanding TF 1, myself commanding TF 2, and Vice Adm. Wilson Brown, commanding TF 3. Every scrap of information that came to him, he passed along to us and to Rear Adm. William L. Calhoun, Commander Base Force, and Rear Adm. Claude C. Bloch, Commandant of the Fourteenth Naval District. I recall with special clarity a conference on the morning of November 27, the day that the famous "war warning" arrived from Washington. Kimmel was always concerned about our picket-line islands—Midway, Wake, Johnston, and Palmyra—which were as

72

inadequately armed and manned as was the fleet. He had sent them all the reinforcements he could spare and had requested Maj. Gen. Charles F. B. Price of the Marines, who was making a tour of the area, to inspect and criticize their defenses. These included, on Wake and Midway, newly completed airfields, which the War and Navy Departments had agreed to stock with Army pursuit planes, to be delivered by the *Enterprise*. The conference was called to decide what types of planes to send, old ones or new ones. The officers present were Lt. Gen. Walter C. Short, commanding the Hawaiian Department; Maj. Gen. Frederick L. Martin, commanding Short's air force; Vice Admiral Brown; Rear Admiral Bellinger, Commander Air Force Scouting Force; myself, and members of Kimmel's staff.

General Short stated that inasmuch as these planes would probably be the first to meet the enemy, we should use the best we had.

I asked General Martin, "Isn't it a fact that your pursuit fliers are forbidden to venture more than 15 miles from shore?"

He nodded. "That is true."

"Then," I said, "they are no good for our purpose. We need pilots who can navigate over water."

We decided to take Marine planes, twelve F4F's. The conference broke up then, but I stayed with Kimmel the rest of the morning, returned after lunch, and remained until six, discussing this project. The utmost secrecy was imperative. We wanted no Japanese agent in the Hawaiians to warn Tokyo that we were arming Wake and Midway with planes. Indeed, except for the officers at the conference and the other members of Kimmel's staff whose duties required the information, only two officers were told—Comdr. Miles R. Browning, my Chief of Staff, and Maj. Paul A. Putnam, commanding Marine Fighting Squadron 211, which had been selected for the assignment. In order to get his pilots onto the *Enterprise* without arousing suspicion, Putnam told them they were going out for two days' experimental work. They landed aboard with overnight kits and the clothes they were wearing. The next time their heroic survivors returned to that longitude was after almost four years in the hellholes of Japanese prison camps.

We fully expected that this cruise would take us into the lion's

73

mouth, and that at any moment an overt act would precipitate war. Before we shoved off, I asked Kimmel, "How far do you want me to go?"

His reply was characteristic: "Goddammit, use your common sense!"

I consider that as fine an order as a subordinate ever received. It was by no means an attempt to pass the buck. He was simply giving me full authority, as the man on the spot, to handle the situation as I saw it, and I knew that he would back me to the hilt.

☆ 6 ☆

TASK FORCE 2 sortied from Pearl Harbor at 0700 on November 28. When we were clear of the channel, I split off the *Enterprise*, three heavy cruisers, and nine destroyers, and designated them Task Force 8. I then directed the second senior in command in TF 2, Rear Adm. Milo F. Draemel, to take charge of our three battleships and remaining cruisers and destroyers and proceed to the drill grounds for normal work, while TF 8 stood to eastward as a feint. The decision to split TF 2 had been threshed out in the conference the day before. Our reasoning was: (1) we had to sortie with the battleships to create an illusion that this was only a routine exercise, but (2) the planes had to reach Wake as soon as possible, and (3) the 17-knot battleships not only would be a drag on the 30-knot *Enterprise*, cruisers, and destroyers, but (4) could give us little protection if we met the Japanese fleet, in which event our greatest safety lay in speed.

When TF 8 was beyond signal distance of TF 2 and Pearl Harbor, I requested the captain of the *Enterprise*, Capt. George D. Murray, to issue Battle Order No. 1, which began

1. The *Enterprise* is now operating under war conditions.
2. At any time, day or night, we must be ready for instant action.
3. Hostile submarines may be encountered. . . .

At the same time I sent a general signal to TF 8, directing that war heads be placed on all torpedoes immediately, that all planes be armed with bombs or torpedoes, and that they carry their full allowance of ammunition. I ordered further that the pilots were to

75

sink any shipping sighted and shoot down any plane encountered. (I had been informed, of course, that no American or Allied shipping was in the waters I had to traverse.)

Miles Browning, Paul Putnam, and I were still the only men along who knew our destination, so my order burst on the task force like a thousand-pounder. My operations officer, Comdr. William H. Buracker, brought it to me and asked incredulously, "Admiral, did you authorize this thing?"

"Yes."

"Do you realize that this means war?"

"Yes."

Bill protested, "Goddammit, Admiral, you can't start a private war of your own! Who's going to take the responsibility?"

I replied, "I'll take it! If anything gets in my way, we'll shoot first and argue afterwards."

Since it was vital for delivery of these planes to be concealed from the enemy, I was prepared to destroy his snoopers, preferably before they could make a radio report of our presence. Accordingly, we maintained rigid radio silence, flew an antisubmarine patrol during daylight hours, and every morning and evening we searched the ocean for 300 miles around. I believed that war was a matter of days, possibly hours, and that if we had to fight, our only chance of survival—and even of getting off an alert to the Commander in Chief before our ships were annihilated—was to strike the first blow. I felt that I would be completely justified in striking it. We did not, in all honesty, expect to encounter any Japanese warships, since the war warning of the day before had indicated that they were probably bound south, not east; but if we *had* encountered them, I would have assumed at once that they were en route to launch one of the sneak attacks with which Japan's history abounds.

At 0700 on December 4, when we reached a position about 200 miles from Wake, I launched the Marine F4F's and turned back toward Pearl. We had planned to enter the channel at 0730 on the seventh, but because head seas delayed the fueling of the destroyers, we were still 200 miles out at dawn that historic morning. At 0600, I sent eighteen of our planes ahead to land at Ford Island, the naval air station, then went below to relax in the flag quarters. (I had been using my emergency cabin in the island structure.) I

76

shaved, bathed, put on a clean uniform, and joined my flag secretary, Lt. H. Douglas Moulton, at breakfast. We were on our second cups of coffee when the phone rang. Doug answered it. I heard him say, "Moulton. . . . *What?* . . . Roger!" He turned to me: "Admiral, the staff duty officer says he has a message that there's an air raid on Pearl!"

I leaped up. "My God, they're shooting at my own boys! Tell Kimmel!"

We had not notified Pearl to expect our planes, which were due to arrive at this very time, so I jumped to the conclusion that some trigger-happy AA gunners had failed to recognize them. I was frantic. Just then my communications officer, Lt. Comdr. Leonard J. Dow, came in and handed me a dispatch:

From: CINCPAC
To: All ships present
AIR RAID ON PEARL HARBOR X THIS IS NO DRILL.

We notified all hands over the loud-speaker and sent the ship to general quarters. That was at 0812. At 0823 we received this:

From: CINCPAC
To: All ships present
ALERT X JAPANESE PLANES ATTACKING PEARL AND AIR FIELDS ON OAHU.

At 0903,

From: CINCPAC
To: All ships present
HOSTILITIES WITH JAPAN COMMENCE WITH AIR RAID ON PEARL.

And at 0921,

From: CINCPAC
To: Task Forces 3-8-12
RENDEZVOUS AS CTF-8 DIRECTS X FURTHER INSTRUCTIONS WHEN ENEMY LOCATED.

TF 3, consisting of the heavy cruiser *Indianapolis* and a few destroyers, was then in the vicinity of Johnston Island. TF 12, consisting of the *Lexington*, three cruisers, and some destroyers, was en route to garrison Midway with Marine fighting planes, just as we had garrisoned Wake. In addition, all available ships at Pearl were ordered to sortie, form TF 2, and report to me, thus giving me operational command of every ship at sea. While we waited for the three task forces to join us, we maneuvered off Kaula Rock, about 150 miles west of Pearl. Presently an old four-stack destroyer came over the eastern horizon at a tremendous rate of knots and ripped past us without a word. I signaled, "Where are you headed?"

She replied, "Don't know. My orders are to steam west at top speed."

"Join up," I said. I never learned who gave her her original orders, but if I hadn't intercepted her, and if her fuel had held out, she probably would have fetched up on the China coast.

I can best describe the rest of the day by quoting from my official war diary, as kept by my flag secretary:

> So many false reports being received from unknown sources concerning presence of enemy ships, carriers, transports, and submarines that it is very difficult to glean the true from the false.

One of the first of these reports stated that a patrol plane had sunk an enemy sub off the entrance to Pearl. This proved true, but the others were false almost without exception. I have always suspected that many of them originated from the Jap force or from espionage centers on Oahu. It was not until several days later, when Intelligence examined charts found on the bodies of Japanese carrier pilots, that their launching point was located, about 200 miles north of Oahu.

> From best information available, some of our planes which were sent to Pearl this morning arrived just in the midst of the Japanese attack and were shot down by their planes and our own antiaircraft on Oahu.

My first assumption had been correct. We learned later that five of the eighteen planes from the *Enterprise* had been shot down. Those who have never experienced a surprise attack may find it hard to understand how AA could shoot down friendly planes, but when you have seen your ships bombed and torpedoed and your comrades killed, no planes look friendly. As the war developed, we had better control and better identification, and such accidents were rare.

At 1100, Admiral Halsey informed Admiral Kimmel that he was depending on him for scouting information.

I could provide little for myself. Half my scouting planes had already been flown into Pearl, and I needed the rest for offensive action if we discovered the enemy.

At 1105, hoisted battle flags and informed CINCPAC accordingly.

During normal cruising, the national ensign is flown from the gaff, but when action is about to be joined, it flies from the foremast and mainmast as well. I believe that this is the first time in its annals that the Pacific Fleet ever hoisted battle flags.

At 1320, changed course to 170 and increased speed, after report of presence of submarines by the [destroyer] *Benham*. Shortly thereafter *Benham* dropped eight depth charges and noted oil slick and debris in the area of the contact.

This was a new *Benham*, of course, not my veteran of World War I.

At 1330, received a message from the Department that Japan announced a state of war exists between herself and the United States—Great Britain.

Japan attacks, kills our citizens, shoots down our planes, sinks our ships; then bows and tells us, "Excuse, please, but have decided to declare war!"

Late in the afternoon, TF 1 joined up—four cruisers and a few destroyers. Milo Draemel, commanding, reported to me and added, "I fear that Anderson's force is incapacitated." Rear Adm. Walter S. Anderson commanded the battleships at Pearl. This was the first I heard of what had happened to them. "Incapacitated" seems mild.

A new dispatch located the enemy to the southwest, so I formed a scouting line of all ships in the combined task forces, except the *Enterprise* and her plane-guard destroyers, and ordered them to search and to open fire on contact. They found nothing. Now came another dispatch: an enemy carrier was south of Pearl. The only weapons I had left were twenty-one planes of Torpedo Squadron 6. I launched them all, accompanied by six smoke planes and six fighters. Again they found nothing. The fighters continued to Pearl, where four of them were shot down by our AA, despite our notification of their arrival. The torpedo planes and the smokers returned to the ship about 2100. That was one of the blackest nights I have ever seen, and not only was TORPRON 6 untrained in night landings, but these planes were carrying torpedoes armed with war heads. Somehow they all got back aboard safely—the first time, to my knowledge, that planes ever landed under such dangerous conditions.

The *Enterprise* and her destroyers proceeded independently that night, with plans to rendezvous with the rest of TF 8 at dawn. The confusing and conflicting reports that had poured in on us all day had succeeded only in enraging me. It is bad enough to be blindfolded, but it is worse to be led around the compass. I waited all night for the straight word, and all night I reviewed my situation. Suppose that the enemy was located, and suppose that I could intercept him: what then? A surface engagement was out of the question, since I had nothing but cruisers to oppose his heavy ships. In addition, we were perilously low on fuel; the *Enterprise* was down to 50 per cent of her capacity, the cruisers to 30 per cent, the destroyers to 20 per cent. On the other hand, my few remaining planes might inflict some damage, and by the next forenoon the *Lexington's* task force would reach a position from which her air group could support an attack. If only someone would give us the straight word!

Well, the milk was spilled, and the horse was stolen; there is nothing to be done about it now. I am sure I made mistakes in judgment during the four years that followed, but I have the consolation of knowing that, on the opening day of the war, I did everything in my power to find a fight.

The war diary continues next day:

At 1100, *Enterprise* with a screen of seven destroyers proceeding to Pearl for fuel. The remainder of this force ordered to operate 50 miles to the northward of the Oahu-Kauai line. Learned that 21-P-1 [a scout plane] had made an unsuccessful and unopposed attack on a Japanese carrier in the vicinity of Johnston Island.

The "Japanese carrier" turned out to be our heavy cruiser *Portland*.

During the early forenoon, Brom Nichol, my former flight instructor at Pensacola and now my assistant operations officer, flew back aboard from Pearl and brought us our first eyewitness account of the disaster. Comdr. Howard L. Young, commanding the *Enterprise* air group, had flown him in the day before to give Admiral Kimmel a verbal report on Wake, which I didn't want to put on the air, and to arrange for the berthing and logistic requirements of TF 8. As they approached Oahu, Brom noticed a lot of AA fire and wondered why the Army was having flak practice on a Sunday. He paid no attention to the planes in the air until one of them dived on their SBD; even then he thought it was a young Army pilot showing off. He glanced at his wings; pieces of metal were shredding away. He glanced at the other plane; there was a Rising Sun on its fuselage. He jumped to unlimber his guns, but by then "Cy" Young was letting down for a landing on Ford Island. Brom dashed to CINCPAC's headquarters. He was standing at the window there when the *Arizona* went up.

I asked him, "How was Admiral Kimmel?"

He answered in one word: "Splendid!"

It was dusk when we entered Pearl Harbor, but I could see enough to make me grit my teeth. The worst was the sight of the *Utah*, sunk at her berth—the berth that the *Enterprise* would have occupied if we had not been delayed.

CAPTAIN MOULTON:

We watched the entry from the bridge. The Admiral was silent for a while, then we heard him mutter, "Before we're through with 'em, the Japanese language will be spoken only in hell!"

I was in such a hurry to see Kimmel that I commandeered the first boat I found. Machine-gunners were firing at everything that moved, and bullets whizzed around us all the way to CINCPAC's landing, but the black-out saved us from damage. In peacetime Pearl, the officers wore whites on Sundays. Kimmel and his staff were still wearing their Sunday uniforms, crumpled, and spotted with mud. Their faces were haggard and unshaven, but their chins were up. Kimmel himself was a marvel of cool efficiency, although the hysteria that surged around him mounted by the minute: eight Japanese transports had been seen rounding Barbers Point; Jap

81

gliders and paratroopers—their uniforms were described—had just landed at Kaneohe. I broke out laughing.

Kimmel wheeled on me. "What the hell is there to laugh at?"

I said, "I've heard a lot of wild reports in my life, but that's the wildest I *ever* heard! The Japs can't possibly tow gliders here from their nearest base, and certainly they're not going to waste their precious carrier decks on any such nonsense. My God!"

Even then, I think everyone present knew that the disaster would be formally investigated, but I'll take my oath that not one of us would have guessed that the blame would fall on Kimmel, because not one of us thought he deserved it—any part of it. I want to emphasize my next statement. *In all my experience, I have never known a Commander in Chief of any United States Fleet who worked harder, and under more adverse circumstances, to increase its efficiency and to prepare it for war; further, I know of no officer who might have been in command at that time who could have done more than Kimmel did.* I also want to repeat and reemphasize the answer I made when the Roberts Commission asked me how I happened to be ready for the Japanese attack. I told them, "Because of one man: Admiral Kimmel."

Who, then, is to blame? Look at it logically: the attack succeeded because Admiral Kimmel and General Short could not give Pearl Harbor adequate protection. They could not give it because they did not have it to give. They did not have it because Congress would not authorize it. Congress is elected by the American people. And the blame for Pearl Harbor rests squarely on the American people and nowhere else. Instead of trying to dodge our responsibility by smirching two splendid officers, we should be big enough to acknowledge our mistakes—and wise enough to profit by them.

We finished fueling the *Enterprise* at 0500 next morning, the ninth, and sortied at once, under orders to patrol northward of the islands in search of enemy submarines, which Intelligence believed were en route to take up raiding positions along the West Coast of the mainland. In fact, an enemy carrier was reported as already operating off California. I have said that Kimmel was cool, but this was far from true of the entire naval establishment. Some of its hysteria we carried to sea with us, as was natural with so many inexperienced youngsters aboard. Our lookouts were spying periscope feathers in every whitecap and torpedoes in every porpoise. These jitters cost us time and fuel, because every time a contact was reported, we had to maneuver the task force away at high speed. However, the *Benham* made a contact that seemed meaty, and was working it out when one of my younger officers shouted, "Look! She's sinking! There she goes!"

I put my glasses on her; she was hull down in a trough but rode up on the next crest. My own nerves must have been a little raw. I told the officer, "If you ever make another report like that, sir, I'll throw you over the side!"

As the day passed, the lookouts' jitters became worse. Finally I sent this signal to the task force: IF ALL THE TORPEDO WAKES RE-PORTED ARE FACTUAL, JAPANESE SUBMARINES WILL SOON HAVE TO RETURN TO BASE FOR A RELOAD, AND WE WILL HAVE NOTHING TO FEAR X IN ADDITION, WE ARE WASTING TOO MANY DEPTH CHARGES ON NEUTRAL FISH X TAKE ACTION ACCORDINGLY.

This rebuke was not intended for our patrols, who were less excitable but equally alert. Next day, indeed, they spotted three enemy subs. One dived before she could be bombed, but the second was classed as "damaged," and the third sank vertically, leaving four of her deck crew struggling in the water.

This same day, the *Enterprise's* radar failed temporarily, just as our lookouts reported the approach of a large flight of planes. We were on the point of opening fire and repeating one of the most painful features of December 7 when the planes were recognized as part of our inner air patrol.

We stayed at sea six days more without incident. When we returned, we found that Admiral Kimmel had been relieved at his own request, and that acting CINCPAC was Vice Admiral Pye. In a conference with him on the eighteenth, I was informed that TF 11, with the *Lexington*, would make a bombing attack on Wotje, while TF 14, with the *Saratoga*, landed reinforcements of men and planes at Wake and attacked enemy ships expected to be found there. My instructions were to proceed with TF 8 to the vicinity of Midway and cover their northern flank.

TF 8 sortied at 1000 on the nineteenth. At 1545 next day, a dispatch ordered TF 11 to cancel its strike on Wotje and TF 14 to hold the *Sara* well away from Wake and to send in the aircraft tender

Tangier instead, without air cover. Wake was our farthest atoll outpost; we had been following the fortunes of its heroic defenders almost hour by hour, and the whole Pacific Fleet was impatient to help them in their desperate fight. When the *Sara's* pilots learned that they were being kept on the deck, many of them sat down and cried. Two days later, they had real reason to cry. On the basis of Wake's famous dispatch, reporting that the enemy was landing and "situation in doubt," CINCPAC ordered TF 11 to return to Pearl, and TF 14, with TF 8 supporting, to deliver its reinforcements to Midway. TF 14 could have been at Wake by then, of course, raising hell with the Jap occupation. Why we were diverted I still don't know. All we knew was that the war was only fifteen days old, and we had already lost Wake and Guam.

Perhaps confusion is to blame. On the thirteenth, a Navy Department bulletin had announced, wrongly, that Jap task forces were operating in the eastern Pacific. Now we were informed that enemy vessels were firing star shells over Johnston Island, and we had steamed toward it for five hours at an expensive 25 knots before we received a correction—it was only a submarine.

We discharged our mission at Midway and reentered Pearl on the thirty-first. What a miserable cruise this was! When I look back on it, the only redeeming feature I can find is this trivial one—for the first and only time in my life, I celebrated a double Christmas. On the afternoon of December 24, we crossed the international date line, westbound, and the following day we recrossed it, eastbound. On the first Christmas I signaled "Merry Christmas" to the force; on the second, I hoisted the same signal with the "first repeater" pennant.

TF 8 sortied again on January 3, to cover the approach of a convoy from the States, but this was a quick job; we were back on the seventh and started fueling and reprovisioning at once. Meanwhile, two extremely important appointments had been made: on December 20, Ernie King became CINCUS (Commander in Chief United States Fleet), and on the thirty-first, Chester Nimitz became CINCPAC, with the rank of admiral. Chester sent for me on the ninth. We usually begin our conversations by swapping a yarn or two, but this time he didn't waste a minute. He said that the Japs had just snapped up the British-governed Gilbert Islands, and if—as it appeared—this was in preparation for a jump to Samoa, 1,300 miles farther southeastward, they would soon be sitting astride our line of communications with New Zealand and Australia, unless we jolted them hard and fast. But how and where? Our amphibious forces were far from ready to seize any Jap territory or to recapture any of our own, so it was up to the fast carrier task forces. The mission chosen for them was half-defensive, half-offensive. The Marine garrison at Samoa was being reinforced, as insurance against the loss of the islands and to develop them as both a base and a possible springboard. These troops were being escorted out from San Diego by Rear Adm. Frank Jack Fletcher, commanding TF 17, which included the *Yorktown*, the heavy cruiser *Louisville*, the light cruiser *St. Louis*, and four destroyers. I would sail for Samoa with TF 8, and as soon as the landing was completed, I would lead both forces in a strike against the Marshalls and Gilberts.

"How does that sound?" Chester asked. "It's a rare opportunity!"

I agreed, but with something less than enthusiasm. We knew very little about the Marshalls except that the Treaty of Versailles had mandated them to Japan, with provisos against fortification. We suspected that Japan had regarded this pledge with contempt, as usual, and had built airfields and submarine bases at Kwajalein, but the whole area had been closed to aliens for so many years that Intelligence could brief us scarcely at all. However, I had a vivid recollection of an exercise on CINCPAC's big game-board, a few weeks before, in which the team attacking Kwajalein had been driven off with heavy losses.

I saw Chester again next day to get my last-minute instructions and to say what I hoped was au revoir. When I left, he walked down to my barge with me, and as I stepped aboard, he called, "All sorts of good luck to you, Bill!"

Good luck? I have never been on an operation cursed with worse luck! Every day brought a new sample, tolerable in itself for the most part, but cumulating to a demoralizing jinx. The day we sortied, January 11, our *bon voyage* present was the news that the *Saratoga* had been torpedoed and would be laid up for months, thereby reducing our carrier strength in the Pacific to three ships —the *Enterprise*, *Yorktown*, and *Lexington*. On the thirteenth, one

MANCHURIA

HOKKAIDO

SEA OF JAPAN

KOREA

SHANTUNG

QUELPART

Shanghai

1400 MILES

Yu-shan

Nimrod Sound

CHINA

OKINAWA

HONSHU

Tokyo

Launched April 18th

999 MILES

J A P A N

SHIKOKU

KYUSHU

RYUKYO IS.

IWO JIMA

BONIN IS.

MARCUS

Mar 4th

FORMOSA

Takao
Koshun

Hong-Kong

HAINAN

CHINA

SEA

LUZON

MARIANAS

SAIPAN

GUAM

PHILIPPINE ISLANDS

Manila

FRENCH INDOCHINA

PALAWAN

Davao

MINDANAO

Brunei
Bay

Brunei

CELEBES

BORNEO

YAP

ULITHI

PALAU
IS.

CAROLINE

TRUK

ISLANDS

EQUATOR

Kavieng
Rabaul

MANUS

NEW IRELAND

Hollandia

BISMARCK
ARCH.

NEW
GUINEA

Lae

NEW BRITAIN

SOLOMON

J A V A

Port
Moresby

TIMOR

Darwin

Battle of
Coral Sea
May 7-8

INDIAN

OCEAN

A U S T R A L I A

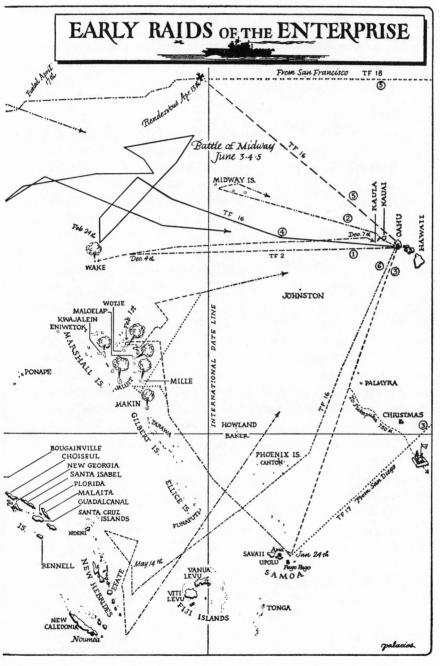

EARLY RAIDS OF THE ENTERPRISE

From San Francisco   TF 18
⑤

Fueled April 17th

Rendezvous Apr 13th

Battle of Midway
June 3-4-5

TF 16

MIDWAY IS.
⑤

KAULA
KAUAI

②
OAHU
HAWAII

TF 16

Feb 24th

④

Dec.7th

Dec. 4th
TF 2
①

WAKE

⑥
③

JOHNSTON

WOTJE
MALOELAP
KWAJALEIN
ENIWETOK

Feb 1st

MARSHALL IS.

PONAPE

JALUIT
MILLE

MAKIN

PALMYRA

To Palmyra 150 M.

CHRISTMAS
③

INTERNATIONAL DATE LINE

TF 16

GILBERT IS.
TARAWA

HOWLAND
BAKER

BOUGAINVILLE
CHOISEUL
NEW GEORGIA
SANTA ISABEL
FLORIDA
MALAITA
GUADALCANAL
SANTA CRUZ
ISLANDS

ELLICE IS.

FUNAFUTI

PHOENIX IS.
CANTON

From San Diego
TF 17

IS.

NDENI

RENNELL

May 14th

NEW HEBRIDES

EFATE

VANUA
LEVU

SAVAII   Apia   Jan 24th
UPOLU
Pago Pago
SAMOA

VITI
LEVU

NEW
CALEDONIA

Noumea

FIJI ISLANDS

TONGA

palacios

of our scout pilots singlehandedly jeopardized the whole expedition by losing his head and breaking radio silence to report engine trouble. On the fourteenth, the destroyer *Blue* lost a man overboard. On the sixteenth, a seaman was killed in a turret accident on the heavy cruiser *Salt Lake City*; an *Enterprise* scout plane crashed on deck, killing a machinist's mate; and one of her torpedo planes failed to return.

The crew of this plane, we learned weeks later, struggled into their rubber raft and drifted for thirty-four days under the tropical sun with virtually no food or water, before they finally fetched up on Pukapuka, 750 miles away. I had the pleasure of seeing the three men decorated, and after the ceremony I asked the captain of the plane, Aviation Chief Machinist's Mate Harold F. Dixon, "Are you still speaking to me, after the way I had to go off and leave you?"

He answered, "Yes, sir. I knew what you were up against."

On the seventeeth, we lost a scout plane, which crashed into the water, killing the radioman and crippling the pilot. On the twentieth, a torpedo plane scored a direct hit on an enemy submarine, but the bomb failed to explode. (Complaints about the inferiority of our bombs and torpedoes became familiar in the next two years.) Early on the morning of the twenty-second, the destroyers *Fanning* and *Gridley* collided in a heavy rain, with such damage to their bows that they had to return to Pearl. That afternoon, a scout plane from the heavy cruiser *Northampton* spotted a small schooner and exchanged messages by blinker, but because the schooner could not give the correct recognition signal, the pilot stupidly ordered her abandoned and then proceeded to bomb and strafe her. It turned out that she was a Britisher from Apia, engaged in searching for the crew of a plane which the *Salt Lake City* had lost on the twentieth but had recovered the next day.

American pilots did not have a monopoly on stupidity. On the twenty-fifth, one of our dive bombers encountered a strange four-engine flying boat which refused to answer any signals. We knew that Jap planes of this type were in the vicinity, so when the stranger ignored a warning burst across his bows, our pilot put a shot through the fuselage. That brought results; the crew belatedly broke out an Australian flag. They were lucky to be alive to do so, because this incident occurred at a time when we were particularly touchy:

88

the landings at Samoa had been completed the day before, and our two task forces were running northwest for the attack.

The original plan called for Frank Jack to hit Makin in the Gilberts, and Jaluit and Mili in the southern Marshalls, while I, with the stronger force, took on Wotje and Maloelap in the northeastern Marshalls. On the twenty-seventh, however, a reconnaissance submarine reported that the whole Marshall group was lightly defended, and Miles Browning urged me to drive straight in and hit Kwajalein too. He argued that although the *Enterprise* would have to be exposed almost within rifle shot of Wotje, the risk was justified by the probability of a rich concentration of ships and planes. It was one of those plans which are called "brilliant" if they succeed and "foolhardy" if they fail. Against my better judgment, I let myself be persuaded to adopt it and I notified Frank Jack that I was adding Kwajalein to my list.

Specifically, I divided TF 8 into three task groups—Rear Adm. Ray Spruance's TG 8.1, the *Northampton* and *Salt Lake City* and the destroyer *Dunlap*, would bombard Wotje; Capt. Thomas M. Shock's TG 8.3, the heavy cruiser *Chester* and the destroyers *Balch* and *Maury*, would bombard Maloelap; and my TG 8.5, the *Enterprise* and the destroyers *Ralph Talbot*, *Blue*, and *McCall*, would hit both Wotje and Maloelap but would focus on Kwajalein.

The attack was set for February 1.* Before I describe it, there are three small things I want to mention. First, we had to fuel the force. The *Enterprise's* turn at the tanker did not come until 2000 and she did not finish until 0130 next day—the first time that a heavy ship ever fueled at night in the open sea. Second, I ordered all ships to rig for towing and for being towed, so that we could pass a hawser to a cripple and tow her away without wasting time. Lastly, on the afternoon of the thirty-first, our radar picked up a Jap patrol plane. We crouched over the screen, watching him close our formation and waiting for his radio to broadcast the alarm. Although he came within 34 miles, the haze evidently hid us, because he serenely continued his patrol. When he had disappeared, I sent for my Japanese language officer and gave him a message:

---

* Editor's note: This is the local, east longitude date. Navy communiques and official records generally use Washington, or west longitude, dates. All dates in Admiral Halsey's narrative are as of his whereabouts at the time.

From the American admiral in charge of the striking force, to the Japanese admiral on the Marshall Islands:

It is a pleasure to thank you for having your patrol plane not sight my force.

This was translated into Japanese, and our planes dropped copies next morning, in the hope that the pilot either would be shot or would have to commit hara-kiri.

At 1830 on the thirty-first, the task groups split up for the run-in to their different stations. The night was clear and calm, and I was the exact opposite. As a commanding officer on the eve of his first action, I felt that I should set an example of composure, but I was so nervous that I took myself to my emergency cabin, out of sight. I couldn't sleep. I tossed and twisted, drank coffee, read mystery stories, and smoked cigarettes. Finally I gave up and went back to flag plot. There, at about 0300, less than 2 hours before we were due to launch, I received a terrifying report. The staff duty officer, Lt. Comdr. S. Everett Burroughs, Jr., came in from the bridge and announced, "Sir, sand has just blown in my face!"

I have already said that the Marshalls area had long been *kapu* (*tabu*, forbidden, keep out). We knew that our charts were old and we were afraid that they were incomplete and inaccurate as well. (Of course, even the best navigation charts don't show mine fields.) When sand blows onto a ship, there is a strong suggestion that land is close aboard; and when the ship is making 25 knots, there is a further suggestion that the situation will clarify quickly and violently.

I could do nothing but tell Evvie to go out and investigate. He returned in a moment, grinning. Suddenly inspired, he had licked his fingers, pressed them against the sand on the deck, and licked them again. The "sand" tasted sweet. On the range-finder platform forward of the bridge, he could dimly make out a sailor stirring a cup.

We began to launch at 0443, under a full moon. Nine torpedo planes, each loaded with three 500-pound bombs, took off for Kwajalein; and thirty-seven dive bombers, each loaded with one 500-pounder and two 100-pounders, took off for Roi, one of the chief islands in the big Kwajalein atoll. At the same time we launched six fighters as a CAP (combat air patrol). The course to

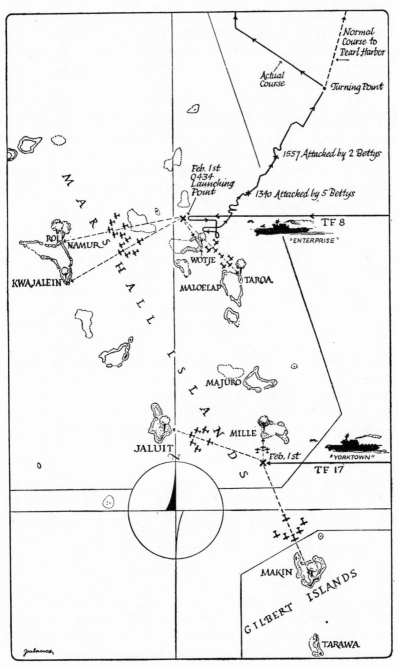

the target and the retirement course were not crowflight, but roundabout, via certain landmarks. This gave us two advantages: enemy planes would be deceived as to the exact position of our task group, and recognition of our own planes would be facilitated by their return on a fixed bearing.

The strike on Roi was timed for 0658, fifteen minutes before sunrise. Although the bombers were in sight of it at 0653, the mist, the darkness, and their inadequate maps, which were no more than photostats of old charts, prevented them from identifying the target until 0705, and the defenders were thus given thirteen minutes' warning. This was ample for them to alert their AA crews and get their fighters into the air, and the war's first bomb to fall on Japanese territory had barely been released by Lt. Comdr. Hallsted L. Hopping, when he was shot down by a burst of AA. Three other bombers were also lost, but our planes succeeded in destroying three fighters and seven bombers, an ammunition dump, two big hangars, a fuel depot, and the radio building.

The pickings at Kwajalein were fatter and softer. The AA was intense, but there was no fighter interception, and shipping was so abundant—a light cruiser, two big merchantmen, five submarines, three tankers, and dozens of smaller vessels—that the strike leader radioed for additional planes to come down and help him flatten them. Accordingly, at 0705 eighteen bombers were dispatched from the squadron over Roi, some 40 miles away, and at 0731, nine more torpedo planes, armed with torpedoes this time, were launched from the *Enterprise*, now 180 miles away. These torpedo planes, TBD's, were not only slow and unwieldy, but were flying without fighter protection into an area which had been thoroughly aroused, yet they pressed home their attack with a vigor that reached my earphones: "Get away from that cruiser, Jack! She's mine!" and, "Bingo!" and, "Look at that big bastard burn!"

I learned later that the masthead level of the attack had panicked the Japs into firing on their own ships and shore batteries. This makes it difficult to assign credit for the destruction, but our estimate was two submarines sunk; the light cruiser, a small carrier, and four auxiliaries either sunk or severely damaged; two four-engine patrol planes destroyed on the water, and a large compound shattered by three direct hits. All our planes returned.

After those three quick strikes on Kwajalein, we let it alone for the rest of the day. Meanwhile, we had sent eleven fighters against Taroa Island, in the Maloelap atoll, and Wotje. Both these fighter sweeps were geared to a bombardment by the other two task groups. Over Wotje, we had control of the air, and Ray Spruance's group was not threatened except by ineffective shore batteries. But Tommy Shock, at Taroa, was bombed three times, one small bomb striking the *Chester's* well deck and killing eight men.

Our surface bombardments were followed by a series of dive-bombing attacks. That day the *Enterprise* launched and landed twenty-one times. The pilots and crewmen would fly off and fight, fly back and take a breather while their planes were being refueled and rearmed, and then fly off and fight again. Three of these strikes were led by Lt. Comdr. William R. Hollingsworth, the skipper of Bombing 6. When he returned from the third, around 1300, he made his usual report to the bridge, then added, "Admiral, don't you think it's about time we got the hell out of here?"

For nine hours we had been maneuvering the *Enterprise* in a rectangle only 5 miles by 20, so close to Wotje that my naked eye could see its AA bursting around our planes and—a more cordial sight—a column of smoke from the burning installations. We had been riding our luck hard enough; we had already dodged a periscope, and enemy planes were bound to pick up our trail soon.

I told Hollingsworth, "My boy, I've been thinking the same thing myself!" And right there we formed a club that later achieved some notoriety. It was called "Haul Out with Halsey."

The club was a little slow in getting organized. At 1340, five twin-engine Jap bombers, of the type subsequently dubbed "Betty," broke through the overcast and glided down on our starboard bow. Our AA guns might as well have been water pistols. We could see the bomb bays open and distinguish each separate bomb as it dropped. Miles Browning yelled, "Down!" but I was already on the deck, "the fustest and the flattest." In fact, the footprints of most of the other men on the bridge were printed on my back. The fifteen bombs fell into the water, but the nearest one was close enough to kill a man in the port after gun-gallery, riddle the side of the ship, and cut a gasoline riser, causing a small fire.

CAPTAIN BROWNING:

The Admiral was wearing an old white sun helmet. We had begged him to swap it for one less conspicuous, but all we could get out of him was a grunt: "Gives 'em something better to shoot at!"

This was the very first time I had ever been under attack, so I reviewed my reactions. I was scared, yes, but I think I am honest in stating that my dominant emotion was rage. I didn't have much time to consider the question. One Betty slid out of the formation and turned back toward us. Although both its engines were afire, the pilot made a perfect approach up the groove, with the evident intention of crashing among the planes parked on the forward end of our flight deck.

Now occurred one of those things that make you doubly proud to be an American. A young aviation mechanic named Bruno Peter Gaida jumped into the rear seat of the rearmost plane, an SBD, grabbed its gun, and opened up. I saw it myself, and everything that followed. It had been my turn to trample, and I had rushed to the inboard bridge rail over the backs of my prostrate staff. The Betty staggered on, straight for us, but the *Enterprise's* skipper, George Murray, threw his helm hard over at the right instant. The Jap couldn't correct his course. His wing dropped and slashed the tail off the SBD, not 3 feet from where Gaida was crouched, then the whole plane struck the port edge of the flight deck and toppled over the side—the first *kamikaze* of the war.

I took a deep breath and stepped into flag plot for a steadying cup of coffee. While I was drinking it, I happened to look up and catch the yeoman of the day grinning at me.

"What are *you* laughing at?" I asked.

The man was embarrassed. He mumbled, "Nothing, sir."

I asked Miles, "Who is this man?"

Miles must have thought I was daffy. "Why, Admiral," he said, "that's Bowman. He's on your staff."

I said, "I don't mean that. What's his rate?"

"Yeoman first class, sir."

"That's where you're wrong," I said. "He's a *chief* yeoman. Any man who can grin like that while my knees are cracking together deserves to be promoted." It gives me pleasure to add that Ira N. Bowman is now a lieutenant.

94

EDITOR's NOTE:

The consensus of Admiral Halsey's staff is that he has caricatured himself under fire here and hereafter. They say, "We always had to watch him before an action to keep him from worrying too much. We'd have to send him out of the chart room and see that he got some sleep. But as soon as the shooting started, he was as cool and quiet as you please."

We had reformed the task force and were retiring at 30 knots when, at 1555, we were attacked by two more Bettys. The first five had glided down to 1,500 feet; these two stayed up at 14,000, and the nearest of their bombs landed well out on our starboard quarter. The skipper of our fighting squadron, Lt. Comdr. Clarence W. McClusky, was flying CAP at the time. The repeated failures of his .50-caliber guns and the Wildcats' inability to overtake the fast Bettys had reduced him to directing the ship's AA fire by radio, which he did well enough for one bomber to be shot down. The other fled for a huge cumulus cloud, with McClusky's section on its tail. We couldn't see them, but we could hear McClusky in our earphones: "Get out of my way, and let me knock that oriental son of a bitch out of the sky!" Presently Betty fragments sprinkled about us.

We were snooped all afternoon, and the night promised no relief. As before, it was clear and cloudless, with a brilliant moon that blazoned our 30-knot wakes as far astern as the horizon. Moreover, the Nips knew we had to follow a groove for a considerable distance, as there were outlying obstacles to be cleared before we had sea room to take a direct course to Pearl. With trailing sure and attack probable, and no night fighters to protect us, our only hope was trickery; when we reached the turning point, instead of taking the direct course of 075, we took a course of 335. It worked. We picked up the Nips on our radar, tracked them to the turning point, and watched them head out on 075. Better yet, my bright-eyed flag lieutenant and signal officer, Lt. William H. Ashford, Jr., spotted a wisp of a cloud which, as we fled toward it, developed into a beautiful overcast and eventually became a front that sheltered us all the way home. The Nips didn't abandon the hunt. We tracked them for two days more, but except for this and occasional submarine threats, the return to Pearl was uneventful.

When we reentered on February 5, flying our largest colors,

such a roar went up that Kailua must have heard it, across the island. The ships in the harbor blew their sirens, the crews yelled, and the troops at Hickam Field and the patients at Hospital Point cheered us all the way to our mooring. (Cheering a ship in is a custom of the Royal Navy; I had never heard it in ours before.) The men of the task force tried to cheer back but choked up. I myself cried and was not ashamed.

Chester Nimitz was down on the dock. He didn't wait for the *Enterprise* to lower a gangway; he came over the side in a bos'n's chair and, pumping my hand, told me, "Nice going!"

After him came COMDESPAC, Rear Adm. Robert A. Theobald, who shook his finger in my face and shouted, "Damn you, Bill, you've got no business getting home from that one! No business at all!"

(The reason we brought off these early raids is that we violated all the rules and traditions of naval warfare. We did the exact opposite of what the enemy expected. We did not keep our carriers behind the battle; we deliberately exposed them to shore-based planes. Most important, whatever we did, we did fast. I have heard that there was a popular saying on the *Enterprise* at this time, "The Admiral will get us in, and the Captain will get us out.")

Frank Jack Fletcher's TF 17 stood in next day, and we were able to round out the story of the operation. The jinx that had dogged us on our way to the Marshalls had transferred to them during the attack. Not only were their targets unproductive, but bad weather had aborted many of their strikes and had contributed to the loss of seven planes. However, they destroyed three four-engine seaplanes and two auxiliary ships, and damaged another auxiliary and a number of shore installations.

When the profit of the two forces is added, the total is not spectacular; but before I am accused of squandering too much space on what was at best a nuisance raid, it should be borne in mind that although it was barren in physical spoils, it was rich in Intelligence material—we had discovered operational airfields on Roi, Taroa, and Wotje—and richer still in morale. We had been whipped in the attack that opened the war and had been on the defensive ever since. When our task forces sortied for the Marshalls raid, you could almost smell the defeatism around Pearl. Now the offensive spirit was reestablished; officers and men were bushy-tailed again. So, presently, was the American public. At last we had been able to answer their roweling question, "Where is the Navy?"

Let me make quite certain that I am not misunderstood. Adm. Thomas C. Hart's Asiatic Fleet, based on Manila, had been fighting offensive actions and fighting them gloriously. But the Asiatic Fleet consisted of only one heavy cruiser, one light cruiser, and thirteen destroyers, plus submarines, PT boats, and some patrol planes. It was the Pacific Fleet, the big fleet, the fleet maimed at Pearl Harbor, that had now paid the first installment on its bill.

Miles Browning's strategy won him a promotion to captain, and he and I were each given a Distinguished Service Medal.

EDITOR'S NOTE:
Admiral Halsey's citation follows:
"For distinguished service in a duty of great responsibility as Commander of the Marshall Raiding Force, United States Pacific Fleet, and especially for his brilliant and audacious attack against the Marshall and Gilbert Islands on January 31, 1942 [west longitude date]. By his great skill and determination this drive inflicted heavy damage to enemy ships and planes."

When I received it, I called in my staff and told them, "This is as much for you as it is for me. You made it possible."

A few nights later, I went to a movie on the *Enterprise*. Before it started, I told the audience, the ship's company, "I want to make a little speech. I just want to say that I've never been so damn proud of anyone as I am of you!"

When we received orders for our next operation, we were appalled to find that not only had we been designated Task Force 13, but our sortie had been set for February 13, a Friday! Miles Browning and my Intelligence officer, Col. Julian P. Brown of the Marines, immediately went to CINCPAC's headquarters and asked his chief of staff, Capt. Charles H. McMorris, "What goes on here? Have you got it in for us, or what?"

"Sock" Morris agreed that no sane sailorman would dare buck such a combination of ill auspices, and changed our designation to TF 16 and our sortie to the fourteenth.

(Woodrow Wilson considered thirteen his lucky number,

curiously enough. When we escorted him to Brest in 1918, the *George Washington* would have made port on December 12 if he hadn't ordered her slowed down to arrive a day later. I have also been told that he believed there was something prophetic in the coincidence of thirteen letters in his name and thirteen states in the original union.)

My new command and my new mission were both substantially the same as before; TF 16 was the former TF 8, with the destroyer *Craven* substituted for the heavy cruiser *Chester;* and once again we were ordered to raid a Jap island base—Wake instead of the Marshalls—in the hope of slowing the enemy's advance, diverting his strength, and gaining information about his dispositions.

This raid was a minor milestone in that, preparing for it, we had the benefit of aerial photography for the first time. Pictures of Wake, taken by a Marine plane from Midway, were flown to Pearl for developing and interpretation, then flown out to us at sea. With the help of what we learned from them, we were able to plan our attacks. The bombardment group, TG 16.7, consisting of the two heavy cruisers *Northampton* and *Salt Lake City*, and a pair of destroyers, the *Maury* and *Balch*, would approach from the west; and TG 16.8, the *Enterprise* and the remaining four destroyers—*Dunlap*, *Blue*, *Ralph Talbot*, and *Craven*—would launch from about 100 miles north.

Our aerologists warned us that a tropical front hung close to our launching point, but they did not lead us to believe that the front would be as bad as it proved. The first plane was scheduled to take off at 0530 on February 24, for the strike to coincide with the bombardment at 0708, ten minutes before sunrise. When 0530 came, however, the wind and the rain were so violent that we postponed the launch until 0544, and even then one SBD crashed into the sea. The thick, low overcast caused a further delay; the planes could not find one another to rendezvous. The result was that the whole timetable was disjointed, and the strike did not arrive over the target until nearly 0800.

Meanwhile, TG 16.7 was waiting a scant 15 miles from Wake. We could not radio them about our difficulties, for fear of disclosing our position. For the same reason, the cruisers, not seeing our planes, postponed launching their scouts, knowing that the flash

98

of the catapult charges would be easily visible at so short a distance. As it turned out, they were spotted anyway, and if Wake had been able to put into the air anything more than three ineffective seaplanes, whose bombs fell wide, TG 16.7 might have had an ugly half hour before we could cover them.

The strike and the bombardment were finally executed. Together they destroyed three four-engine flying boats and three small craft, and damaged hangars, shore batteries, and fuel and ammunition dumps. Our losses were three planes, one to AA and the other two to the foul weather. The real profits from this raid were long range. Thanks in part to recommendations based on our experience, the strength of our carrier fighter squadrons was increased, incendiary ammunition was issued to our planes, and the installation of leakproof tanks was rushed.

We were retiring to the northeast to pick up TG 16.7 and our tanker, the *Sabine*, with her escort, the destroyer *McCall*, for the return to Pearl when, the following evening, a dispatch from CINCPAC caught us: DESIRABLE TO STRIKE MARCUS IF YOU THINK IT FEASIBLE.

Three mileages have always stuck in my head—Wellington, New Zealand, is 1,234 miles from Sydney; Espiritu Santo is 555 miles from Guadalcanal; and Marcus Island is 999 miles from Tokyo. That figure comprised our knowledge of Marcus, except that it was within easy range of planes from Iwo Jima and was supposed to be well-defended. This would be another morale raid. By venturing so near the home islands of the Empire, we would presumably disconcert the Japs and stimulate the Allies more than ever.

We reformed the task force next morning, the twenty-sixth, fueled the destroyers, and headed out on a course of 275. I remember the exact course because my staff officers made a point of glancing at the compass from time to time and muttering, "Two-seven-five. . . . Two-seven-five. . . . Why do we always seem to retire to the westward?"

We had intended to complete fueling by the twenty-seventh, but fueling is not a foul-weather operation, and here is the entry for that date in my war diary:

Overcast, low visibility, high wind, and heavy seas. As forecast indicates the continuation of these conditions in this area, course was changed to the southward to find conditions favorable to fueling heavy ships tomorrow.

The situation was more anxious than it may sound. The *Sabine* could supply enough fuel to take us to Marcus and back only if we shoved off by March 1. Here is the entry for the twenty-eighth:

Weather and sea conditions this morning preclude possibility of fueling.

We steamed at our most economical speed all night, watching the skies. Just before daybreak we saw the stars; the wind moderated, and that night the war diary read,

Completed fueling about 1700. *Enterprise, Northampton,* and *Salt Lake City* commencing run-in for air attack.

The destroyers were too light to match our speed through the heavy seas, and I was afraid they might delay both the attack and the retirement, so I ordered them to stay behind with the tanker.

We launched our strike—thirty-two bombers and six fighters— from 125 miles northeast of the target at 0447 on March 4 and guided it in by radar. The Japs were sound asleep. Their radio had just begun to yell when a direct hit knocked it off the air. This brought a plane over from Iwo to investigate, and during our withdrawal we had the satisfaction of hearing it make a report that caused an alert and a black-out in Tokyo. Our strike met no air opposition, but a bomber was lost to AA. On the credit side, we set fire to a fuel tank and destroyed several buildings flanking the airfield. If we accomplished nothing else, it was because there was little else to accomplish, either tactically or strategically. CINCPAC summed it up, "The raid against Marcus caused some concern as to the defenses of the Japanese homeland, but the exact amount of diversion from Japanese effort in the southwest cannot be measured at this time."

When the *Balch* had moored at Pearl on our return, she sent for a Marine guard to take custody of four prisoners salvaged from a gunboat she had sunk at Wake. Just as the first prisoner was brought topside, a pneumatic riveter cut loose on an adjacent ship, and I am told that the three Japs still below decks tried to scream the bulk- heads down: they thought their comrade was being welcomed with a machine gun.

A few days later, Miles Browning and I were called to CINC-PAC' sheadquarters for a conference with Rear Adm. Donald B. Duncan, from CINCUS. (Ernie King, not liking the implication of "CINCUS," may have changed his title to "COMINCH" by then; I'm not sure.) "Wu" Duncan told us that something big was in the air, something top-secret: Lt. Col. James H. Doolittle, with Navy cooperation, had trained sixteen Army crews to take B-25's off a carrier's deck, and the Navy had promised to launch them for Tokyo. They might not inflict much damage, Wu said, but they would certainly give Hirohito plenty to think about.

Chester Nimitz asked me, "Do you believe it would work, Bill?"

I said, "They'll need a lot of luck."

"Are you willing to take them out there?"

"Yes, I am."

"Good!" he said. "It's all yours!"

I suggested that the operation would run more smoothly if Miles and I could discuss it man-to-man with Doolittle, whom I had never met. Chester agreed and gave us orders to proceed to San Francisco. Our conference took place on March 31, and our talks boiled down to this: we would carry Jimmy within 400 miles of Tokyo, if we could sneak in that close; but if we were discovered sooner, we would have to launch him anyway, provided he was in reach of either Tokyo or Midway.

That suited Jimmy. We shook hands, and I wished him luck. The next time I saw him, he was Lieutenant General Doolittle, wearing the Medal of Honor.

The sixteen B-25's landed at the Alameda Air Base, near San Francisco, on April 1, taxied down to the dock, and were hoisted onto the flight deck of our newest carrier, the *Hornet*, Capt. Marc A. Mitscher commanding. To accommodate them, the *Hornet's* own planes had to be packed into her hangar deck. Her handling crews worked fast. In company with the rest of TF 18—the heavy cruiser *Vincennes*, the light cruiser *Nashville*, the destroyers *Gwin, Grayson, Meredith,* and *Monssen,* and the tanker *Cimarron*—she stood out of San Francisco next morning, under orders to take a circuitous route to the rendezvous with my ships on the twelfth.

Miles and I had expected to be back in Pearl on the second,

in ample time to polish our plans for the mission, but strong westerly winds grounded all westbound planes. We telephoned the air operations officers at Alameda and Pan American every day, and every day we were given the same report. On the fifth, we had to notify the *Hornet* to postpone our rendezvous for twenty-four hours. On the sixth, already sore and sour, I added a touch of flu to my other worries and took to my bed, loaded with dynamite pills. Naturally this was the afternoon that the winds died and our flight was scheduled. When I boarded the plane, I was so full of pills that I rattled, but I slept until a nosebleed woke me as we lost altitude for our landing, and I stepped off at Honolulu with the flu licked.

We sortied at noon next day, the eighth. Again my task force was substantially the same—the *Enterprise*, *Northampton*, and *Salt Lake City*, the destroyers *Balch*, *Benham*, *Fanning*, and *Ellet*, and the tanker *Sabine*. But this time it kept the same designation, TF 16, whereas mine was changed; I became Commander Carriers Pacific Fleet, with additional duty as COMCARDIV 2. We made our appointed rendezvous with TF 18, at a point as close to Kamchatka as it was to Pearl, and as soon as I felt that no word could leak back through a disabled ship, I announced our destination: "This force is bound for Tokyo."

Never have I heard such a shout as burst from the *Enterprise's* company! Part of their eagerness came, I think, from the fact that Bataan had fallen four days before.

We fueled the heavy ships on the seventeenth, 1,000 miles east of Tokyo, and at 1400 they commenced their run-in at 23 knots, with the destroyers and tanker left behind, as at Marcus. Everything went smoothly until 0300 on the eighteenth, when our radars began getting blips from what we assumed were picket vessels. These outliers we managed to dodge, but at 0745 another was sighted, 12,000 yards on our port bow. I directed the *Nashville* to sink it. Before she succeeded, we intercepted a radio transmission which, showed, by its strength, that it was originating close aboard, and our inference was that the picket had given the alarm. Although we were then 650 miles from Tokyo, instead of the 400 we had hoped for, the fact that our force had been reported left me no choice. At 0800 I sent "Pete" Mitscher a signal: LAUNCH PLANES X TO COL DOOLITTLE AND HIS GALLANT COMMAND GOOD LUCK AND GOD BLESS YOU.

Jimmy's original plan had been to take off alone at 1400 on the eighteenth, carrying incendiaries to light up the target area for the rest of his squadron, which would follow a few hours later. He believed that this would help them slip through the gantlet, since the Japs' AA was not radar-controlled, so far as our Intelligence knew, and therefore was less accurate at night. I disagreed. Jimmy's hopes of pushing on to the nearest friendly airfield, at Yu-Shan, China, some 1,400 miles beyond Tokyo, struck me as fragile at best, and I felt that the added safety factor of crossing the target at night did not compensate for the comparative haphazardness that night bombing then entailed. However, the whole argument was a dead donkey now, killed by the necessity for this premature launch.

The wind and sea were so strong that morning that green water was breaking over the carriers' ramps. Jimmy led his squadron off. When his plane buzzed down the *Hornet's* deck at 0825, there wasn't a man topside in the task force who didn't help sweat him into the air. One pilot hung on the brink of a stall until we nearly catalogued his effects, but the last of the sixteen was airborne by 0924, and a minute later my staff duty officer was writing in the flag log, "Changed fleet course and axis to 090, commencing retirement from the area at 25 knots."

During the next three hours, our patrol planes attacked a total of sixteen enemy vessels, including a submarine. The *Nashville* again assisted in sinking one and picked up four prisoners. The youngest talked volubly, despite a bullet wound in his cheek. He said he had roused his skipper just after dawn to look at some planes. The skipper wasn't interested; he stayed in his bunk. Presently the sailor roused him again and reported, "Two of our beautiful carriers ahead, sir!"

The skipper came on deck and studied them through his glass. "They're beautiful," he said, "but they're not ours." He went below and put a bullet through his head.

Meanwhile we had our radios tuned to Tokyo. One of their glibbest liars came on and began describing, in English, the wonders of life in Japan. Of all the warring countries in the world, he said, Japan alone was free from enemy attack. Moreover it would continue so, as its indomitable navy would demolish any foe that dared approach its shores. With that conviction, the happy inhabitants

103

today were enjoying not only the Festival of the Cherry Blossoms, but two splendid baseball games as well. Indeed Japan was blessed among nations!—And right there we heard the air-raid sirens. Jimmy's boys had arrived.

Here let me say that, in my opinion, their flight was one of the most courageous deeds in all military history. For those crews to make that dangerous take-off, fly 650 miles over stormy water in land planes, fight their way across an alerted and viciously defended area, and fly 1,400 miles more to an inadequate landing field in a strange country—all that took guts and a hell of a lot of 'em! My cap is off to Jimmy and his brave squadron!

CAPTAIN ASHFORD:

I happened to be with the Admiral when he got word that three of General Doolittle's men had been executed. It was the first time I ever noticed that he has a birthmark on his neck. I noticed it because it turned purple. He stuck out that ram-bow jaw and he ground his teeth. Those eyebrows of his began to flail up and down. I wouldn't swear that St. Elmo's fire didn't play about his ears. All he could choke out was, "We'll make the bastards pay! We'll make 'em pay!"

The Japs chased us all the way home, of course. Whenever we tracked their search planes with our radar, I was tempted to unleash our fighters, but I knew it was more important not to reveal our position than to shoot down a couple of scouts. They sent a task force after us; their submarines tried to intercept us; and since the war, I have seen statements by Japanese officers that even some of their carriers joined the hunt; but with the help of foul weather and a devious course, we eluded them and reentered Pearl on the morning of April twenty-fifth.

Eluding the Japs was nothing to the difficulty of eluding the insistent queries of our associates ashore. The raid was on every tongue, but nobody had any facts to chew. President Roosevelt announced that the jump-off had been from "Shangri-La," and let it go at that. Many of my civilian friends in Honolulu charged me with being implicated, as they knew I had been at sea then. I took the "Who, me?" line. Every man jack of us realized the necessity of preserving absolute secrecy, in order to deceive the Japanese into believing that our B-25's were superplanes, capable of flying

3,600 miles nonstop—2,200 miles from Midway, our nearest land base, to Tokyo, and from Tokyo on to Yu-Shan. Considering the number of men involved, the secret was kept better than any other in my experience. When the truth was disclosed many months later, a great many high-ranking officers were as surprised as was the public.

I reported to Chester Nimitz immediately on my return. The South Pacific theater, he said, was warming up; the Japs were renewing their threats against New Guinea and the Solomons. The *Lexington's* task force was already on guard there; so was the *Yorktown's*. We were to go down and reinforce them, and at the same time put a squadron of Marine fighters on the island of Efate, in the New Hebrides.

TF 16 sortied on April 30—the *Enterprise* and the *Hornet*, four heavy cruisers, eight destroyers, and two tankers. On May 7, when we were still 1,000 miles away, the Battle of the Coral Sea was fought, and the *Lexington* was sunk, reducing our Pacific carrier strength to four, one of which, the *Saratoga*, was still under repair on the West Coast. (In the Atlantic, we had the *Wasp* and the *Ranger*.) By May 11, we were close enough to send two planes ahead, to see if the Efate field was ready to receive the squadron. It was not, so we flew them off to Nouméa instead, then turned north along the 170th meridian, scouting for 200 miles on each side as we cruised. The Jap forces that had been engaged in the Coral Sea Battle had disappeared immediately afterwards, and I wanted to make sure that they weren't reforming to break through between the New Hebrides and Fijis, as I would have done in their place. Under the date-time of May 14 at 2000, this entry appears in my war diary:

Dispatch has been received from CINCPAC quoting COMINCH which states it is inadvisable for Task Force 16 to operate beyond the coverage of our shore-based air or within range of enemy shore-based air. This greatly restricts the operations of this force.

It did indeed! I was mad as the devil! At that moment, our position was almost exactly 600 miles from each of three air bases: ours at Nouméa to the south, and Nandi in the Fijis to the southeast, and the Japs' at Tulagi, off Guadalcanal, to the northwest. I could see nothing from where I was, yet if I ran farther north for

105

a better view, I would violate both of COMINCH's orders; I would lose our air cover and be well under the Japs'. I was hamstrung and hobbled.

Back in World War I, Adm. Sir Louis Bayly had always given his destroyer skippers full discretion at sea, on the theory that the man on the spot knows the local situation better than the man back at headquarters. I thought of this now, and I deemed it a lot more important to scout a potential breakthrough area than to risk the surprise and loss of our bases. I headed north.

Next day another significant entry was made in my war diary:

1015. From this time on throughout the morning and most of the afternoon, had radar contacts with enemy planes to the westward, thought to be patrol planes operating from Tulagi [then about 450 miles due west of us]. These planes approached only to 60 miles, and whenever our VF [fighters] were sent to intercept, they turned and ran. Although visibility was excellent, our forces being visible from the air from a distance of 70 miles, the accuracy of the enemy pilots' reports, and their success in evasion, indicated the possibility that their VP [patrol planes] carry aircraft radar.

The events of this day are important for three reasons: (1) The fact that our scouts sighted no enemy ships made me almost certain that a breakthrough was not imminent; (2) the fact that the enemy sighted our ships might discourage the attempt permanently; and (3) from now on our operations would have to recognize that the enemy shared the benefits of radar.

That afternoon we steamed eastward at 20 knots, to open the range from Tulagi, and that night we turned southeastward, to retire under air cover from Nandi and to occupy the Samoa-Fijis-New Caledonia line. The following afternoon, however, brought us another dispatch from CINCPAC, directing us to return to Pearl. Before we could do so, we had to collect our tankers and other scattered ships in the area, and while we were waiting for the last of them to join up, we received a third despatch: EXPEDITE RETURN.

That could mean only one thing: trouble was brewing somewhere else in the Pacific. My speed to Pearl was limited by the speed of my tankers, but we reentered on May 26, for me to face the most grievous disappointment in my career. The trouble brew-

106

ing was the Battle of Midway. Instead of being allowed to fight it—and I would have been senior officer present—I was sent to the hospital.

The doctors diagnosed my affliction as "general dermatitis." To me it was simply a skin eruption that itched until I nearly went out of my mind. I'm sure that scratching was *kapu*, but not to scratch took more will power than I seemed to possess, and giving in made me even more irritable. It had begun in March, when I went Stateside to meet Jimmy Doolittle. What brought it on I don't know. Possibly the combination of nervous tension and tropical sun was to blame, since I had been on the bridge for six straight months, except for a few short stays in port. I tried every remedy in the pharmacopoeia, including oatmeal-water baths, but nothing gave me relief. I lost 20 pounds and had reached the stage where I was lucky to get two hours' sleep in twenty-four.

When they told me I had to go on the sick list, I stalled them long enough for a quick conference with Chester Nimitz, in which I recommended that command of the fleet be turned over to Ray Spruance. Bill Ashford stayed with me; the rest of my staff went with Ray. And from the Naval hospital at Pearl, "itching"—as Chester put it—"to get into the fight," I watched them sortie on May 28 to win the crucial carrier duel of the war.

☆
☆ 7 ☆
☆ ☆

MY WAR CAREER was divided into three phases. From the outbreak until May 28, 1942, when I was put on the sick list, I commanded a task force at sea. From October 18, 1942, until June 15, 1944, I commanded an area and the forces within it. During the rest of the war, I commanded a fleet.

The first phase was now finished. Between it and the second, I had to spend an impatient two months in hospitals at Pearl Harbor and Richmond, Virginia, waiting for my dermatitis to abate. When the doctors finally certified me fit for active duty again, I was able to spend a few days with my family in Wilmington, before reporting back to Pearl. Some friends were having cocktails with us on a Sunday afternoon when one of my young grandsons, Halsey Spruance, burst into the room, popeyed with excitement. "Look, Granddaddy!" he shouted. "You're famous! Here you are in the funny papers!"

This stimulating realization I took with me to Pearl early in September. Because of the secrecy surrounding the movements of senior officers, only my staff and a very few other men knew that I had returned. On the twelfth, Chester Nimitz invited me to a ceremony on the *Saratoga*, where he was presenting decorations. All hands were lined up on the flight deck. Chester stepped to the microphone, beckoned me forward, and said, "Boys, I've got a surprise for you. Bill Halsey's back!"

They cheered me, and my eyes filled up.

My new job, commander of a carrier task force built around my old flagship, the *Enterprise*, was not quite ready for me, so I decided to improve the interim with a tour of the area where we would operate—the South Pacific. I wanted to familiarize myself with our bases there, meet the men I would work with, consult the leaders in New Zealand, and pay my respects to General MacArthur, over in SOWESPAC.

Our Coronado took off from Pearl on October 15, with Miles Browning, Julian Brown, two rear admirals, and myself as passengers. Our intended itinerary was Canton Island, in the Phoenixes, to Funafuti, in the Ellices, to Guadalcanal; but at Canton I received a dispatch from COMSOPAC (Commander South Pacific Area and Force), Vice Adm. Robert L. Ghormley, suggesting that we by-pass Guadalcanal in view of the tactical situation. I replied that I expected to continue as planned, unless otherwise directed, and sent copies of both dispatches to CINCPAC. I was wakened at 0200 next morning for CINCPAC's answer: PROCEED SUVA AND NOUMEA.

We settled down on Nouméa Harbor at 1400 on the eighteenth. Our four propellers had barely stopped turning when a whaleboat came alongside. As I stepped aboard, Admiral Ghormley's flag lieutenant saluted and gave me a sealed envelope. Inside was a second envelope, marked "SECRET" and also sealed. I would have been aboard the flagship in a few minutes, so I realized that the message must be highly important. It was another dispatch from CINCPAC: YOU WILL TAKE COMMAND OF THE SOUTH PACIFIC AREA AND SOUTH PACIFIC FORCES IMMEDIATELY.

COLONEL BROWN:
The Admiral read the dispatch twice, then showed it to me. His exact words were, "Jesus Christ and General Jackson! This is the hottest potato they ever handed me!"

My reactions were astonishment, apprehension, and regret, in that order.

I was astonished because I had not had the slightest inkling of the appointment. Nimitz's instructions to cancel my trip to Guadalcanal might have served as a warning to someone more percipient than myself, but I hadn't read them that way, and this second dispatch dumfounded me.

109

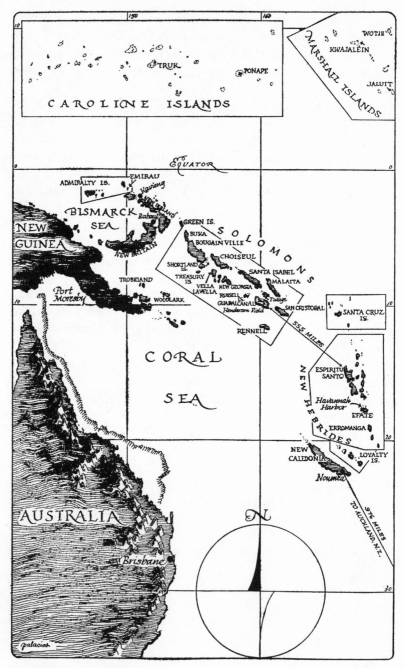

CAROLINE ISLANDS

TRUK

PONAPE

MARSHALL ISLANDS

WOTJE

KWAJALEIN

JALUIT

EQUATOR

ADMIRALTY IS.

EMIRAU

Kavieng

NEW IRELAND

BISMARCK SEA

Rabaul

NEW BRITAIN

NEW GUINEA

GREEN IS.

BUKA

BOUGAINVILLE

CHOISEUL

SHORTLAND IS.

TREASURY IS.

VELLA LAVELLA

NEW GEORGIA

SANTA ISABEL

MALAITA

RUSSELL IS.

GUADALCANAL

Henderson Field

Tulagi

SAN CRISTOBAL

SOLOMONS

RENNELL

555 MILES

SANTA CRUZ IS.

TROBRIAND

Port Moresby

WOODLARK

CORAL

SEA

NEW HEBRIDES

ESPIRITU SANTO

Havannah Harbor

EFATE

ERROMANGA

NEW CALEDONIA

Noumea

LOYALTY IS.

AUSTRALIA

Brisbane

N

976 MILES TO AUCKLAND, N.Z.

palacios

COLONEL BROWN:

I too was astonished at first, but later I remembered something that had occurred when we came through San Francisco early in September. The Admiral and Miles and I went to a meeting one afternoon. Nimitz and King were there; so was Randall Jacobs, the Chief of BuPers [the Bureau of Personnel]. Jacobs made a gesture toward the Admiral and asked King, "Can we tell him now?"

King said, "No, not yet."

At the time, Miles and I thought they meant that the Admiral was slated for four stars, or possibly for COMAIRPAC [Commander Aircraft Pacific], but after we had been in Pearl for a month, doing nothing but sitting on our dead duffs, we gave up guessing. I still don't know for certain what they were referring to, but it may well have been the COMSOPAC job.

I was apprehensive for two reasons. First, I knew nothing about campaigning with the Army, much less with Australian, New Zealand, and Free French forces. Second, although I knew little about the military situation in the South Pacific, I knew enough to realize that it was desperate. That sunny afternoon in spring—October is spring in those latitudes, of course—the hopes of the area were icebound. Japan was grasping island after island, always southward. New Zealand had begun to clamor for its regiments to be rushed back from Africa for home defense. Australia was prepared to withdraw halfway down the continent to "the Brisbane Line." At sea, the Pacific Fleet had lost a carrier, three heavy cruisers, five destroyers, and four transports in the area since August. Ashore on Guadalcanal, our troops were locked in a savage struggle to maintain their foothold. A crisis was obviously imminent, and we would have to meet it.

EDITOR'S NOTE:

One of these heavy cruisers was the *Astoria*, which in 1939 had carried the ashes of Ambassador Hirosi Saito home to Japan. Emperor Hirohito in person thanked her then captain, R. Kelly Turner (see page 116 *ff.*), for President Roosevelt's courtesy.

Lastly, I was regretful because Bob Ghormley, whom I was relieving, had been a friend of mine for forty years, since the days when we had played on the same football team at the Naval Academy.

COMSOPAC's headquarters were on the *Argonne*, a merchant-man converted to a repair ship. The whaleboat took us across to her, and Bob met me as I stepped on the quarterdeck. He was as cordial and friendly as ever, but we both were ill at ease.

Bob said, "This is a tough job they've given you, Bill."

I said, "I damn well know it!"

We went to his cabin. He briefed me on the area and the problems facing me, then the ship's company was called to quarters, and we read them our new orders, changing the command.

The second phase of my war career had begun. In fact, it began with a bang. Within forty-eight hours after I took command, and despite my ignorance of the terrain, I had to make two important decisions.

Let me sketch in the strategic situation. As early as January, the Japanese had occupied Rabaul and Bougainville, both under Australian mandate, and had started their march down the stepping-stones of the Solomons, with the obvious intention of jumping to the New Hebrides and New Caledonia, from which they could easily hack through our thin life line to New Zealand and Australia.

Although their progress was unopposed, it was slow. By April they had reached only as far as Tulagi, across Sealark Channel from Guadalcanal, but they were assembling an invasion force there when planes from the *Yorktown* found it and shattered it on May 4 and, with planes from the *Lexington*, turned back their battle force in the Coral Sea on the seventh and eighth. The enemy lost a carrier, the *Shoho*, and we lost the *Lexington*, but we gained a breathing spell. It lasted two months. On July 4, the Japs moved into Guadalcanal, and presently our reconnaissance planes reported that construction of an airstrip had started near Lunga Point, the strip that later became famous as Henderson Field.

The presence of land-based air only 555 miles from Espiritu Santo, which we had occupied in March, was a threat that we had to parry at once. The Joint Chiefs of Staff had envisaged the Japs' program and had issued a counterdirective in April. It was not popular, even among themselves. Two- and three-starred officers in both the Navy and the Army opposed it. The probability of success was too remote, they argued. Too many advantages lay with the enemy—he was thoroughly prepared for war (with the help of the fuel and scrap iron we had sold him); his fighting was confined to one ocean; he had the initiative and was on the offensive; his lines of communication and supply were internal; he had many more bottoms available; and three of his major bases—Rabaul, Truk, and Kwajalein—were within 1,200 miles, whereas our own nearest major base—Pearl Harbor—was 3,000 miles away.

All this was true, and it was all disheartening, but there was another consideration which outweighed the rest: our life line *had* to be held, whatever the handicaps, whatever the cost. COMINCH, Admiral King, grasped this vital fact and never relaxed his grip. His adamant insistence—bless him for it!—that we meet the enemy at Guadalcanal finally wore down his opponents, and they authorized the directive.

The code name of Guadalcanal Island was CACTUS, and God knows it was a thorny spot. I don't remember the code name of the operation, but it should have been called SHOESTRING. The Navy and Army commanders charged with seeing it through made repeated requests for additional troops and ships, but Europe was Washington's darling; the South Pacific was only a stepchild. None the less, the Marines landed on Guadalcanal and Tulagi on August 7. They might have won a reasonably quick victory if we had been able to protect them, supply them, and reinforce them, but we weren't. We didn't have the ships, either cargo or combat, and the enemy did.

The disproportion rapidly became more acute. Early on the morning of the ninth, a force of five Japanese heavy cruisers, two light cruisers, and a destroyer steamed down "the Slot"—New Georgia Sound—to pick off our transports, whose unloading had been delayed by air attacks on the seventh and eighth. To screen them, we had five heavy cruisers—the *Chicago, Quincy, Vincennes, Astoria,* and *Canberra* (of the Royal Australian Navy)—and six destroyers— the *Bagley, Patterson, Helm, Wilson, Ralph Talbot,* and *Blue.* The Battle of Savo Island lasted eight minutes. When it was over, we had lost all the cruisers except the *Chicago,* and she and the *Ralph Talbot* were damaged. Although the Japs had no losses, for some strange reason they did not follow through and attack our helpless transports; instead, they returned north, mission uncompleted.

113

I forbear to comment on this battle since I had no part in it. Nor, for the same reason, will I comment on the next two battles.

Savo Island was followed by a two weeks' lull, during which the enemy, at will and almost with impunity, bombarded our positions, reinforced and supplied his troops, and reduced our own support to a trickle. We had three carriers in the area, the *Enterprise*, *Wasp*, and *Saratoga*, but they were being held well south of the combat zone, out of range of search planes, until the enemy should commit an important part of his strength to the business of dislodging us from our foothold.

His attempt began on August 23, when one of our long-range patrol planes from Guadalcanal sighted four transports escorted by four destroyers, 250 miles north, on a southerly course. This was the occupation force. About 100 miles to its eastward, later sightings discovered a striking force of five carriers (one for seaplanes), eight battleships, six cruisers, and twenty-one destroyers. Since the battle that was joined on the twenty-fourth was a carrier duel, it would be superfluous to itemize our surface force, beyond the statement that only the air groups from the *Enterprise* and *Saratoga* were engaged; a combination of fuel requirements and confused Intelligence reports had resulted in the *Wasp's* being withdrawn to the south. But for this, our victory in the Battle of the Eastern Solomons might have been more decisive. As it was, our two air groups, with the help of eight Marine dive bombers from Guadalcanal (Henderson Field was now operational) and eight Army B-17's from Espiritu Santo, sank the carrier *Ryujo*, a destroyer, and a transport, and scored damaging hits on one battleship and a cruiser. Marine fighters shot down twenty-one planes at the cost of three F4F's, and Navy planes and AA shot down seventy more, at a cost of seventeen planes. The *Enterprise* took three direct hits and several near misses which killed about seventy men and required her return to Pearl Harbor for repairs. But we had beaten off the Japanese and gained another reprieve.

A few days after the *Enterprise* left, the *Hornet* arrived, so our carrier strength was back to three. It stayed at that figure for two days. On the thirty-first, the *Saratoga* was torpedoed by a submarine, for the second time. Fortunately there were no fatalities, and damage was slight, but she too had to go to the yard at Pearl. Her departure

114

may have keyed the enemy to his next assault: on September 14, one of our scout planes reported a large force again standing down toward Guadalcanal. Something alarmed it, because the *Wasp's* and *Hornet's* planes never made contact, and both carriers were retiring to cover a northbound transport group next afternoon, when three torpedoes suddenly smashed into the *Wasp*. Nearly 200 men were killed, and the fires were so fierce that she had to be abandoned and sunk. Now we had one carrier in the whole South Pacific.

Our transport group, carrying the 7th Marine Regiment, reached Guadalcanal safely; and early in October another group, carrying elements of the Army's American Division, started up from Nouméa. Protecting its left flank was a small task force assigned to block "the Tokyo Express," the enemy's nightly raiders from the northern Solomons. The American force comprised the heavy cruisers *San Francisco* and *Salt Lake City*, the light cruisers *Boise* and *Helena*, and the destroyers *Duncan, McCalla, Farenholt, Buchanan,* and *Laffey*. The Tokyo Express comprised three heavy cruisers and two destroyers. They met at midnight on October 11, off Cape Esperance, the northern tip of Guadalcanal. The battle was almost a duplicate of the Battle of Savo Island: a small number of cruisers and destroyers were opposed; they were fairly evenly matched; they fought in darkness; and the action was short and furious—only thirty-four minutes between "Open fire!" and "Cease fire!" Moreover, the two scenes were only a few miles apart. But there was this considerable difference: in the Battle of Cape Esperance, we surprised the Japanese, and at the price of the *Duncan* sunk and *Boise* damaged, we sank a heavy cruiser and a destroyer, and crippled another heavy cruiser.

Contrasting our naval resources with the enemy's, Cape Esperance was an American victory, but it was not a disastrous Japanese defeat. Although we landed the American Division, the enemy landed two divisions under cover of his shore-based air and his surface superiority. Worse, before his escorts withdrew, they subjected our positions to fire so obviously unhurried that it was contemptuous. At times we had only one dive bomber at Henderson Field able to leave the ground. At times the pilots were so weak from incessant combat, sleepless nights, and scanty rations that they would land after a battle and crawl under the wings of their planes and sob. Brig. Gen. Roy S. Geiger, Commander of the Marine Air Force on Guadalcanal, had to kick them—literally kick them—back into their cockpits.

Deterioration of morale kept pace with attrition of personnel and matériel. Our beleaguered troops knew that their predicament was critical, and they knew that these bombardments from the sea and air were only a preliminary to the all-out assault which was massing at Rabaul, Bougainville, and Truk. They began to echo the question that the public had asked in the weeks following Pearl Harbor, "Where is the Navy?"

As of October 18, it was my grim task to give them an answer.

Lt. Comdr. John E. Lawrence, an Air Combat Information Officer who was on Guadalcanal at this time, and later on Admiral Halsey's staff:

We were living off captured rice and driving our trucks on captured gas. Our AK's [cargo ships] were loaded with the stuff we needed, but every time there was a Condition Red [enemy air raid], they had to up-anchor and get out. First the planes pounded us, and then the battleships. During thirty-six hours on October 13 and 14, the *Kongo* and the *Haruna* gave us 1,000 rounds of 14-inch. But it wasn't that; it was the hopelessness, the feeling that nobody gave a curse whether we lived or died. It soaked into you until you couldn't trust your own mind. You'd brief a pilot, and no sooner had he taken off than you'd get frantic, wondering if you'd forgotten to tell him some trivial thing that might become the indispensable factor in saving his life . . . .

Lt. Comdr. Roger Kent, also an Air Combat Information Officer on Guadalcanal:

Then we got the news: the Old Man had been made COMSOPAC. I'll never forget it! One minute we were too limp with malaria to crawl out of our foxholes; the next, we were running around whooping like kids. I remember two Marines working up to a brawl. One of them was arguing that getting the Old Man was like getting two battleships and two carriers, and the other was swearing he was worth two battleships and *three* carriers. If morale had been enough, we'd have won the war right there.

I began my new job under the crippling handicap of never having seen Guadalcanal, the keystone of the area I was defending. My information about it was not even secondhand, since Bob Ghormley and his Chief of Staff, Rear Adm. Daniel J. Callaghan,

116

had never had an opportunity to see it either. It was impossible for me to leave headquarters this early for a trip to the front, so I asked the men who knew the local situation best to fly down and describe it to me in person.

We met in my cabin on the *Argonne* on the night of October 20 —Maj. Gen. A. Archer Vandegrift, commanding the 1st Marine Division; Maj. Gen. Alexander M. Patch, who later commanded the Army troops that took over from the Marines; and Maj. Gen. Millard F. Harmon, the senior Army officer in the South Pacific. Also present, in addition to my skeleton staff and Ghormley's subordinate commanders, were Lt. Gen. Thomas Holcomb, the Commandant of the Marine Corps, who happened to be in Nouméa on an inspection tour, and Maj. Gen. C. Barney Vogel, who had just arrived as Commander of the I Marine Amphibious Corps.

Archie Vandegrift and "Miff" Harmon told their bitter stories. It was quite late when they finished. I asked, "Are we going to evacuate or hold?"

Archie answered, "I can hold, but I've got to have more active support than I've been getting."

Rear Adm. Kelly Turner, commanding the Amphibious Forces Pacific, protested that the Navy was already doing its utmost. He correctly pointed out that the few bottoms we had were becoming fewer almost daily; we did not have the warships to protect them; there were no bases at Guadalcanal where they could shelter, no open water permitting evasive tactics; and enemy submarines were thick and active.

When Kelly had finished, Archie looked at me, waiting. What Kelly had said was of course true. It was also true that Guadalcanal *had* to be held.

I told Archie, "All right. Go on back. I'll promise you everything I've got."

Some pages ago I wrote, "Within forty-eight hours after I took command, and despite my ignorance of the terrain, I had to make two important decisions." Supporting Guadalcanal was not one of them; here I was merely a willing mouthpiece for the Joint Chiefs of Staff. My first independent decision was whether or not we should proceed with construction of an airfield on the island of Ndeni, the largest of the Santa Cruz group. Not only was Henderson our sole

117

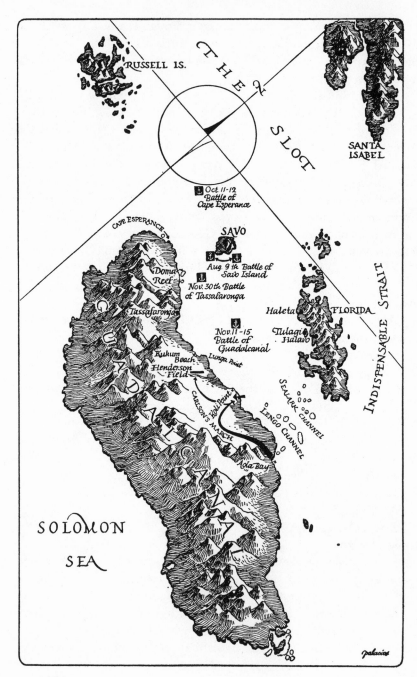

THE SLOT

RUSSELL IS.

SANTA
ISABEL

Oct. 11-12
Battle of
Cape Esperance

CAPE ESPERANCE

SAVO

Aug. 9th Battle of
Savo Island

Doma
Reef

Nov. 30th Battle
of Tassafaronga

Tassafaronga

Haleta

FLORIDA

Nov. 11-15
Battle of
Guadalcanal

Tulagi
Halavo

Kukum
Beach

Lunga Point

Henderson
Field

GUADALCANAL

CARLSON'S MARCH

Koli Point

SEALARK CHANNEL

LENGO CHANNEL

Aola Bay

INDISPENSABLE STRAIT

SOLOMON

SEA

palacios

118

advanced field, but it was at the weather's mercy as well as the enemy's; an hour's rain turned it into a marsh. Ndeni was 330 miles from Henderson, but at that it was 205 miles closer than our nearest field, on Espiritu. The plan for the Ndeni field had been approved, and Army troops were on their way to occupy the island, when the situation at Guadalcanal became so desperate that I intercepted them and rushed them into the defenses. This decision brought me considerable adverse criticism, but I never had reason to regret it; Ndeni's importance soon evaporated.

A supplementary field was still needed, however, and Kelly Turner recommended that one be built at Aola Bay, about 30 miles east of Henderson. Now I had to make my second decision. I had no personal information about Aola Bay and no time to consult COMAIRSOPAC, Rear Adm. Aubrey W. Fitch, or Roy Geiger, both of whom were at the front. I submitted Kelly's recommendation to a conference on the *Argonne*, accepted the vote of approval, and ordered a Seabee battalion to begin construction, with the support of the 14th Infantry and Lt. Col. Evans F. Carlson's 2d Marine Raider Battalion.

The reaction from Fitch and Geiger was immediate and violent; both notified me that the terrain at Aola Bay was utterly unsuited to a field. I canceled the order, of course, but the men were already ashore, and I was confronted with the problem of evacuating them. They could not join up with the troops fighting around Henderson, because the Japs had just landed 1,500 men at Koli Point, between our two forces; and they could not withdraw, because air attacks had made our transports retire. We eventually sent them back in and moved the Seabees and the infantry to Henderson, but the Raiders chose the hard way out. They went overland, joined up with some other Marines and an infantry regiment, fell on the Jap force at Koli Point, nearly annihilating it, and made a brilliant thirty-day march behind the Jap lines in which they killed 600 men and lost two. However, I couldn't take that performance as standard for all troops. From then on, I waited until I had all available information before I put a plan in motion.

Frequently, to be sure, "all available information" was hardly a handful, as in the case of the battle now looming. We knew the enemy's program only in broad outline. The mounting ferocity of

119

his efforts to recapture Henderson Field implied his intention to use it first as a staging point for his carrier planes in the mop-up of our presumably shattered troops, and then as a base from which his bombers could support the final, crushing assault on our ships, after which he would sever us from our South Pacific allies and engulf them at leisure.

So Guadalcanal, with its potential facilities, was the key to the whole campaign. To turn it and lock us out, the enemy poured in men and matériel almost nightly and sent his submarines, planes, and light surface units to harry our supply lines while he assembled a powerful fleet to the northward. At a minimum it comprised four carriers, four battleships, possibly two score cruisers and destroyers, and an armada of transports and other auxiliaries. To oppose them, I had the Third Fleet, which then consisted of two small task forces. One, commanded by Rear Adm. Norman Scott, was the survivors of the Battle of Cape Esperance—one heavy cruiser, one light cruiser, and three destroyers, plus the battleship *Washington*. The other, commanded by Rear Adm. George D. Murray (the former skipper of the *Enterprise*) was built around the *Hornet* and included the heavy cruisers *Northampton* and *Pensacola*, the light cruisers *San Diego* and *Juneau*, and the destroyers *Morris*, *Anderson*, *Hughes*, *Mustin*, *Russell*, and *Barton*. A third task force, built around the *Enterprise* and including the battleship *South Dakota*, the heavy cruiser *Portland*, the light cruiser *San Juan*, and the destroyers *Porter*, *Mahan*, *Shaw*, *Cushing*, *Preston*, *Smith*, *Maury*, and *Conyngham*, was enroute from Pearl, where the *Enterprise* had gone for repairs after the Battle of the Eastern Solomons. I directed Rear Adm. Thomas C. Kinkaid, commanding this force, to expedite his return, but I knew he could not arrive by October 23, which Intelligence had picked as Zero Day.

However, the twenty-third passed with the enemy's fleet still poised, waiting for word that his troops had driven the Marines from Henderson, at the moment the "key-to-the-key" of Guadalcanal. The Marines bought time with blood, but they never got a better bargain; at 1245 on the twenty-fourth, the *Enterprise's* task force met the *Hornet's*, northeast of the New Hebrides. Carrier power varies as the square—two carriers are four times as powerful as one. Until the *Enterprise* arrived, our plight had been almost hopeless. Now we had a fighting chance.

120

I sent the combined carrier forces northward, to a position off the Santa Cruz Islands where they would be beyond reach of the enemy's land-based air, yet able to hit his flank when he closed Guadalcanal. Meanwhile, our submarines patrolled the Solomon Sea; we channeled eighty-five patrol planes and heavy bombers into Espiritu; and bombers from the SOWESPAC command hacked for three nights straight—although ineffectually—at the concentration of shipping in Rabaul Harbor and at the air bases on New Britain.

The crescendo of the fighting ashore made it plain that the climax was rushing toward us. I thought that the twenty-fifth would precipitate it. Before dawn that morning, a Japanese heavy cruiser and four destroyers landed troops and supplies on Guadalcanal, then stood off and added their broadsides to the artillery. Rain had made a bog of Henderson; our dive bombers could not retaliate until noon, when six Espiritu B-17's joined them in scoring two hits on the light cruiser and two on a destroyer. Almost at the same minute, our patrol planes reported two large forces steaming southward. The *Enterprise* launched a search and a strike, but no contact was made; the enemy had retired. On the chance that he was biding the cover of darkness, I ordered Scott to make a night sweep around Savo Island. Again nothing developed, but action was now so obviously a matter of hours that I sent a final dispatch to all my combat commands: ATTACK REPEAT ATTACK. The rest was in their hands.

The Battle of Santa Cruz was another carrier duel. Scott's task force had no part in it; and except for one torpedo attack by an enemy submarine, ships' fire was strictly defensive, against planes. The preliminary skirmishes began at 0804 on the twenty-sixth, when the enemy attempted to shoot down four *Enterprise* scouts who were reporting his movements and composition—an advance force of two battleships, a carrier, five cruisers, and eleven destroyers; a carrier striking force of three carriers, a heavy cruiser, and seven destroyers; and a battleship striking force of two battleships, three cruisers, and eight destroyers.

The opposing carriers, 250 miles apart, launched their attacks at approximately the same time. Seventy-four fighters, dive bombers, and torpedo planes from the *Hornet* and the *Enterprise* fought their way through vigorous interception and intense antiaircraft, and the survivors struck the enemy at 1040. They sank none of his

121

ships, but they put two carriers out of commission and damaged a cruiser and two destroyers. Meanwhile, at 1010, the *Hornet* had been subjected to an air attack so violent that within five minutes she was smashed by four bombs, two torpedoes, and two suicide planes; and within another five she was dead in the water, afire, with communications disrupted and all power lost. At 1101, the destroyer *Porter*, in the *Enterprise's* task group, was torpedoed by a submarine and eventually had to be abandoned. The explosion had hardly subsided when twenty-four dive bombers plunged at the *Enterprise*. One bomb struck the forward end of her flight deck, penetrated the fo'c'sle deck, and burst in the water. Another twisted her forward elevator and caused a number of casualties. A third was a near miss, but the shock tossed a parked plane overboard and also ruptured a seam in one of her fuel tanks, so that she left a trail of oil across the ocean. Despite her injuries, she took aboard the *Hornet's* planes and fought on.

In the next two hours, her task group withstood three more attacks. A torpedo plane crashed on the deck of the destroyer *Smith;* a bomb put the *South Dakota's* No. 1 turret out of commission and wounded her skipper, Capt. Thomas L. Gatch; the *San Juan* was damaged by a direct hit and five near misses; and the *Enterprise* herself was slightly damaged by a near miss. The *Hornet*, however, was the focus of five attacks, spaced over six hours. One of them was fatal; a torpedo in her starboard side increased her list to 20 degrees, and at 1727 she was ordered abandoned and sunk.

Our surface-ship losses in the Battle of Santa Cruz were thus a carrier and a destroyer sunk, with 283 men killed or missing, as against mere crippling to the enemy's ships and unknown casualties. Tactically, we picked up the dirty end of the stick, but strategically we handed it back; our carrier-plane losses *from all causes* were seventy-four, of which only twenty were combat losses, whereas the enemy lost a minimum of 100 planes in combat alone, and presumably a great many more in operational accidents. Even this minimum meant that the four air groups on his carriers had been cut to pieces, and with two of the carriers themselves damaged, we had weakened him so much that he was unable to provide effective air support in the Battle of Guadalcanal, sixteen days later.

Our damaged ships retired to Nouméa. Before they arrived, I

122

called in the senior officers of all branches of all services and directed them to pool their available mechanics in a repair force. Our shoestring had held at Santa Cruz but it had been badly frayed, and it had to be patched up as quickly as possible for the tougher fight we felt sure was coming.

While the repair force worked around the clock, I took advantage of the lull to make my postponed trip to Guadalcanal, accompanied by the chief of my war plans section, Brig. Gen. Dewitt Peck of the Marine Corps, and my new flag lieutenant, Lt. William J. Kitchell, who had come down from Pearl on the *Enterprise*, with the rest of my staff. Archie Vandegrift met our plane and took us on a tour of the front.

COMMANDER KITCHELL:

The Admiral's purpose was to familiarize himself with the spot situation, but the staff had another purpose: we wanted him to let the men in the front lines see him in person. Our purpose was not served. Since the Admiral's informal costume was almost indistinguishable from a pfc's, we begged him to stand up in his jeep, to wave, to make some gesture that would help them identify him. He refused. He said, "It smells of exhibitionism. The hell with it!"

It was at a press conference on this trip that he gave his recipe for winning the war: "Kill Japs, kill Japs, and keep on killing Japs!"

Archie put us up in his shack that night, November 8. Soon after we turned in, an enemy destroyer somewhere near Savo Island began lobbing over shells, and our artillery started an argument with the Japs'. It wasn't the noise that kept me awake; it was fright. I called myself yellow—and worse—and told myself, "Go to sleep, you damned coward!" but it didn't do any good; I couldn't obey orders.

Early next morning we flew down to Efate, where I stopped to visit the base hospital. One of the patients was a Navy doctor, with his head in bandages. I asked, "What happened, son?"

"I don't know, Admiral," he said. "Last thing I remember, I was talking to you at the 'Canal last night."

That's how the Navy takes care of its men. They get wounded, and twelve hours later, they're safe in a hospital 700 miles behind the lines.

123

☆
☆ 8 ☆
☆ ☆

W E RETURNED to Nouméa on the afternoon of November 9. Miles Browning was waiting for me, with news that another enemy offensive was brewing, one that would employ a vast number of ships and planes on a schedule which Intelligence estimated as follows: planes would bomb Guadalcanal on the eleventh; ships would bombard Henderson Field on the night of the twelfth; and after a day-long carrier attack on the thirteenth, troops would land.

First reports credited this combined assault and invasion fleet with two carriers, four battleships, five heavy cruisers, about thirty destroyers, and possibly twenty transports and cargo vessels. To intercept it, I had a fleet that would have been inferior even if two of its heaviest units were not crippled; moreover, not only was it dispersed, but it was already committed, in part, to delivering the support I had promised Archie Vandegrift. The exact situation was as follows:

Rear Admiral Scott's force—one light cruiser and four destroyers—was escorting three cargo vessels from Espiritu to Guadalcanal, where it was due to arrive on the eleventh.

Rear Admiral Turner's force—one heavy cruiser, one light cruiser, and four destroyers—was escorting four transports from Nouméa to Guadalcanal, where it was due to arrive on the twelfth.

Rear Admiral Callaghan's force—two heavy cruisers, one light cruiser, and six destroyers—would sail from Espiritu on the tenth and rendezvous with Turner on the eleventh.

Rear Admiral Kinkaid's force—the *Enterprise*, the battleships

124

South Dakota and *Washington*, one heavy cruiser, one light cruiser, and eight destroyers—was still at Nouméa, where the *Enterprise* and *South Dakota* were under repair for damages suffered in the Battle of Santa Cruz.

If the enemy kept to his probable schedule, our supply ships would have to discharge and be clear of the area before the night of the twelfth, so that the warships escorting them could join the battle free of responsibility. Meanwhile, Kinkaid's force would be sent forward the moment it was able to sail. The *South Dakota's* No. 1 turret was completely out of commission, but the *Enterprise* was crippled far worse. When we sent her back to sea, eighty-five repairmen were still aboard, one of her tanks was still leaking oil, and her forward elevator was still jammed, as far as we knew, at flight-deck level. I say "as far as we knew," because we didn't dare test it. If we had lowered it and had been unable to raise it again, she would have been useless. As it was, she could conduct flight operations at slow speed, and this was a time when even half-ships counted.

Norm Scott's force reached its anchorage off Lunga Point at 0530 on the eleventh and began to unload at once. The enemy gave him four hours' grace, then attacked with dive bombers. All were shot down, but not before the three cargo vessels had been damaged, one of them seriously enough to require its return to Espiritu, with a destroyer. While the other two continued unloading through the night, Scott took his remaining warships into Indispensable Strait and joined Callaghan's force, which had sprinted ahead of Turner's. They made two sweeps east and west of Savo Island, but found nothing, and retired at dawn on the twelfth to protect the unloading of Turner's four transports, off Kukum Beach.

That morning our scouts reported a strong enemy force bearing down on Guadalcanal and already close enough to arrive during the night. No transports were sighted; this was a bombardment force. Turner rushed his unloading and might have completed it by nightfall, if he hadn't had to suspend for two hours to beat off an attack by torpedo planes. Even so, his transports—all credit to their captains and the unloading crews—were 90 per cent empty when he withdrew them, accompanied by three destroyers and two fast mine sweepers.

125

Callaghan, Scott's senior, was now left with a total strength as follows: the heavy cruisers *San Francisco* (flagship) and *Portland;* the light cruisers *Atlanta* (Scott's flagship), *Helena*, and *Juneau;* and the destroyers *Aaron Ward, Barton, Monssen, Fletcher, Cushing, Laffey, Sterett*, and *O'Bannon*. (In addition to the four destroyers detached to escort the transports, three more and a heavy cruiser had been sent to reinforce Kinkaid.) This was little enough with which to face two battleships, a light cruiser, and fifteen destroyers, so all we hoped for was an action that would delay the enemy long enough for him to be within reach of the *Enterprise's* planes next morning, Friday the thirteenth.

Callaghan entered Lengo Channel at midnight. At 0124, the *Helena's* radar picked up three groups of ships, the nearest group 27,100 yards away. The moon was down, near-by land masses confused the radar readings, and TBS (Talk Between Ships) transmission was poor. Almost before Callaghan was aware, his column had steamed between two of the groups. Searchlights suddenly pinned him from both sides, and he was under fire at the point-blank range of 3,000 yards.

The action lasted twenty-four minutes. In Admiral King's opinion, it was "one of the most furious sea battles ever fought." Back on the *Argonne*, in Nouméa, all we knew was that the battle was raging. I had sent Callaghan and Scott into it, and now I could do nothing but wait for the results. The waiting was hard, as always. I walked the decks, re-examined reports and charts, and conferred with my staff. I must have drunk a gallon of coffee and smoked two packs of cigarettes. When the tension became unbearable, I skimmed through the trashiest magazine I could find.

It was broad daylight when a communications watch officer brought me the first official word. As in all battles, the bad news came first. This was a dispatch from the *Portland:* STEERING ROOM FLOODED AND RUDDER JAMMED HARD RIGHT BY TORPEDO HIT STARBOARD QUARTER X CANNOT STEER WITH ENGINES X REQUEST TOW.

Half an hour later the *Atlanta* reported, HELP NEEDED. Then, about 0900, came this one, from the *Helena:* HELENA SAN FRANCISCO JUNEAU OBANNON FLETCHER STERETT IN COMPANY PROCEEDING COURSE ONE SEVEN FIVE [toward Espiritu] X HELENA SENIOR SHIP X ALL SHIPS ARE DAMAGED SO REQUEST MAXIMUM AIR COVERAGE.

Where were the *Portland* and *Atlanta?* What had happened to the five other destroyers? And why was the *Helena* the senior ship when Dan Callaghan's *San Francisco* was present? The implication was plain: Dan was either dead or badly wounded.

Late in the afternoon, Guadalcanal began to round out the story: TEN MILES NORTH SAVO ISLAND FIVE ENEMY DDS [destroyers] ATTEMPTING ASSIST KONGO-CLASS BB [battleship] WHICH HAS BEEN HIT BY SEVEN TORPEDOES AND 1000 LB BOMB X AFTER PART OF SHIP BURNING FIERCELY X SHIP BELIEVED HOSTILE DD BEACHED AND SMOKING NORTH COAST OLEVUGA ISLAND X LARGE VESSEL BURNING INDISPENSABLE STRAIT X USS CUSHING BURNING FIVE MILES SE SAVO ISLAND AND USS MONSSEN DEAD IN WATER BOTH ABANDONED X ATLANTA AND PORTLAND BADLY DAMAGED X USS LAFFEY HAS SUNK X 700 SURVIVORS PICKED UP 25% OF THESE WOUNDED.

And ten minutes later the *Portland* stated, ATLANTA UNABLE TO CONTROL WATER X ABANDONING AND SINKING HER WITH DEMOLITION CHARGES X I AM PROCEEDING UNDER TOW TO TULAGI.

Presumably the *Atlanta* could not speak for herself for the same reason that the *San Francisco* had not spoken; like Dan Callaghan, Norm Scott was dead or wounded. We eventually learned that both these splendid men were dead. Dan was killed when the battleship *Hiyei's* third salvo smashed into the *San Francisco's* bridge. Norm was killed at some subsequent time, never established. I had known and loved Norm Scott for years; his death was the greatest personal sorrow that beset me in the whole war.

But Guadalcanal had been saved. As Archie Vandegrift expressed it in a dispatch to me: TO SCOTT, CALLAGHAN, AND THEIR MEN GOES OUR GREATEST HOMAGE X WITH MAGNIFICENT COURAGE AGAINST SEEMINGLY HOPELESS ODDS, THEY DROVE BACK THE FIRST HOSTILE STROKE AND MADE SUCCESS POSSIBLE X TO THEM THE MEN OF GUADALCANAL LIFT THEIR BATTERED HELMETS IN DEEPEST ADMIRATION.

Our loss of the *Atlanta* and the *Barton, Cushing, Laffey,* and *Monssen* (and, hours later, the *Juneau*) was balanced by the enemy's loss of the *Hiyei* and two destroyers. What made this opening phase of the battle an American victory had been excellently described in CINCPAC's official report:

"This action, in which a brave and gallant leader . . . took in brave men against superior forces, was a turning point in the

127

Solomons Islands campaign. Had the powerful enemy fleet succeeded in its mission of bombarding our airfield on Guadalcanal, the task of preventing a major enemy attack and landing of large-scale reinforcements would have been much more difficult, if not impossible. . . . The resolution with which Rear Admirals Callaghan and Scott led the ships in, the well-directed fire and courage of our personnel, merit the highest praise."

The Battle of Guadalcanal was fought in three stages. The main action in the first stage ended about 0225 on the thirteenth, but there were sporadic skirmishes for a few hours more, and air attacks on the stricken *Hiyei* all through the day. One of these attacks marked the first participation of the *Enterprise* and therefore opened the second stage.

When we sent Kinkaid to sea on the eleventh, we hoped that his force would be able to break up the invasion which we expected to begin on the night of the thirteenth. We knew that his speed of advance was geared to the *Enterprise*, and that the *Enterprise's* depended on the wind. If it was southerly, she would have to reverse course whenever she launched or landed her planes; but if it was northerly, she could log a steady speed. The force was keeping radio silence. No data reached us. Nevertheless, I was so confident of the wind's loyalty that I sent Kinkaid a dispatch on the afternoon of the thirteenth, ordering him to put his two battleships and four of his destroyers under command of Rear Adm. Willis A. Lee, Jr., with instructions to lay an ambush that night east of Savo Island.

This plan flouted one of the firmest doctrines of the Naval War College. The narrow, treacherous waters north of Guadalcanal are utterly unsuited to the maneuvering of capital ships, especially in darkness. The shade of Mahan must have turned even paler. But if any principle of naval warfare is burned into my brain, it is that the best defense is a strong offense—that, as Lord Nelson wrote in a memorandum to his officers before the Battle of Trafalgar, "No Captain can do very wrong if he places his Ship alongside that of an Enemy."

My explanation—my excuse, if historians prefer—is that a dilemma confronted us. The dispatches I had received that morning made it obvious that the remnants of Callaghan's force were in no condition to fight another battle. Yet if I did not take positive action, if I let the enemy enter the combat zone unmolested, to bombard our troops and their positions and their airfield and to land reinforcements, not only would he increase his strength at the expense of ours but our morale would be riddled. Lee's ships were my only recourse, so I ordered them in.

EDITOR'S NOTE:

After the Battle of Guadalcanal, Admiral Nimitz said of Admiral Halsey, "He has that rare combination of intellectual capacity and military audacity, and can calculate to a cat's whisker the risk involved."

Kinkaid's acknowledgement of my order was a shock: FROM LEE'S PRESENT POSITION IMPOSSIBLE FOR HIM TO REACH SAVO BEFORE 0800 TOMORROW. The wind had betrayed us, and Guadalcanal was in for a savage bombardment.

Sure enough, before dawn next morning, the fourteenth, I received this dispatch from Archie Vandegrift: BEING HEAVILY SHELLED. The shelling was concentrated on Henderson Field and lasted an hour and twenty minutes, then stopped abruptly. None of us at Nouméa could imagine why. Later we learned that a squadron of PT boats, Lt. Hugh M. Robinson commanding, had dashed out from Tulagi and harried the enemy ships—six cruisers and five destroyers—until they broke off and fled. Three planes at Henderson had been wrecked and seventeen damaged.

Five hours later, Henderson struck back. A mixed formation of twenty planes, including three *Enterprise* torpedo planes which had landed there after attacking the *Hiyei* the day before, found the fleeing bombardment group and hit two of the cruisers. At about the same time, more *Enterprise* planes—these from her dawn search —sighted the same group and inflicted further damage, which was increased by a concerted attack by sixteen of her SBD's.

I had ordered the *Enterprise* north early that morning, in response to information that the enemy's invasion group had started its run down the Slot. Actually, this proved to be two groups—one, consisting of eleven transports and thirteen destroyers, following the other, consisting of three heavy cruisers, a light cruiser, a carrier, and a destroyer. Our instructions were for the *Enterprise* to keep 100 miles westward of the axis of the Solomons, while "Ching" Lee's

129

force took a parallel course inboard, midway between her and the chain, thereby permitting her planes to strike across the screening battleships. We told her, YOUR OBJECTIVE TRANSPORTS.

Documents captured later suggest that there may have been as many as 13,500 troops aboard these transports. All we knew when we struck was that the pickings would be rich, and we threw in every plane that could take the air—planes from the *Enterprise*, Marine planes from Henderson, Army B-17's from Espiritu, fighters, bombers, dive bombers, and torpedo planes. Their attacks began at 1000 and continued until twilight. They would strike, return to base, rearm and refuel, and strike again. When "the Buzzard Patrol," as they dubbed themselves, had finished its work, one heavy cruiser and six transports had been sunk, and the three other cruisers had been damaged, as had four more transports and two destroyers. The prize of the day fell to a division of Marine fighter pilots who discovered a sleek speedboat spurting away from one of the sinking ships, presumably attempting to salvage the high command. The Marines dove on it, opened up with all their guns, and chewed it in half.

The four damaged transports straggled down to Guadalcanal and beached themselves near Tassafaronga next morning, to be shelled by our artillery, bombed and strafed by our planes, and finally riddled at leisure by the destroyer *Meade*, which took them under fire at popgun range. Some of their troops may have reached shore, but having no food or other supplies, they must have succeeded only in adding to the misery of the destitute troops already there.

Many hours elapsed between these actions and my receipt of reports about them, but it gradually became obvious that we had rattled Hirohito's protruding teeth. As the damage mounted, so mounted our spirits. As Rising Suns sank, our sun rose. The attack on the transports was the climax. I showed the dispatch to my staff and told them, "We've got the bastards licked!"

The Japanese, however, did not seem to realize it. Despite their appalling losses in ships and men on the fourteenth, they doggedly, or rashly, sent another force against us that same night. We sighted it in the afternoon, when it was still 150 miles north of Guadalcanal, so I had ample time to get Ching Lee into position

Official USN photo

"The *Big E*, the galloping ghost of the Oahu coast" (*U.S.S. Enterprise*), 1942

Official USN Photo
RAY THURBER
Operations

Official USN photo
MILES BROWNING
Chief of Staff

Amos Carr photo
DOUG MOULTON
Air Operations

Official USN photo
HAROLD STASSEN
Flag Secretary

Official USN photo
BILL KITCHELL
Flag Lieutenant

Official USN photo
MICK CARNEY
Chief of Staff

Official USN photo
ROLLO WILSON
Operations

Official USN photo
DEWITT PECK
War Plans

Official USN photo
JULIAN BROWN
Intelligence

SOME MEMBERS OF MY STAFF

Official USN pho

Bougainville, 1943. The man in the jungle suit is Frank Tremaine, of the United Press

PING WILKINSON*

NORM SCOTT*

DAN CALLAGHAN*

TIP MERRILL

PUG AINSWORTH

ARCHIE VANDERGRIFT

MIFF HARMON

NATE TWINING

SANDY PATCH

ROY GEIGER*

OSCAR GRISWOLD

JOHN HODGE

SOUTH PACIFIC COMMANDERS

ased

Official USN photo
SLEW McCAIN*

Official USN photo
PETER MITSCHER*

Official USN p
RAY SPRUANCE

Official USN photo
RALPH DAVISON

Official USN photo
JOCKO CLARK

Official USN pl
TED SHERMAN

Official USN photo
ARTHUR RADFORD

Official USN photo
JERRY BOGAN

British Information Services p
BERT RAWLINGS

Official USN photo
CHING LEE*

Official USN photo
JACK SHAFROTH

Task force and ta
group commanders
the Third Fleet, a
Ray Spruance, Co
mander Fifth Fleet

* Deceased

A Japanese carrier of the Zuiho class, afire and her flight deck buckled, maneuvers violently in her death throes at the Battle for Leyte Gulf, October 25, 1944

A *kamikaze* crashes the *U.S.S. Essex*, November 25, 1944

At the White House, March, 1945, with my wife

Press Association, I

near Savo Island for an interception around midnight. The enemy force consisted of two heavy cruisers, two light cruisers, nine destroyers, and the battleship *Kirishima*, a sister ship of the sunken *Hiyei*. Ching had, as before, the *Washington* and *South Dakota* and the destroyers *Walke*, *Benham*, *Gwin*, and *Preston*.

The action of the third stage opened at 0016 and lasted fifty minutes. We lost the *Walke*, *Benham*, and *Preston*, and the *Gwin* was damaged, as was the *South Dakota*. But the enemy lost a destroyer and the *Kirishima*. Though I am a destroyer man, I will gladly exchange two of my destroyers for an enemy battleship whenever the chance is offered. (Incidentally, of twelve battleships that Japan possessed eleven were sunk, eight by forces under my command.)

This engagement of Sunday, November 15, concluded the five-day Battle of Guadalcanal. The complete score follows:

| | ENEMY | | OURS | |
	Sunk	Damaged	Sunk	Damaged
Battleships.................	2			1
Heavy cruisers..............	1	2		2
Light cruisers...............		1	3	
Destroyers..................	3	6	7	4
Transports and cargo ships.....	10			
Totals...................	16	9	10	7

This battle was a decisive American victory by any standard. It was also the third great turning point of the war in the Pacific. Midway stopped the Japanese advance in the Central Pacific; Coral Sea stopped it in the Southwest Pacific; Guadalcanal stopped it in the South Pacific. Now, nearly five years later, I can face the alternative frankly. If our ships and planes had been routed in this battle, if we had lost it, our troops on Guadalcanal would have been trapped as were our troops on Bataan. We could not have reinforced them or relieved them. Archie Vandegrift would have been our "Skinny" Wainwright, and the infamous Death March would have been repeated. (We later captured a document which designated the spot where the Japanese commander had planned to accept Archie's surrender.) Unobstructed, the enemy would have driven south, cut our supply lines to New Zealand and Australia and enveloped them.

But we didn't lose the battle. We won it. Moreover, we seized the offensive from the enemy. Until then he had been advancing at his will. From then on he retreated at ours.

EDITOR'S NOTE:

When news of the Battle of Guadalcanal was released in the United States, the Mayor of Elizabeth, New Jersey, Admiral Halsey's native city, proclaimed November 20 as "Halsey Day" and ordered public buildings decorated, schools closed early, and church bells rung.

President Roosevelt, Secretary Knox, Admiral King, Admiral Nimitz, and others sent me messages of congratulations. I had no illusions about who deserved them, so I passed them on to the men who had done the fighting, along with a tribute of my own:

From: HALSEY
To: ALL SHIPS SOPAC, ALL COMD'G GENERALS SOPAC
TO THE SUPERB OFFICERS AND MEN UNDER THE SEA AND ON THE SEA AND IN THE AIR WHO HAVE IN THE PAST FEW DAYS PERFORMED SUCH MAGNIFICENT FEATS FOR THE U.S.: YOUR NAMES HAVE BEEN WRITTEN IN GOLDEN LETTERS ON THE PAGES OF HISTORY AND YOU HAVE WON THE EVERLASTING GRATITUDE OF YOUR COUNTRYMEN X NO HONOR FOR YOU COULD BE TOO GREAT X MY PRIDE IN YOU IS BEYOND EXPRESSION X MAGNIFICENTLY DONE X TO THE GLORIOUS DEAD: HAIL HEROES, REST WITH GOD X GOD BLESS YOU ALL.

VICE ADM. WILLIAM L. CALHOUN, FORMER COMMANDER BASE FORCE SOPAC:

On November 18, President Roosevelt nominated Bill for four stars. The news astonished us as much as it pleased us. Unwritten law forbade the Navy to have more than four full admirals on the active list at the same time, and we already had them—"Betty" Stark, Ernie King, Chester Nimitz, and Royal Ingersoll. However, Congress ignored the law and approved the nomination at once.

The word found Nouméa short of four-star pins, as it was of almost everything else in those days, so I obtained four two-star pins from a major general of Marines and had them welded in pairs, while regulation Navy pins—our stars are smaller than the Marines'—were being cut on a repair ship in the harbor.

When I gave Bill the makeshifts, he handed me his old three-star pins and told me, "Send one of these to Mrs. Scott and the other to Mrs. Callaghan. Tell them it was their husbands' bravery that got me my new ones."

It was my privilege to recommend a large number of decorations after Guadalcanal, but few gave me as much pleasure as recommending the *Enterprise* for the Presidential Unit Citation. This was the Big E's eighth operation in less than a year, and the Japanese had reported sinking her so many times that she had acquired an additional sobriquet, "the Galloping Ghost of the Oahu Coast." She helped open the war, and she helped close it. She is obsolete now, but, as Secretary Forrestal said of her, "She is the one ship that most nearly symbolizes and carries with it the history of the Navy in this war." Thank God that someone had the sentiment not to anchor her at Bikini!

I cannot close this account of the Battle of Guadalcanal without adding my confession of a grievous mistake. I have already confessed it officially; now I do so publicly.

Early on the morning of November 13, the light cruiser *Juneau*, bringing up the rear of Callaghan's column, was torpedoed and badly damaged. The first I knew of it was that afternoon, when the *Helena's* dispatch included her among the ships limping down to Espiritu. When Espiritu reported their arrival, however, her name was no longer on the list.

I called Miles Browning and asked, "Where's the *Juneau?*"

"I don't know, sir," he said. "I'll have to check."

It transpired that she had been torpedoed again and had sunk so suddenly, in such a hail of debris, that the other ships at first thought they were under a high-altitude bombing attack. The senior officer present, Capt. Gilbert C. Hoover of the *Helena*, now faced a grim decision. Although few men if any, in his opinion, could have survived the terrific explosion, common humanity urged him to search for them. (Capt. Lyman K. Swenson of the *Juneau* was one of Hoover's closest friends.) On the other hand, the *O'Bannon* had been sent off on a special mission, so he now had only the *Fletcher* and the crippled *Sterett* as escorts for his crippled force; rescue operations would almost certainly invite a second torpedo attack; and at that critical stage, the loss of another ship—and possibly more—might jeopardize the whole campaign. Hoover chose to continue his withdrawal toward Espiritu. He notified a patrol plane that he was doing so and gave it all pertinent informa-

133

tion. This information never went through. As a result, of some 120 men left alive in the water (it developed), only ten made the beach.

When the *Helena* eventually reached Nouméa, Hoover reported to my headquarters. After interrogating him thoroughly, my advisers—Jake Fitch, Kelly Turner, and Bill Calhoun—agreed that he had done wrong in abandoning the *Juneau*, and recommended his detachment. Reluctantly, I concurred. Hoover's record was outstanding—he had won three Navy Crosses—but I felt that the strain of prolonged combat had impaired his judgment; that guts alone were keeping him going; and that his present condition was dangerous to himself and to his splendid ship. In this conviction, I detached him with orders to CINCPAC.

Much later, when I reviewed the case at the instigation of Rear Adm. Robert B. Carney, who had become my Chief of Staff, I concluded that I had been guilty of an injustice. I realized that Hoover's decision was in the best interests of victory. I so informed the Navy Department, requesting that he be restored to combat command, and adding that I would be delighted to have him serve under me. The stigma of such a detachment can never be wholly erased, but I have the comfort, slight as it is, of knowing that Hoover's official record is clean. I deeply regret the whole incident. It testifies to Captain Hoover's character when I say that he has never let it affect our personal relations.

Our most reliable barometer of enemy intentions was the amount of shipping in the Shortlands-Southern Bougainville area. After the Battle of Guadalcanal, this barometer fell rapidly and stayed low until November 24, when it began to rise again. By the twenty-seventh, reconnaissance was reporting the presence of more than twenty-five ships, not counting small craft. Another attempt either to attack or to reinforce was imminent.

The strength of our surface forces, too, had been increasing. The *Enterprise*, the *Washington*, and the light cruiser *San Diego* were at Nouméa. At Nandi in the Fijis were the *Saratoga*, the battleships *North Carolina*, *Colorado*, and *Maryland*, and the light cruiser *San Juan*. And at Espiritu were the heavy cruisers *Northampton*, *Pensacola*, *New Orleans*, and *Minneapolis*, with the light cruiser *Honolulu*, and the destroyers *Drayton*, *Fletcher*, *Maury*, and *Perkins*. On the night of the twenty-ninth, we sent the Espiritu group toward Guadalcanal, under Rear Adm. Carleton H. Wright. Two more destroyers, the *Lamson* and *Lardner*, joined him a few hours before the action, which began close to midnight on the thirtieth.

As usual, the scene was the waters southeast of Savo Island—"Iron Bottom Bay," as it was becoming known. The title to the nickname was strengthened by the Battle of Tassafaronga. One enemy destroyer was sunk by gunfire, and our *Northampton* by a torpedo. Our other three heavy cruisers were also torpedoed, but managed to make port and lived to fight again. For an enemy force of eight destroyers, as it was estimated, to inflict such damage on a more powerful force at so little cost is something less than a credit to our command. But once again the tactical loss was overbalanced by strategic profit. This was the enemy's last surface offensive against Guadalcanal. Except for desultory help brought his troops by the Tokyo Express, they were abandoned to die from disease or starvation, or at the hands of the United States Army and Marine Corps.

9

I N MY FIRST six weeks as COMSOPAC, our surface forces had to
fight three savage battles. In addition, our troops on Guadalcanal were fighting daily and no less savagely. Tassafaronga,
however, was followed by a lull, during which I was able to turn
my attention, for the first time, to organizing my command and
settling in for the long struggle ahead.

I have said that Miles Browning and Julian Brown were the
only two officers on my staff who accompanied me to the South
Pacific. The rest were aboard the *Enterprise*, which delivered them
and certain key enlisted personnel at Nouméa on October 25, the
day before the Battle of Santa Cruz. As I dug into my new job, I
realized that the tremendous burden of responsibility which Bob
Ghormley had been carrying was far beyond my own capacity. I
have known too many commanding officers whose epitaph could be

> I am a cook and a captain bold
> And the mate of the *Nancy* brig,
> And a bo'sun tight and a midshipmite
> And the crew of the captain's gig.

I believe in delegating all possible authority. I called in my staff and
told them, "There's a lot to be done. Look around, see what it is,
and do it." Able as they were, the job swamped even them, and I
had to supply them with more assistants. Before we were running
smoothly, Operations alone was getting the full-time attention of
twenty-five of my officers.

The *Argonne* was hopelessly inadequate for this increase. Not only was she overcrowded, but she was not air conditioned, and the tropical summer was on top of us. I have always insisted on comfortable offices and quarters for my staff. Their day's work is so long, their schedule so irregular, the strain so intense, that I am determined for them to work and rest in whatever ease is available. Bob Ghormley had told me that he had wanted to move ashore but had been unable to find accommodations. I was going to find them or else.

Being well aware of the importance that French officials attach to decorations, I told Julian Brown to array himself in all his ribbons, with special emphasis on the Croix de guerre and its *fourragère*, and sent him to call on the Governor of New Caledonia, M. Montchamps. Julian made his politenesses, then explained our need for larger quarters.

Montchamps asked, "What do we get in return?"

Julian answered coldly, "We will continue to protect you as we have always done."

Montchamps reluctantly promised to see what he could do, and Julian took his leave. Nothing happened. Next day Julian received more empty promises. This continued for a month. Finally Julian told him, "We've got a war on our hands and we can't continue to devote valuable time to these petty concerns. I venture to remind Your Excellency that if we Americans had not arrived here, the Japanese would have."

Montchamps shrugged. When I heard that, we simply moved ashore.

The offices "put at our disposal" had been the headquarters of the High Commissioner for Free France in the Pacific, Rear Admiral d'Argenlieu, who was enroute to San Francisco at the moment. This extraordinary character had served in the French Navy in World War I and had then become a Carmelite monk. He rejoined the Navy in World War II, was captured but escaped, was seriously wounded in the abortive Dakar coup in July, 1940, and arrived in Nouméa a year later. Here his insistence on the formal maintenance of French sovereignty so antagonized the New Caledonians—not to mention the British and Americans—that they put him under confinement in May, 1942. Maj. Gen. Alexander M. Patch, commanding the Americal Division, rescued him, however, and De

137

Gaulle made him acting head of the Fighting French naval forces. Still later, he became Assistant Chief of the General Staff of the Navy and when I last heard of him, was Governor of French Indo-China.

We were still overcrowded in our new offices, but not so badly as on the *Argonne*. Next we looked for living quarters and eventually established ourselves in a cluster of buildings constituting a miniature International Settlement—two Quonset huts, which we christened "Wicky-Wacky Lodge"; one ramshackle French house, "Havoc Hall"; and, of all anomalies, the former Japanese consulate. Here we lived for the next nineteen months.

The consulate was one of the few brick houses in Nouméa, and its cool, airy hilltop commanded one of the most superb views I have ever seen. The consul himself had been sent to Australia for internment at the outbreak of war, but his household furnishings were still there, including the usual watercolor of Fujiyama, the usual embroideries of goldfish and geishas, and the usual dwarf pine in a pot. The chairs were so squatty that we felt as if we were sitting on the deck, and the tables hardly reached our knees. My Filipino mess attendants never became accustomed to my response when they broke a piece of the consul's china. Instead of bawling them out, I told them, "The hell with it! It's Japanese." But my deepest satisfaction came from a simple ceremony every morning, when the Marine guards raised the American flag over this bit of property which had once belonged to a representative of Japan.

The Joint Chiefs of Staff had fixed the original boundary between the South and Southwest Pacific areas at the 160th east meridian, but because this intersects Guadalcanal and would divide responsibility for that campaign, they later chose the 159th. To maintain equilibrium between the services, they appointed an Army officer, General MacArthur, Supreme Commander of the Southwest Pacific, and a Navy officer Supreme Commander of the South Pacific.

I emphasize "Supreme Commander" to establish the realization that MacArthur and I commanded everything in our respective areas—Army, Navy, Marines, and Allies; troops, ships, planes, and supplies. MacArthur reported only to General Marshall; I, only to CINCPAC and, through him, to COMINCH. This was my first experience with a composite command, and I was determined that our job should not be slowed by interservice friction. I need not have worried. Archie Vandegrift was my other self, and the cooperation given me by Miff Harmon and his Chief of Staff, Brig. Gen. Nathan F. Twining, was ready and whole-hearted.

To make sure that this spirit penetrated the ranks, I summoned all my subordinate commanders and told them, "Gentlemen, we are the South Pacific Fighting Force. I don't want anybody even to be thinking in terms of Army, Navy, or Marines. Every man must understand this, and every man *will* understand it, if I have to take off his uniform and issue coveralls with 'South Pacific Fighting Force' printed on the seat of his pants."

I had already ordered all Navy men and Marines in the area to leave off their neckties. They were a discomfort in that climate, and tying and untying them consumed time; my real reason, though, was that the Army was not required to wear them, and I hoped that uniformity of appearance would encourage uniformity of action.

When the South Pacific campaign was over and we returned to Pearl, we found that CINCPAC's uniform of the day still included ties. Indoors at our quarters, though, we reverted to our old informality. Our staff poet, Capt. Ralph E. Wilson, had a plaque lettered and posted in our front hall:

> Complete with black tie
> You do look terrific,
> But take it off here:
> This is still South Pacific!

CAPT. HAROLD E. STASSEN, WHO SUCCEEDED CAPTAIN MOULTON AS FLAG SECRETARY:

It was in 1943, I think, that the Navy Department introduced gray uniforms for officers and chief petty officers; anyhow, that's when they first appeared in the South Pacific. Most of us disliked them on sight. In fact, the Admiral always referred to them as "bus-driver suits." Their unpopularity in our theater was so general that Washington issued a special bulletin, pointedly stating that grays had been authorized as an alternate uniform for the entire Navy, including *every theater* of the war.

139

When the Admiral saw this bulletin, he hitched up his khaki trousers, pulled down the sleeves of his khaki shirt, and remarked to no one in particular, "The Department is absolutely right. Any Navy uniform should apply to the whole Navy, and officers and chiefs in my command are wholly at liberty to wear the damn things—*if*, that is, they are so lacking in naval courtesy and have such limited intelligence as to prefer dressing differently from the commander of the force."

We stuck to our khakis.

The lull that followed Tassafaronga gave us a chance to relieve the 1st Marine Division, which, with elements of the 2d and of the Army's Americal Division, had withstood the enemy, the jungle, and malaria on Guadalcanal for four fearful months. (The Americal was the first American division to arrive in New Caledonia; hence its name.) On December 9, Archie Vandegrift turned over Guadalcanal to "Sandy" Patch of the Americal, and the Marines were transferred to Australia for the rest they had earned if ever men earned it.

In exchange, General MacArthur diverted to my area the Army's 25th Infantry Division, then en route from Oahu to Sydney, under Maj. Gen. J. Lawton Collins. I had known Joe Collins in Honolulu when he was a colonel—a small man, quick on his feet, and even quicker in his brain—and I was delighted to see him when he reported to me in Nouméa. He had great pride in his men. "The finest regular division in the Army," he said. "Give me three weeks to unload my transports and combat-load them, and I'll be ready to go anywhere. . . . Why, what are you laughing at?"

I told him, "Your division is leaving for Guadalcanal tomorrow!"

Joe took it in his stride. Reinforced by the 147th Infantry and the unblooded 6th and 8th regiments of the 2d Marine Division, the 25th went into Guadalcanal and not only made a splendid record, but equaled it later in New Georgia and again in the Philippines. My respect for Joe Collins' men is as high as his own.

As December wore on, the New Georgia area attracted our attention more and more frequently. We had been warned at the end of November that the Japanese were constructing an airfield at Munda, on the southwest tip of the island, and on December 9 photographic reconnaissance showed that it was nearly completed.

140

An airfield less than 200 miles from Henderson could not be ignored. Although our planes pounded it regularly, it was brought to operational shape, and "Zekes" began to use it. (Zekes are Japanese fighter planes, earlier known as "Zeros.") On the morning of December 24, we mustered our small air strength and shot the works. I put the results into a dispatch to CINCSOWESPAC, CINCPAC, COMINCH, and all my task-force commanders: 9 SBD'S WITH 9 P-39'S PLUS 4 F4F'S ATTACKED MUNDA THIS MORNING X 4 ATTACKING ZEKES SHOT DOWN X ABOUT 20 MORE CAUGHT ATTEMPTING TAKE-OFF X 10 OF THESE SHOT DOWN IN AIR BY F4F'S AND REMAINING 10 OR 12 GROUPED AT END OF RUNWAY DESTROYED BY DIVE BOMBERS X 2 OTHERS STRAFED IN REVETMENTS X WEAK AA FIRE SILENCED BY SBD'S X ALL PLANES RETURNED SAFELY X AT 1800 9 SBD'S COVERED BY 4 EACH F4F'S AND P-39'S BOMBED 13 LANDING BARGES LOADED WITH TROOPS AND SUPPLIES NEARING MUNDA X 4 BARGES REACHED SHORE BUT FEW JAPS ESCAPED X AIRPORT FLOWN OVER AT 50 FEET NO PLANES SEEN NO AA FIRE RECEIVED X THIS BY WAY OF CHRISTMAS GREETING.

It is true that not only fighters but medium bombers were using Munda Field again within a week. Still, having hung up a record that day, we hung up our stockings that night with extra cheeriness. My staff procured some small, imitation Christmas trees, and our Filipino mess attendants festooned them with "flowers" carved from radishes and carrots.

Now I approach an incident which needs, I gather, some explanation. On New Year's Eve, the correspondents in Nouméa asked me to give them an interview and to make a few predictions for 1943. I did so. I said that we now had the initiative, that the Japs would keep on retreating, and that the end of 1943 would see us in Tokyo. I also made several passing references—some rather indelicate, perhaps—to Hirohito, Tojo, and others.

The "intemperate" tone of my remarks brought me considerable criticism. Even so, the remarks that appeared in print were a diluted version of what I actually said; Miles, Julian, and the SOPAC chief censor edited them and watered them down. The State Department may be right in its argument that it doesn't become an American admiral to sling billingsgate at the Japanese Emperor and his Prime Minister, but the correspondents had

141

asked for my opinion, not for my guess at what State hoped it was. So I said what I thought: the Japanese are bastards.

The severest criticism was centered on my prophecy about Tokyo. The production leaders at home put up a bellow that I could hear in Nouméa. They were terrified that labor would take my word as gospel and quit their war jobs. The draft authorities also complained, as did a lot of other officials. They accused me of everything from recklessness to drunkenness. God Almighty, I knew we wouldn't be in Tokyo that soon! I knew we wouldn't be there even by the end of 1944. I may be tactless, but I'm not a damned fool!

What the civilian bigwigs didn't consider is this: my forces were tired; their morale was low; they were beginning to think that they were abused and forgotten, that they had been fighting too much and too long. Moreover, the new myth of Japanese invincibility had not yet been entirely discredited. Prior to Pearl Harbor, the United States in general had rated Japan as no better than a class-C nation. After that one successful sneak attack, however, panicky eyes saw the monkeymen as supermen. I saw them as nothing of the sort, and I wanted my forces to know how I felt. I stand by the opinion that the Japs are bastards, and I stand by this one, too.

In fact, I stood by it, repeated it, and strengthened it two days later, in New Zealand. Ever since my arrival in the South Pacific, the New Zealand government had been pressing me to make a visit, but crises were recurring too frequently for me to risk being caught 1,000 miles behind my headquarters. Toward the end of December, Intelligence reported that no major actions seemed imminent, so I accepted the invitation, in order both to pay my official respects and to look over American personnel and equipment at our depots there.

Julian Brown, Bill Kitchell, and I took off from Nouméa in my Coronado on January 2 and reached Auckland that afternoon. The Prime Minister, Peter Fraser, courteously met me at the dock and accompanied me to our hotel. On the way, he told me that his country was still apprehensive about a Japanese breakthrough and was urging him to bring its divisions back from Africa, whereas Mr. Churchill and President Roosevelt were no less insistent that he leave them; they had warned him that General Montgomery's slender forces might not be able to survive the depletion and that the Allies had no ships to spare as transports. Mr. Fraser expressed reluctance to jeopardize the Allied cause, but feared he would have to yield unless he could go before the war cabinet backed by a strongly reassuring statement from me.

I asked him, "What do you want me to say, and when and where?"

He told me that a number of editors and reporters were waiting at my hotel; if I would give them an interview in which I reiterated my New Year's Eve statement, they would circulate it throughout New Zealand, and his position would be fortified. I did so gladly, on condition that the interview be withheld, for the sake of security, until my return to Nouméa.

EDITOR'S NOTES:

1) Following are extracts from this interview as printed in *The New Zealand Herald* for January 7, 1943:

"Interviewed at Auckland during the visit he has just made to New Zealand, the Commander-in-Chief of the South Pacific Area, Admiral William F. Halsey, stood confidently to his recently cabled prediction of a complete Allied victory in 1943. 'That is right,' he said. 'We have 363 days left to fulfill my prediction and we are going to do it.'

". . . Questioned whether he was satisfied with the progress of operations against the Japanese, he replied, 'We have their measure in the air, on and under the water, and on the land. When we first started out against them I held that one of our men was equal to three Japanese. I have now increased this to twenty. They are not supermen, although they try to make us believe they are.'

"Asked whether Japanese naval tactics were difficult to meet, Admiral Halsey said, 'Like everything else about them, they are tricky, but not too hard to fathom. There is nothing to be worried about in their tactics. Any normal naval officer can lick them.'

"'What do you expect Japan's next move will be?' Admiral Halsey was asked.

"'Japan's next move will be to retreat,' he said. 'A start has been made to make them retreat. They will not be able to stop going back.'

". . . Questioned whether the forces in the combat area under his command were now confident of the future, Admiral Halsey characteristically said, 'I would not say that they are now confident. There is a feeling of continuing confidence.'

143

". . . Throughout his interview Admiral Halsey did not bombast. Even when making what the Japanese would consider the most outrageous statements of their character and their fate, his tone did not rise above a level of firmness.

"His confidence was clearly immense, but the expression of it was even and not in declamatory statements. It was so great and so obviously no bigger than his conviction that it was infectious, and as statement succeeded statement it became very clear why it is said of Admiral William 'Pudge' Halsey by his officers and men that they would follow him to Hell. He is a man whose confidence could clearly win battles."

2) Following is an extract from an editorial in the same issue of the same newspaper:

"Few people can live up to their reputations. Admiral Halsey is one of them. The bold actions fought in the Gilberts, the Marshalls, and the Solomons had made of him a legend for enterprise and hard hitting. His recent visit to Auckland showed all who were privileged to meet him the embodiment of the legend. For all his unassuming manner and quiet speech, none could fail to identify in him the leader, the man of action, the fighter. The pity is that more could not have the tonic experience of seeing and hearing him, of being fired and steeled by his free spirit. Yet the main impression he made will be spread from those who met Admiral Halsey. Some of it is communicated in the interview published this morning. It is one of robust confidence—not the idle confidence that breeds complacency and slackness, but rather the faith that issues in works. The men he commands are fortunate in their leader. So is New Zealand and she should strive in every way to be worthy of her good fortune in having such a man appointed to match and out-match her nearest enemy. Admiral Halsey sticks to his prediction of complete victory this year, as he sticks to everything he starts. He has the right way of it, for we shall certainly not conquer in 1943 unless we believe we can, and plan and work to do it. The willing must precede the doing, and the action will be fortified by faith. . . ."

3) On February 20, 1945, Captain Stassen gave an interview which he prefaced by saying, "The Admiral doesn't like alibis, but I'll take a chance and tell why he made that wrong prediction." Following is an extract from this interview, as reported by *The New York Times*:

"He made it [the prediction] during the darkest period of the Pacific War. We had very little Navy afloat. Australia was very much concerned. The Japanese Navy was still strong. It was a pretty gloomy situation.

144

Halsey knew that if the Jap Navy had attacked our force, it was doubtful if our fleet, even with its magnificent fighting spirit, could hold the line. So he made this bold assertive statement both to mislead the Japs and to cheer up our force. It worked. The Japanese didn't attack for six months. Instead they tried to find out what in the world Admiral Halsey had that led him to make that statement."

Next day I made a tour of various military installations at Auckland, including our naval hospitals, which were filled with wounded from Guadalcanal, then flew to Wellington for a similar tour. We returned to Nouméa on January 7. A few days later, word of my Auckland interview reached Japan, and Tokyo Rose went on the air with a grisly description of the tortures being prepared for me. When I came into my quarters that night, I found my two guests, Jake Fitch and Bill Calhoun, enacting a mysterious pantomime.

I was bewildered. I asked them, "What the hell goes on here?"

"We're stirring a caldron," they said.

"A caldron? Why?"

"Boiling oil! Boiling oil!"

I had no time to waste on these well-wishers. A dispatch informed me that Secretary Knox, Chester Nimitz, and Rear Adm. John Sidney McCain were expected at Espiritu, so I left at once. We met aboard the aircraft tender *Curtiss* and had just settled into our beds when bombs started falling. Their total effect was a few craters in the beach, but since this was Espiritu's first raid in several weeks, we couldn't help wondering whether its coincidence with our arrival was luck or leakage. The following night, at Guadalcanal, we were bombed again, from 2030 until daybreak, and our wonder increased to a strong suspicion. It was never verified, but I learned later that it was shared. When our plane took off from Henderson, and a communications officer sat down to file the routine departure dispatch, his shaken assistant begged him, "Do me a favor, will you? Send it in Japanese. I want 'em to know for sure that the high-priced hired help has left here!"

I have very little stomach for bombs. There were no foxholes on the *Curtiss*, but there were plenty on Guadalcanal. When I heard the first *boom!*, I left my comfortable hut and dove into the ground, with Mr. Knox and "Slew" McCain. But not Chester.

145

He said he hadn't had any sleep the night before; he was going to catch up; besides, he said, he was scared of mosquitoes. Chester spent the night under a sheet, behind screens. The other three of us spent it half-naked, out in the open. And Chester was the only one who caught malaria!

His resistance may have been weakened by something I told him. Back in November, the Commander of the Guadalcanal Naval Base had been taken ill and I had to find a relief for him at once. The name of Comdr. Oliver Owen Kessing, an excellent officer and an old friend of mine, jumped at me from the Navy Register, so I requested the Bureau of Personnel to order him to my command with the temporary rank of captain, which the duty required. BuPers replied coldly, REGRET HIS SERVICES UNAVAILABLE. This was nonsense, and I knew it. There was not the slightest reason why "Scrappy" Kessing shouldn't be assigned to the important job I had for him. Somebody in BuPers was simply being hoity-toity. I sent another dispatch: MAKE HIS SERVICES AVAILABLE. Finally, after six or seven ill-tempered exchanges, they notified me that Scrappy was on his way, but said nothing about his promotion, although Chester, a former Chief of the Bureau, had approved my request for it.

When I saw Chester on this trip, I told him that I was thoroughly fed up with such obstructionism, and that if the promotion had not been confirmed when I returned to Nouméa, I would send Scrappy the following dispatch, with an information copy to BuPers: YOU WILL ASSUME RANK UNIFORM AND TITLE OF CAPTAIN US NAVY.

Chester had a fit. "No! For God's sake, don't do it! You'll foul up everything!"

"You wait and see," I said. But when I reached Nouméa, Scrappy's promotion had come through.

EDITOR'S NOTE:

When Secretary Knox returned from this trip, he brought back a story which he told to many of his friends in Washington:

Two enlisted men were sauntering along a passageway on Admiral Halsey's flagship. One said, "Halsey? I'd go through hell for that old son of a bitch!"

Just then a finger jabbed his back. It was Halsey himself. "Young man," he said, "I'm not so old!"

December had shown us faint signs that the tide was turning. By January no one could doubt that it had begun to run with us. New ships and aircraft arrived, and we were able to withdraw our old worn ones for the overhauls they needed so badly. The shoestring was still frayed; the total forces available were still so sparse that we had to strip the planes from three new escort carriers and send them to beef up the shore-based squadrons at Guadalcanal; but now for the first time we felt strong enough to attempt a modest offensive.

Our early moves consisted chiefly in developing port and training facilities nearer and nearer to the front—first on Efate, then on Espiritu Santo, and eventually in the Tulagi-Purvis Bay area, next to Guadalcanal itself. As soon as these forward ports were ready, we sent in our ships—PT's, destroyers, and even cruisers—not only to block off the Tokyo Express and to discourage submarine and air raids on our Guadalcanal shipping, but to make occasional offensive forays up the Slot, such as Rear Adm. Walden L. Ainsworth's bombardment of Munda on the night of January 4/5.

By the end of the month, I had at my disposal six major task forces. One, commanded by Rear Adm. Robert C. Giffen, was covering a convoy to Guadalcanal when, on January 29, a flight of enemy planes burst out of the darkness and put a torpedo into the heavy cruiser *Chicago*. She was taken under tow, but she had made only 70 miles toward Espiritu before another dozen torpedo planes attacked her and finished her off. The destroyer *Lavallette* was also hit but managed to limp into port.

The loss of the *Chicago* would have been a blow at any time, and just now we felt it with special severity. On February 5, an Army B-17 from Espiritu, at the extreme limit of its 800-mile search, spotted a powerful enemy force standing down from Truk —two carriers, four battleships, six heavy cruisers, two light cruisers, and twelve destroyers. I had been expecting this development. The enemy's obstinacy, the desperate plight of his troops on Guadalcanal, and the long lull since his last assault—long enough for him to replenish his carrier groups and task forces—all had led me to anticipate a final, supreme effort. Accordingly, I had disposed my own task forces south of Guadalcanal, ready to move

147

forward at the word. While we waited, the Tokyo Express made three runs and evacuated all except a few scattered troops. We knew what was happening, but although we had a veteran group of cruisers and destroyers within range of the Express's track, we considered it wiser to hold them against, the major threat. It proved to be only a threat. The main force never closed us.

The Express' last run was on the night of February 7—exactly six months since our Marines had landed at Haleta, Gavutu, and Tulagi. Next day Sandy Patch informed me, ORGANIZED RESIST-ANCE ON GUADALCANAL HAS CEASED; and Miles Browning replied over my signature, WHEN I SENT A PATCH TO ACT AS TAILOR FOR GUADAL-CANAL, I DID NOT EXPECT HIM TO REMOVE THE ENEMY'S PANTS AND SEW IT ON SO QUICKLY X THANKS AND CONGRATULATIONS.

The grim, ugly, bloody, expensive campaign was finished.

Before I leave it, I want to mention two lighter incidents, both of which occurred toward its end. To appreciate the first, it is neces-sary to understand the Navy's alphabet: *Able* represents the letter A; *Baker*, B; *Charlie*, C; and so on, with *Option* representing O, and *Sail*, S. Around the middle of January we learned that a Jap sub-marine would land a certain high official at Cape Esperance at a certain time. We sent the data to our surface-force commander and added, IMPORTANT SAIL OPTION BAKER ABOARD X GET HIM. Soon afterward we received his terse answer: SANK SUB X IMPORTANT SAIL OPTION BAKER STILL ABOARD.

The other incident involved the New Zealand corvette *Kiwi*. (A corvette is roughly equivalent to a gunboat.) Three of the *Kiwi's* officers—the captain, the medical officer, and the chief engineer— were famous from the Solomons to Auckland. Everyone knew them, at least by sight. Not only were they the most mastodonic men I ever laid eyes on—their combined weights were close to 800 pounds—but whenever the *Kiwi* put into Nouméa, these monsters would stage a three-man parade through the town, one of them puffing into a dented trombone, another tooting a jazz whistle, and the third playing a concertina.

On January 29, the *Kiwi* was patrolling off Guadalcanal when a big Japanese sub suddenly surfaced close aboard. The skipper immediately put his helm over and rang up full speed on his tele-graph, which so astonished the chief that he yelled up the speaking tube, "What's the matter, you bastard? Have you gone crazy?"

"Shut up!" the skipper yelled back. "There's a week-end's leave in Auckland dead ahead of us! Give me everything you've got, or I'll come below and kick hell out of you!"

The big sub turned out to be the I-1, half again as long as the *Kiwi* and with twice the fire power. None the less, the *Kiwi* charged in, with her little guns popping, and rammed the I-1 amidships.

"Hit her again!" the skipper yelled. "It'll be a *week's* leave"!

They hit her again.

"Once more, for a fortnight!"

The third time the *Kiwi* rammed her, the I-1 sank.

It was a bold attack, bold enough to deserve recognition, so I notified the skipper and the chief that I was recommending them for Navy Crosses, our Navy's highest award. When they reported to my office to be decorated, it was in a spirit that might be described as "picnic." In fact, I had to support them with one hand while I pinned on the Crosses with the other. They thanked me, saluted, and rumbled away. The last I saw of them, they had picked up the medical officer and their musical instruments, and were forming another parade.

The North African campaign had top priority on New Zealand's man power, and the number of troops she could lend us was limited. One exacting and invaluable duty, however, the "New Zealanders" shared exclusively with the Australians. This duty was coast watching. Paratroopers, Rangers, and underwater demolition experts already enjoy a wide reputation for fearlessness, but no list of hazardous services would be complete without the coast watchers. Before the war, most of them had been interisland traders or managers of coconut plantations, so they knew the Solomons intimately, the trails and channels, the natives and their languages. The establishment of our front at Guadalcanal put a premium on the special information which these men possessed and their special facilities for acquiring more. Equipped with radios and a few supplies and weapons, they returned to their islands, dove into the jungle, and stayed there, sometimes hundreds of miles within the enemy's lines and sometimes for six months on end.

Each of them developed his own spy system, to supplement his personal observation. His native scouts, moving freely among the Japanese, would report what they had learned, and the coast

149

watcher would pass us the word by radio—how far construction of the airfield at Vila had progressed; where the enemy's barges were lying up at night; how many planes had flown over on their way to strike Guadalcanal, and how many had returned. In addition, the coast watchers organized rescue parties to pick up our downed fliers and keep them safe until we could send for them. One of them showed me his "guest book," with the signatures and thanks of some thirty pilots and crewmen who had been returned to their bases by his guts and ingenuity.

It was a lonely, desperately dangerous life, and only real men could endure it. The Japs knew about the coast watchers and tried every means of capturing them. They bribed and tortured the natives, combed the islands with patrols, and even tried to hunt them down with dogs. A coast watcher on Bougainville discovered the exact location of the kennel and radioed it to us, with a request for a bomb. Our pilot's direct hit was acknowledged with THANKS X WILL NOT BE BOTHERED FURTHER.

Most of the natives were loyal to the Allies, but the Japs occasionally managed to corrupt a village. As soon as we heard of it, we would bomb the village, then drop pidgin English messages on the villages near by, warning them not to invite bombs on themselves. I have kept a copy of a message we dropped on Bougainville in January, 1943, and I append it here as a curiosity:

SITROG PELA TOK BILOG NAMBAWAN KIAP BILOG OLMASTA,
A serious warning from the big white chief,
OL IUPELA MAN BILOG BUKAPASIS NA BILOG BUIN NA KIETA:
to all natives of Buka Passage, Buin, and Kieta:
DISPELA TOK MIGIVIM IU I STRAITPELA TOK. MOBETA IU HARIM GUT.
This is straight talk.   You must listen.
PLES KANAK OLIKOLIM SORUM I AMBAG TUNAS LOG KIAP TRU BILOG IU NAU
The village of Sorum has been disloyal, has
HARIM TOK BILOG JAPAN NAU ALPIM JAPAN.
taken orders from the Japs, and has helped the Japs.
ORIAT TROWEI BOM OLSEM DAINAMAIT LOG IN NAU.
We have now bombed them.
MIPELA TROWEI PINIS BOM LOG PIDIA LOG POKPOK LOG TOBEROI NAU LOG
We also bombed Pidia, Pok Pok, Toberoi, and
SADI TAIM OLIAMBAG TUMAS LOG MIPIA NA ALPIM JAPAN.
Sadi when they helped the Japs.

150

SIPOS NADAPELA PLES KANAK I ALPIM JAPAN ORAIT MIPELA TROWEI BOM
If any villages help the Japs, we will bomb
LOGIM TU NA KWITKAIM I BAGARAP OLGETA.
them and destroy them altogether.
MIPELA I GOT PLANTI BALUS PLANTI BOM PLANTI SOLJA.
We have many planes, many bombs, and many soldiers.
MIPELA NO KEN LIAS LOG DISPELA WOK.
We will not hesitate to carry out this work.
I NO LONGTAIM NA MIPELA OLGETA IKAM WANTAIM OL SOLJA BILOG
Before long we will come with all the American
AMERIKA NA RAUSIM OL JAPAN NA KILIM OLGETA NAU MEKIN
soldiers to dislodge the Japs and kill them all and punish
SAVE OLMAN I ALPIM JAPAN.
all natives who helped them.

> TOK I PINIS.
> That is all.
> IUPELA I LUKAUT.
> You have been warned.

Each of our pilots carried a pidgin English paper to read to the natives in case of a forced landing. Here is a copy of that, too, with the translation:

1. DISPALA MASTA I GIFIM PAS LONG YU I PEREN BILONG GAVMAN.
   The white man holding this paper is a friend of the Government.
2. BALUS BILONG EN I BAGARAP TRU NAU YUPALA MAS LUKAUT GUT LONG EN INAP LONG MASTA IKAMAP LONG MIPALA GEN.
   His plane has crashed and you must look after him so that he reaches safety.
3. IM INO SAVE GUT LONG TOK PISIN NAU YUPALA MAS TING LONG OL LIKLIK SAMTING BILONG EN.
   He is not able to ask in pidgin for everything he needs, so you must anticipate his wants.
4. GIFIN WARA BILONG DRING OLSEM KULAU.
   Bring drinking water and drinking coconuts.
5. GIFIM KAIKAI OLSEM KOKURUK NAU KIAU NAU BANANA MAU NAU POPO NAU OL GUTPALA KAIKAI.
   Give him food, such as fowls, eggs, bananas, pawpaws, and other suitable foods.
6. SAPOS JAPAN IKAM KILOSTU YUPALA HAITIM MASTA NAU GIAMONIM OL JAPAN.

151

If the Japanese come, hide the white man and give them false information.

7. WANPALA BOI IGOT TAUNAM OLSEM KALAMBO I GIFIM LONG MASTA.

If anyone has a mosquito net, give it to the white man.

8. SAPOS PILES INO GAT AUSKIAP OLARIT MAKIM WANPALA NUPALA AUS BILONG IM I SILIP. WOKIM GUT BET BILONG IM OLSEM PASIN BILONG WOK BUS.

If there is no resthouse in the village, allot him a newly built house to sleep in. Make a bush bed for him.

9. SAPOS MASTA INO INAP LONG WOKABAUT YUPALA MEKIM BET NAU KARIM.

If he is unable to walk, make a stretcher and carry him.

10. DOKTA BOI LUKAUT LONG SOR BILONG EN.

The village medical orderly should attend to any wounds or sores.

11. SAMPALA BOI I WOKABAUT WANTAEM LONG MASTA NAU KARIM LIKLIK SAMTING BILONG EN. YUPALA BRINGIM LONG KIAP NO LONG OL MASTA NO LONG OL SOLDIA BILONG INGLIS.

Some natives are to travel with him, to carry his effects and to guide him to a Government officer or to our lines or to other whites.

12. BIAEN IGAT PE IKAMAP LONG OL DISPALA SAMTING.

Later you will be paid for all these services.

13. YUPALA KISIM PAPA NA PENSIL LONG MISIN BOI BILONG YUPALA NAU-MASTA I WOKIM PAS NAU GIFIM LONG YUPALA. TAEM KIAP IKAMAP GIFIM PAS LONG KIAP NAU KISIM PE. SAPOS JAPAN ILAIK KAMAP HAITIM PAS GUT INAP LONG OL INO KAN LUKIM.

Get a pencil and paper from your native mission teacher, and the white man will write a note to leave with you. When a Government officer visits you, show him this, and he will pay you. If the Japanese come to your village, do not let them see this note.

GAVMAN I TOK YUPALA MAS ARIM.

These are the instructions of the Government, and you must obey them.

That last sentence became very popular with our pilots. If one of them grumbled about being assigned to a tough mission, another was sure to tell him, "*Gavman i tok, yupala mas arim!*"

152

10

THE FALL of Guadalcanal on February 8, 1943, ended the first phase of the Solomons campaign. Geographically, this was the southern phase; militarily, it was the defensive phase. The second phase, which would be fought in the Central Solomons and fought offensively, opened on February 21, when we made an unopposed landing on the Russell Islands, 55 miles northwest of Henderson Field. The purpose of our move was to establish an airfield that much closer to the enemy's base at Munda on New Georgia. Munda was blocking our path to Bougainville, Bougainville was blocking our path to Rabaul, and Rabaul was the keystone of the whole Japanese structure in the southern Pacific.

Rabaul's peacetime blessing, a magnificent natural harbor at the entrance to the Solomon Sea, was its wartime doom. The Japanese had overwhelmed the small Australian garrison only seven weeks after Pearl Harbor and immediately had begun to develop the town into a major base. They built five airfields, fortified the surrounding mountains, and poured in troops and supplies. By the end of the year, Rabaul had become a bastion second in strength and importance only to Truk, 700 miles northward. It dominated both my area and General MacArthur's, and until we captured it or neutralized it, our part of the war would be deadlocked.

The problem was this: Rabaul was 436 miles from MacArthur's base at Port Moresby, on New Guinea, and 515 miles from the Russells—too far for our fighter planes to provide adequate cover for our heavy bombers. Munda was 125 miles closer than the Russells. We would have to capture it eventually, since it was one of the few sites in the Solomons that permitted construction of a bomber field, but it was too heavily defended for quick seizure, and we were eager to step up our attacks on Rabaul as soon as possible. However, halfway between Munda and Port Moresby, in the center of the south Solomon Sea, lay Woodlark Island, only 300 miles from Rabaul, and just over 200 from Bougainville. Fighters based there could hit Rabaul, Bougainville, or Munda, as we pleased.

One obstacle prevented my moving in. Woodlark's longitude was 153 degrees East, which meant that it was in General Mac-Arthur's area, and the protocol and punctilio of command forbade me to collaborate with him directly. I had to outline my plan in a dispatch to COMINCH, through CINCPAC, with a request that he submit it to the Joint Chiefs of Staff, and not until they approved it, with MacArthur's concurrence, could I take a positive step. This consisted of sending him the 112th Cavalry Regiment as an occupation force, some Seabees as a construction force, some shore-based Navy to organize and administer the port facilities, and some fighter planes.

Meanwhile, we were building two airfields in the Russells, amassing stock piles of fuel and ammunition, and training troops for the eventual assault on New Georgia. This, too, was SOWES-PAC territory—the Russells marked SOPAC's extreme western limit—but whereas the over-all strategy of the whole area was in MacArthur's hands, the Joint Chiefs of Staff had put tactical command of the Solomons subarea in mine. Although this arrangement was sensible and satisfactory, it had the curious effect of giving me two "hats" in the same echelon. My original hat was under Nimitz, who controlled my troops, ships, and supplies; now I had another hat under MacArthur, who controlled my strategy.

To discuss plans for New Georgia with him, I requested an appointment at his headquarters, which were then in Brisbane, Australia, and I flew across from Nouméa early in April. I had never met the General before, but we had one tenuous connection: my father had been a friend of his father's in the Philippines more than forty years back. Five minutes after I reported, I felt as if we

154

were lifelong friends. I have seldom seen a man who makes a quicker, stronger, more favorable impression. He was then sixty-three years old, but he could have passed as fifty. His hair was jet black; his eyes were clear; his carriage was erect. If he had been wearing civilian clothes, I still would have known at once that he was a soldier.

The respect that I conceived for him that afternoon grew steadily during the war and continues to grow as I watch his masterly administration of surrendered Japan. I can recall no flaw in our relationship. We had arguments, but they always ended pleasantly. Not once did he, my superior officer, ever force his decisions upon me. On the few occasions when I disagreed with him, I told him so, and we discussed the issue until one of us changed his mind. My mental picture poses him against the background of these discussions; he is pacing his office, almost wearing a groove between his large, bare desk and the portrait of George Washington that faced it; his corncob pipe is in his hand (I rarely saw him smoke it); and he is making his points in a diction I have never heard surpassed.

He accepted my plan for the New Georgia operation, and L Day was set for May 15, to coincide with his own advances in New Guinea and his occupation of Woodlark and the Trobriand Islands. The combined operation on both fronts was known as ELKTON.

I returned to Nouméa in time to sit in on an operation that was smaller but extremely gratifying. The Navy's code experts had hit a jack pot; they had discovered that Admiral Isoruku Yamamoto, the Commander in Chief of the Imperial Japanese Navy, was about to visit the Solomons. In fact, he was due to arrive at Ballale Island, just south of Bougainville, precisely at 0945 on April 18. Yamamoto, who had conceived and proposed the Pearl Harbor attack, had also been widely quoted as saying that he was "looking forward to dictating peace in the White House at Washington." I believe that this statement was subsequently proved a canard, but we accepted its authenticity then, and it was an additional reason for his being No. 3 on my private list of public enemies, closely trailing Hirohito and Tojo.

Eighteen P-38's of the Army's 339th Fighter Squadron, based

155

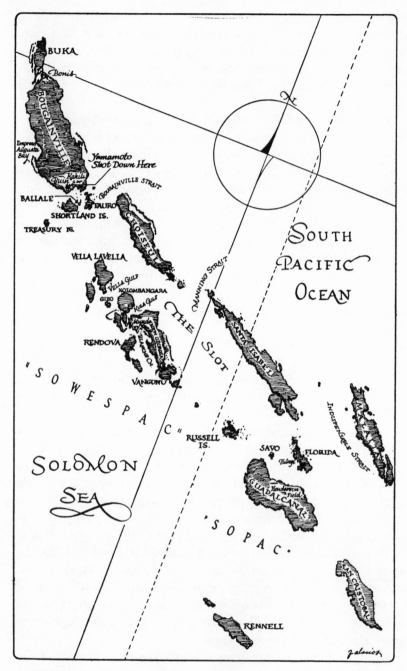

BUKA

Bonis

BOUGAINVILLE

Empress Augusta Bay

Yamamoto Shot Down Here

Kahili
Buin

BALLALE

FAURO

BOUGAINVILLE STRAIT

SHORTLAND IS.

TREASURY IS.

CHOISEUL

VELLA LAVELLA

Vella Gulf

KOLOMBANGARA

GIZO

Kula Gulf

Munda

RENDOVA

Blanche C.

VANGUNU

"SOWESPAC"

SOLOMON

SEA

THE SLOT

MANNING STRAIT

SANTA ISABEL

SOUTH

PACIFIC

OCEAN

INDISPENSABLE STRAIT

RUSSELL
IS.

SAVO

FLORIDA

Tulagi

GUADALCANAL

Henderson Field

MALAITA

"SOPAC"

RENNELL

SAN CRISTOBAL

at Henderson Field, were assigned to make the interception over Buin, 35 miles short of Ballale. Yamamoto's plane, a Betty, accompanied by another Betty and covered by six Zekes, hove in sight exactly on schedule, and Lt. Col. Thomas G. Lanphier, Jr., dove on it and shot it down in flames. The other Betty was also shot down for good measure, plus one of the Zekes.

When the news was announced at my regular conference next morning, Kelly Turner whooped and applauded. I told him, "Hold on, Kelly! What's so good about it? I'd hoped to lead that scoundrel up Pennsylvania Avenue in chains, with the rest of you kicking him where it would do the most good!"

We bottled up the story, of course. One obvious reason was that we didn't want the Japs to know that we had broken their code. The other reason was for Lanphier's personal sake. His brother was a prisoner of war, and if the Japs had learned who had shot down Yamamoto, what they might have done to the brother is something I prefer not to think about. I have in mind the nuns they caught on Guadalcanal and raped for forty-eight hours before cutting their throats; and the two Marines whom they vivisected; and the young girl on New Guinea whom they forced to watch her parents being beheaded, before her own turn came; and the execution of General Doolittle's pilots; and the Marine pilot in a parachute, whose feet were chopped off by the propeller of a Zeke.

Unfortunately, somebody took the story to Australia, whence it leaked into the papers, and no doubt eventually into Japan. (The usual route was via a broadcast from South America.) But the Japs evidently did not realize the implication any more than did the tattletale; we continued to break their codes, and Lanphier's brother received only routine mistreatment.

About two weeks after the ELKTON conference, MacArthur notified me that he could not meet the date for L Day, and directed its postponement to June 1, and later to the thirtieth. This made little difference to us. Our plans, and even our preliminary attacks, had been under way since December, when we began bombing Munda's newly discovered airfield. It was shelled for the first time on January 4/5 by Rear Adm. "Pug" Ainsworth's light cruisers and destroyers; on March 5/6 by Capt. Robert P. Briscoe; and on May 12/13 by Capt. Colin Campbell. Across Kula Gulf from

157

Munda was the supporting area of Vila-Stanmore, on Kolombangara Island. This, too, was frequently shelled—on January 23/24 by Ainsworth; on March 5/6 by Rear Adm. Aaron S. Merrill, who sank two Jap destroyers on the way in to his firing position; on March 15/16 by Comdr. Francis X. McInerney; and on May 12/13 by Ainsworth again. Between shellings, our bombers worked over both areas, and on the four days immediately preceding L Day, they pounded Munda with special ferocity. Even the heaviest air or surface bombardment will render a coral airfield unusable for no more than a few hours, but it tears up planes, destroys supplies, and kills, cripples, or unnerves personnel. In addition, these operations served notice on the enemy that we were now strong enough to move aggressively, and not merely defensively as before.

As soon as the Japs realized that we were mounting a major attack, they tried to beat us to the punch, with cruisers, destroyers, submarines, and planes. On June 16, they sent against Guadalcanal a strike of more than 120 planes, half of them fighters, the rest bombers. We launched around 100 fighters to meet them—Army, Navy, and Marine—and when the air had cleared, our pilots had shot down 107 enemy planes at a cost of six of ours. *One hundred and seven* for *six!*

Five months before, in Auckland, I had told the reporters, "When we first started out against them, I held that one of our men was equal to three Japanese. I have now increased this to twenty."

I seem to have been slightly off in my estimate. The actual ratio was 1 to not quite 18. The only comparable air battle in the Pacific was the "Turkey Shoot" that prefaced the Battle of the Philippine Sea, when fighters from Pete Mitscher's carriers shot down 402 Japs at a cost of twenty-seven, or 1 to not quite 15.

Our preparations for ELKTON also included thorough close reconnaissance by trained scouts. We had learned during the Guadalcanal campaign that though the coast watchers and the natives were bold and willing, they did not have the military background necessary to providing all the information we needed: type of defenses, caliber of guns, equipment of units, and so on. Accordingly we organized a combat reconnaissance school on Guadalcanal with experienced Marine and Army personnel as instructors. About 100 men took the course; teams were chosen; and beginning with ELKTON, we never made a forward move without their help.

The curtain raiser to ELKTON was a landing on June 21 at Segi Point, 40 miles from Munda, on the opposite end of New Georgia. Two companies of the 4th Marine Raider Battalion occupied it without squeezing a trigger; the Army reinforced them next day; construction of a fighter strip was started on the thirtieth, and on July 11 planes took off from what had been virgin jungle only eleven days before. The officer in charge of this project was Comdr. William Painter, "the Henry Kaiser of the Solomons." We would give Bill a piece of level ground, a coral quarry, and a bulldozer. He would do the rest.

On the night of June 29, Rear Admiral Merrill led an attack covering force of light cruisers, destroyers, and mine layers up the Slot, past New Georgia, and into the Buin-Shortland area, 200 miles farther. Two of the destroyers dropped off and turned into Kula Gulf, to shell Vila-Stanmore; the mine layers set their traps across the southern entrance to Bougainville Strait, to seal it against raids on our Munda forces; and the other ships blasted the enemy's anchorages and installations at Shortland, Faisi, Poporang, and Ballale.

The commander of MacArthur's Fifth Air Force, Lt. Gen. George C. Kenney, had promised to cover "Tip" Merrill's retirement with a heavy strike against Rabaul and Buin-Shortland. (The Japs had a float-plane base at Faisi and airstrips at Ballale and Kahili.) However, the weather thickened that night and grounded his planes. It also grounded the Japs', and Tip wasn't bombed, but if Kenney had been able to carry out his promised strike, he might have saved us some grief on the afternoon of the landing.

L Day dawned with low, scattered clouds that soon burnt away. Coast watchers and air reconnaissance had warned us that Munda was protected by an impassable barrier of reefs, so we had picked Rendova Island, 7 miles offshore, as a staging point for our troops and a site for our artillery. Two hours after our six transports began unloading, our 105-millimeter howitzers had been emplaced and were exchanging counterbattery fire with the enemy. The landing proceeded smoothly, under an umbrella of thirty-two fighters from Guadalcanal and the Russells, which beat off attempted attacks

159

twice during the morning. The transports completed unloading by 1500 and were standing down Blanche Channel, on their way back to Guadalcanal, when the third attack came in—between twenty-four and twenty-eight torpedo planes. Ships' fire and the combat air patrol shot down every one of them, but not before a torpedo had smashed into the transport *McCawley*, formerly the Grace liner *Santa Barbara* and now Kelly Turner's flagship.

She was taken under tow and survived another attack an hour later, but continued to settle by the stern and was ordered abandoned. Suddenly, three more torpedoes struck her, and she slid under in thirty seconds. Rear Admiral Theodore S. Wilkinson, who would relieve Kelly in a few days, had stayed aboard her. "Ping" Wilkinson was afraid that a submarine had sneaked through his screen. It hadn't. A PT skipper had mistaken the poor old "Wacky Mac's" silhouette for an enemy's.

EDITOR'S NOTE:

Following is an extract from Radiotokyo's account of the landing:

"The enemy, when discovered by Imperial air units, was attempting to force a landing on the northern shore of Rendova Island. . . . Swinging into action at once, our air units in gigantic formations pierced the enemy's defense line to attack the transports and escort vessels. The results accomplished, as announced by Imperial Headquarters, are either the sinking or heavy damage of six transports, three cruisers, and one destroyer. . . . "

The main body of our invasion force went ashore on Rendova: the 43rd Infantry Division, reinforced, plus a Marine antiaircraft battalion. Two lesser landings were made at the same time: units of the 169th Infantry occupied Sasavele and Baraulu Islands, 6 miles east of Munda, just offshore; and two more companies of the 4th Marine Raider Battalion occupied the vicinity of Wickham Anchorage, off Vangunu Island, to establish a staging refuge for small craft operating between Munda and Guadalcanal. A fourth landing was made the following morning at Viru, 8 miles up the coast from Segi.

On L-plus-2, we were ready to close in. Scouts found a good beach on the mainland at Zanana, directly opposite Sasavele and Baraulu, and landing craft began ferrying our troops across from Rendova. A line was established along the Barike River, and at

160

dawn on L-plus-9, the 43rd moved forward on a 1,300-yard front, behind a bombardment from four of our destroyers in Blanche Channel. Our advance gained more than a mile the first day but slowed almost to a standstill when it reached the enemy's main defense, a series of formidable, concealed pillboxes.

The jungle was so thick that it isolated every man from the man beside him. The rain was incessant. Most important, the 43rd was not only unblooded, but certain units were feebly led. Two of its regiments, each commanded by a colonel of the regular Army, were composed of troops from the same part of the United States. One colonel's brother was killed in front of his eyes, and he was wounded twice himself. Nevertheless, he accepted only emergency medical attention and pressed forward with his determined men. The accompanying regiment sent 360 men back to Guadalcanal as "war nerves" casualties after one day's fighting. General Harmon met them there, promptly returned 300 of them to the combat zone, and relieved their colonel on the spot. From then on they fought magnificently.

The ground forces' real weakness, however, was not in the lower echelons. This became evident as day succeeded day, yet our advance was measured in yards instead of miles. We controlled the air and the sea; we outnumbered the enemy 4 or 5 to 1; we bombed his positions every day and supported our troops with ships' fire on request. Rugged as jungle fighting is, by now we should have been within reach of our objective, the airfield. Something was wrong, so I sent Miff Harmon up with authority to take such steps as he saw fit. On the fifteenth, he replaced the commanding general of the ground forces with Maj. Gen. Oscar W. Griswold, the commanding general of the XIV Corps, and presently the advance gathered momentum again. (Even before the campaign started, I had had to recommend the relief of the major general commanding the I Marine Amphibious Corps. Our original plan allotted 15,000 men to wipe out the 9,000 Japs on New Georgia; by the time the island was secured, we had sent in more than 50,000. When I look back on ELKTON, the smoke of charred reputations still makes me cough.)

Meanwhile, on July 5, two battalions of infantry from the 37th Division, and the 1st Marine Raider Battalion, had been put ashore

161

at Rice Anchorage, on the north coast of New Georgia, with orders to occupy the Bairoko-Enogai area and thereby prevent the enemy garrisons on Kolombangara from reinforcing the Munda garrison. A task force being commanded by Pug Ainsworth, and consisting of the light cruisers *Honolulu*, *Helena*, and *St. Louis*, and the destroyers *Nicholas*, *O'Bannon*, *Strong*, and *Chevalier*, smoothed the way with a bombardment of positions on both sides of Kula Gulf. Although the return fire was accurate, Pug's only loss, the *Strong*, was caused by a "mystery" torpedo; no one in the task force knew what type of craft had fired it.

Pug's cruisers and his remaining destroyers—except the *Chevalier*, which had ripped her bow in going alongside the sinking *Strong*—were steaming home next afternoon when they were ordered to turn back at full speed and intercept a run of the Tokyo Express. He picked up the destroyers *Jenkins* and *Radford* en route and met the Express at the entrance to the gulf soon after midnight. The enemy force could not be itemized in the darkness, but it seemed to comprise nine ships, all destroyers, or destroyers with one or two light cruisers. The Battle of Kula Gulf lasted four hours and resulted in our loss of the *Helena* to a torpedo, and the enemy's loss of two destroyers and damage to four others.

A week later, Pug caught the Express again, in almost the same waters at almost the same hour. This time he had six additional destroyers—the *Taylor*, *Ralph Talbot*, *Buchanan*, *Gwin*, *Maury*, and *Woodworth*—and the Australian light cruiser *Leander* had replaced the sunken *Helena*. Although it was again impossible to be certain of the number and type of enemy ships, most observers agreed on one light cruiser and five destroyers. The Battle of Kolombangara was comparatively short, but it was long enough for the *Gwin* to be sunk and our three cruisers damaged, all by torpedoes, whereas the enemy escaped with the loss of only his cruiser.

These two engagements were expensive, but they served to protect our landings on the northwest coast of New Georgia, and to deny the Japs further use of Kula Gulf as a supply route to their garrisons.

Let me return to the *Strong* for a moment. About three-fourths of her company were rescued by the *Chevalier*, but nearly all the rest were lost—some to the torpedo and to hits by shore batteries, others to her own depth charges when she sank, still others by drowning. Six men, however, drifted ashore four days later on an island between New Georgia and Kolombangara. One died of his injuries on the tenth, and another on the thirteenth; and by the fifteenth, the only officer left, Lt. Hugh Barr Miller, Jr., a former All-American quarterback from the University of Alabama, had become so weak from internal bleeding caused by the depth charges that, convinced he was going to die, he gave most of his clothes and equipment to the three bluejackets and ordered them to try to make their way to our lines.

It is hard to imagine a more desperate plight than that of a seriously injured man, naked except for a jacket, unarmed except for a broken pocket knife, and alone in a hostile jungle, but Miller survived. In fact, he did far more than survive. A heavy rain on the seventeenth gave him a flicker of strength. Two days later he split open a coconut and was able to retain its meat—the first solid food he had kept down since the *Strong* sank. Next he found a dead Jap and took his grenades, rations, and uniform. The stripped corpse tipped off Miller's presence, but the first Jap patrol that approached him, on August 5, he annihilated with a grenade—all five men. By the time he was finally picked up by an amphibious plane, after forty-three days, he had not only killed at least twenty-five more Japs but had amassed a large amount of valuable intelligence material.

This is, of course, only the skeleton of Miller's heroic story, as I heard it from him in a hospital at Nouméa, but it is enough to show that he deserved the Navy Cross for which I recommended him, and that as long as America continues to breed boys like him, she can never be beaten.

Between L Day and July 31, we funneled 28,748 men into New Georgia through Rendova alone: three Army divisions—the 43rd, 37th, and 25th—plus Navy and Marines. On August 5, I received from General Griswold the dispatch we had been waiting for: OUR GROUND FORCES HAVE WRESTED MUNDA FROM THE JAPS AND PRESENT IT TO YOU AS THE SOLE OWNER X OUR MUNDA OPERATION IS THE FINEST EXAMPLE IN ALL MY EXPERIENCE OF A UNITED ALL-SERVICE ALL-AMERICAN TEAM.

I replied, CONSIDER THIS A CUSTODY RECEIPT FOR MUNDA AND FOR

A GRATIFYING NUMBER OF ENEMY DEAD X SUCH TEAMWORK AND UNRE-
LENTING OFFENSIVE SPIRIT ASSURES THE SUCCESS OF FUTURE DRIVES
AND THE IMPLACABLE EXTERMINATION OF THE ENEMY WHEREVER WE
CAN BRING HIM TO GRIPS X KEEP EM DYING.

I was watching the operation from my headquarters at Nouméa. Two days after the fall of Munda, another piece of good news came to me—my son Bill. The *Saratoga* had put into Havannah Harbor at Efate, and Bill, her Aviation Supply officer, had been sent down to pick up some spare parts. He spent the night with me and started back the next afternoon, August 8, as a passenger on a flight of three of the *Sara's* torpedo planes.

Bill had hardly left when an attack of flu put me to bed. I must have been sicker than I realized, because not until the tenth was my Operations officer, Capt. H. Raymond Thurber, allowed to tell me, "Admiral, we have had three torpedo planes missing for two days."

I knew at once. "My boy?"

"Yes, sir."

Ray described the searches being made, then asked if I could suggest any additional measures.

I told him, "My son is the same as every other son in the combat zone. Look for him just as you'd look for anybody else."

Another day passed, and another, with no word of the planes. Usually I shared my problems with my staff, but this was personal, and I kept it to myself. I didn't give up hope, but I knew that hope was a double-edged sword. When the families of missing men begged me to hold out hope of their return, I always refused. I considered it too cruel. I would tell them frankly, "Only a miracle can bring him home."

By the afternoon of the twelfth, four days after he had disappeared, this was my feeling about Bill. That evening, though, a search plane reported spotting several rubber rafts ashore on the island of Eromanga, between New Caledonia and Efate, and next day all ten men were recovered, suffering from nothing worse than fleabites, diarrhea, and sore feet. It turned out that they had missed their course and had been forced to make a water landing.

The day they were picked up was Friday, August 13. From then on—for awhile—I spit in the eye of the jinx that had haunted me

165

on the thirteenth of every month since the *Missouri's* turret explosion thirty-nine years before.

A fresh anxiety arose within a week. I was informed that Mrs. Roosevelt was making an air tour of the South and Southwest Pacific, and would reach Nouméa on the twenty-fifth. Among an area commander's worst problems are the politicians, admirals and generals, "special" correspondents, and "do-gooders" who present themselves in the assurance that their visit is a "morale factor," or that they are entitled to "see it from the inside." Mrs. Roosevelt I classed as a do-gooder, and I dreaded her arrival.

This opinion was strictly COMSOPAC's, not Bill Halsey's. I had known Mrs. Roosevelt for many years and had always liked and admired her; but I could find no excuse for her entering my area and monopolizing planes, crews, and fuel that were needed for military purposes. Secondly, large delegations from the Australian government and from General MacArthur insisted on coming over to give her an official welcome, and Nouméa had no accommodations for them. Thirdly, a series of contradictory messages were pouring into my headquarters, announcing, canceling, and changing her future itinerary, and it was impossible for me to arrange transportation for her until her schedule crystallized. Lastly, I'd have to wrench my attention from New Georgia, put on a necktie, and play the gracious, solicitous host. I had no time for such folderol, yet I'd have to take time.

She was wearing a Red Cross uniform when she stepped from her plane. I asked her at once if she would tell me her plans.

"What do you think I should do?" she asked.

"Mrs. Roosevelt," I said, "I've been married for thirty-odd years, and if those years have taught me one lesson, it is never to try to make up a woman's mind for her."

We decided she should stay in Nouméa for two days, then fly over to Australia, and spend two more days with us on her way home. I had begun to breathe more easily when she handed me a letter from the President, requesting permission for her to go to Guadalcanal, if I considered the trip feasible. That set me back on my heels. I told her rather curtly, "Guadalcanal is no place for you, Ma'am!"

"I'm perfectly willing to take my chances," she said. "I'll be entirely responsible for anything that happens to me."

166

I said, "I'm not worried about the responsibility, and I'm not worried about the chances you'd take. I know you'd take them gladly. What worries me is the battle going on in New Georgia at this very minute. I need every fighter plane I can put my hands on. If you fly to Guadalcanal, I'll have to provide a fighter escort for you, and I haven't got one to spare."

She looked so crestfallen that I found myself adding, "However, I'll postpone my final decision until your return. The situation may have clarified by then."

This cheered her up, and we drove into town.

I billeted her in Wicky-Wacky Lodge, where she would be more comfortable and would have more privacy than in our other quarters adjoining. Of course, we had a cordon of MP's around the house the whole time she was there. That night I gave a small reception and dinner for her (I put on a tie), and early next morning she started her rounds. Here is what she did in twelve hours: she inspected two Navy hospitals, took a boat to an officers' rest home and had lunch there, returned and inspected an Army hospital, reviewed the 2d Marine Raider Battalion (her son Jimmy had been its executive officer), made a speech at a service club, attended a reception, and was guest of honor at a dinner given by General Harmon.

When I say that she inspected those hospitals, I don't mean that she shook hands with the chief medical officer, glanced into a sunparlor, and left. I mean that she went into every ward, stopped at every bed, and spoke to every patient: What was his name? How did he feel? Was there anything he needed? Could she take a message home for him? I marveled at her hardihood, both physical and mental; she walked for miles, and she saw patients who were grievously and gruesomely wounded. But I marveled most at their expressions as she leaned over them. It was a sight I will never forget. (At one hospital, I arranged for her to pin the Navy Cross and two Purple Hearts on my "one-man army," Lieutenant Miller of the *Strong*.)

The New Georgia campaign was finished by the time she returned from Australia, and I consented—though with misgivings—to her visiting Guadalcanal. When I saw her off, I told her that it was impossible for me to express my appreciation of what she had done, and was doing, for my men. I was ashamed of my original surliness. She alone had accomplished more good than any other person, or any group of civilians, who had passed through my area. In the nine months left to me as COMSOPAC, nothing caused me to modify this opinion.

Incidentally, my misgivings about her Guadalcanal trip were very nearly warranted. The night before her plane arrived, the enemy sent his first bombing attack against the island in two months, and sent another the night after her departure. I was there at the time, on a tour of our northern positions, and again I wondered if our team was the only one with code-breakers.

My reluctance to let Mrs. Roosevelt junket through my area at the expense of aviation fuel and a fighter escort reminds me of the similar trouble I had with correspondents. An essential part of their job is, of course, seeing the battle zone and describing it for their readers. I realized this, but I too had a job—to fight the war— and where my job conflicted with theirs, mine took precedence. The point of conflict was air transportation to the front. At one time during the Guadalcanal campaign, we had only 3,500 gallons of aviation fuel on the island, or enough for only two ten-plane strikes. Ammunition was also low; so were bombs, torpedoes, food, and medicine. When the situation reached the stage where even a dribble of supplies was vital, we grounded all passengers, took over the transport planes, loaded them until they were bowlegged, and flew them up the line. (The combat pilots were glamor boys, but save a cheer for the transport pilots who hauled fuel and live ammunition in unarmed planes, without escort, and landed them under fire!)

Those critical weeks were naturally the weeks that the correspondents wanted to cover. Miles Browning usually had the unpleasant duty of refusing their requests for a flight, but occasionally one would elude Miles and appeal to me. I always asked, "How much do you weigh?" and when he told me, I said, "I'd like to send you up, but I feel that an equivalent weight of gas, bombs, and mail is needed more at this moment than you are. If you are willing to go by ship, we can arrange it, but we can't book you on a plane."

Most of them took my refusal in good part and were of a character too high to let resentment color their stories. This group includes Frank Morris, of *Collier's;* Frank Tremaine, of the United Press; Joe Driscoll, of *The New York Herald-Tribune;* Bob Trumbull, of *The New York Times;* and a great many others. One, however, was a conspicuous exception. The first I knew of his duplicity was when I received a dispatch from the Secretary of the Navy requesting permission, on this man's behalf, to quote a tribute I had paid his article about a night surface engagement off Guadalcanal, which he had witnessed (he said) from a foxhole on the beach, and which I was supposed to have acclaimed as "not only superb, but breathless, and marvelously accurate"—or something equally extravagant.

I was astonished. Far from having made any such statement, I had never even seen the story. I sent for it, read it, and replied to the Secretary, PRIOR TO RECEIPT OF YOUR MESSAGE I HAD NOT READ ARTICLE IN QUESTION X HAVE NOW DONE SO AND FIND IN IT LITTLE OF FACTUAL VALUE X I WILL NOT ENDORSE IT.

Here the scoundrel was merely presumptuous. In the New Georgia campaign, he became vicious. One of his stories declared, among other brazen lies, that we were burying our casualties without bothering to make sure that they were dead! Julian Brown sent for him at once and asked his authority for such an accusation. Having none, he took refuge behind a screen of equivocation about his "duty to educate the American public in the psychology of jungle warfare."

Julian interrupted him with what I am afraid was an ugly word and went on to suggest that his true motive was quite different— yellow sensationalism and nothing else.

"I resent that!" the man shouted.

"I hoped you would," Julian said, and took off his blouse.

There was no fight. The correspondent's yellowness extended to his back.

An arrant fabrication like this was so remote from the honest stories our other correspondents filed, so shameless and so dangerous, that we requested Public Relations headquarters at CINCPAC to reexamine his credentials, and returned him there under guard. While he was en route, we were informed that a camera and some photographs had been discovered in his gear, although he had pledged himself, as had all correspondents, not to bring films or a camera into our area. Now there was no further doubt about his sincerity. His credentials were revoked, and he never annoyed us again.

Inevitably, we were pestered with freaks as well as knaves.

I recall a lieutenant colonel of Marines—the former secretary of a Congressman, I believe—who paraded around Nouméa wearing two identical rows of ribbons, although no one else wore any ribbons at all. What he had done to earn them, if anything, I have no idea, but I know that we infuriated Julian Brown by acclaiming this creature as representing the highest type of Marine officer.

Then there was the lieutenant commander sent me by General Donovan's Office of Strategic Services—a wild-eyed young professor who was an authority on Tibet and therefore, presumably, indispensable to the South Pacific campaign. He was so wrapped in his cloak-and-dagger role that he whispered even in my office, and I had great difficulty learning why he was there. I finally gathered that he was promoting a one-man collapsible rubber submarine. When I asked him to describe it, he whispered, "I'd rather not. It's highly confidential."

I assured him that he could trust my discretion, and finally he admitted, "The fact is, we haven't got one yet, but I'll tell Washington to develop it."

I told him, "Get out of here!"

Another hour was shot to hell.

(I don't mean to discredit the OSS. It did a splendid job in Europe and elsewhere, but there was simply no place for it in our part of the world.)

Isolated pockets on New Georgia continued to resist until August 25; after that, the whole island was ours. We had not waited for the extermination of the last Jap. We had already picked our next handhold on the ladder of the Solomons. The nearest island north of New Georgia, Kolombangara, had a fighter strip at Vila-Stanmore and—as confirmed by a combat reconnaissance team—a garrison of 10,000 troops dug into positions as nearly impregnable as Munda's. The undue length of the Munda operation and our heavy casualties made me wary of another slugging match, but I didn't know how to avoid it. I could see no victory without Rabaul, and no Rabaul without Kolombangara. Besides, ELKTON called for the capture and occupation of Kolombangara, the Shortland Islands, and Kahili airfield on Bougainville.

It was here that my staff first suggested the by-pass policy—

jump over the enemy's strong points, blockade them, and leave them to starve. We looked at our charts. Next above Kolombangara is Vella Lavella, 35 miles nearer the Shortlands and Kahili. According to coast watchers, its garrison numbered not more than 250, and its shore line would offer at least one site for an airstrip. That was all we needed. On July 12, I canceled Kolombangara from ELKTON and wrote in Vella Lavella.

Ten days later, a PT boat landed a combat reconnaissance team of six Army, Navy, and Marine officers on Vella's southeast coast. When we took them off a week later, they reported finding a potential airstrip along the beach at Barakoma and another beach near by suitable for a PT base. The enemy garrison, they added, was concentrated on the northwest coast, so we could expect little or no resistance.

By L Day, August 15, this garrison had been swelled to 700 by refugees from Kolombangara and by the few Jap survivors of the Battle of Vella Gulf, on the night of the sixth, when six of our destroyers—the *Dunlap, Craven, Maury, Lang, Sterett,* and *Stack*—under Comdr. Frederick Moosbrugger, waylaid four of the enemy's, carrying supplies and 950 Army troops to Vila-Stanmore, and in a short, brilliant action sank three of them and damaged the fourth without damage or casualties of their own. However, the only opposition to our landing came from the air, and this was ineffective. Planes from Kahili made four attacks that resulted in fewer casualties for us than for the enemy's pilots and aircrewmen.

By sunset of L Day, Ping Wilkinson, my new Amphibious Forces Commander, had put ashore 4,600 troops, under Brig. Gen. Robert B. McClure of the Army. The Seabees began work on the airstrip at once; the site was cleared by September 3, and planes were operating from it by the twenty-seventh. Meanwhile, on the eighteenth, the Army troops on Vella had been relieved by elements of the 3rd New Zealand Division, whose commanding officer, Maj. Gen. H. E. Barrowclough, then became Island Commander—the first time in my area that Americans served under any but American officers. We had already expanded our perimeter until Vella was free of Japs except on its northwest coast, and Barrowclough set about eliminating these last forlorn few hundreds. By the night of October 6, he had them penned on a narrow strip of

171

beach. At dawn his New Zealanders rushed in for the kill. The only Japs they found were dead ones.

What had happened is worth explaining in some detail. In July and August, the enemy's main concern was reinforcing and supplying Kolombangara. In September, his concern was evacuating it. Almost nightly he sent barges to sneak out his men by fifties and hundreds, and almost nightly our destroyers and PT's chopped them up and sank them. What our surface craft left, our aircraft scuttled in the morning. On September 9, Corsairs alone sank nine barges. On the fourteenth, PT's sank five. The hunt intensified as the month turned. On the twenty-eighth, our destroyers sank four; on the twenty-ninth, we sank three; on the thirtieth, six. The nights of October 1 and 2 were moonless, so the enemy redoubled his efforts. On the first, we sank twenty barges; on the second, twenty more; on the fourth, sixteen. These last sixteen brought our total up to 598 barges sunk in three months, and 670 believed seriously damaged. We have no way of knowing how many Japs were killed by gunfire or were drowned, but our estimate is between 3,000 and 4,000. It was rich, rewarding, beautiful slaughter.

Intelligence warned us that on the night of October 6/7, the Tokyo Express would probably make a final attempt to rescue the troops cornered on Vella or to complete the evacuation of Kolombangara. Three of our destroyers—the *Selfridge*, *Chevalier*, and *O'Bannon*, under Capt. Frank R. Walker—at once stood north and presently engaged ten of the enemy's, in the night Battle of Vella Lavella. Early in the action, the *Chevalier* was mortally torpedoed and, out of control, was rammed by the *O'Bannon*. Five minutes later, the *Selfridge* lost her bow to another torpedo. Although the enemy had also lost a ship, his proportionate strength was now far greater; yet instead of pounding our cripples to pieces, he broke off and fled toward Rabaul. The New Zealanders discovered the explanation next morning: under cover of the engagement and the flight, barges had crept in and evacuated the Vella garrison.

Our occupation of this important offensive base was now complete. The central Solomons campaign was finished. Vella had cost us fewer than 150 dead and had abundantly justified our strategy of by-passing. The next campaign, the northern Solomons, would see this strategy win us the war in the South Pacific.

172

BOUGAINVILLE was the last major obstacle on the road to Rabaul. It is the largest of the Solomon Islands—150 miles long, fiddle-shaped, and split down the back by the Crown Prince Range, which features two active volcanoes. In the twenty-one months that the Japanese had occupied it, they had made it a formidable fortress. They had built a seaplane base and four air-fields; a fifth was on Ballale, a small island a few miles southward; a sixth was under construction. Their ground forces were estimated at 35,000 and included the infamous 6th Division, which had raped Nanking in December, 1937.

Our first plan for invading Bougainville called for a direct assault on its southern coast, including Ballale and the near-by Shortland Islands. However, there was evidence that the defenses of these areas were being strengthened; and with the successful by-pass of Kolombangara fresh in our minds, we decided to by-pass again—to establish a beachhead where opposition would be weak and difficult of reinforcement, and to carve out our own airfield.

Submarines, seaplanes, and PT boats put combat reconnais-sance teams ashore at several likely points. These teams reported that Cape Torokina, in Empress Augusta Bay, about halfway up the southwestern coast, offered the best possibilities. Strategically, it would bring all the Bougainville airfields within a radius of 65 miles and Rabaul itself within 215 miles—a range that our fighters could easily cover; it would also put behind us the three main airfields to the south. Tactically, Torokina appeared to be a natural defense region about 7 miles square; it was held by a mere 1,000 troops; and once we had denied them access to the sea, their prob-

173

lem of supply would be acute, since they could be reached overland only by narrow trails. (We figured it would take the Japs four months to bring up heavy equipment from their nearest forward base; this proved correct almost to the week.)

Torokina had its disadvantages too. It faced the breadth of the Solomon Sea and therefore was open to the probability of heavy surf; our knowledge of the terrain was derived from missionaries and traders, who are not expert topographers; and there was a chance that the sites of our fighter and bomber strips would be dangerously swampy. The question was debated back and forth, day after day. Talk took the place of action. The South Pacific was suffering from the inertia of consolidation; the natural tendency was to snug down in Vella Lavella and catch a breath, instead of pushing forward again so soon. MacArthur wanted Bougainville secured by the end of December, to anchor his right flank before his left moved forward, yet the arguments went on: should we land at Torokina, or on the east coast at Kieta, or where?

I became impatient. One morning at a conference in Nouméa, I announced flatly, "It's Torokina. Now get on your horses!"

The operation was christened CHERRYBLOSSOM, and November 1 was set as L Day. Certain phases of CHERRYBLOS-SOM were cursed with luck as bad as the opening phases of ELKTON. The hoodoo struck first on October 20. Maj. Gen. Charles D. Barrett of the Marines, who was slated as over-all commander of the operation, fell from the window of his quarters in Nouméa and was killed. This was a double blow, since we had no one to replace him. The only Marine officer in SOPAC who could have done so, Archie Vandegrift, had recently left for Washington to become Commandant of the Corps. I sent a dispatch requesting his return and meanwhile I discussed a substitute with my War Plans officer, Brig. Gen. William E. Riley of the Marines. Bill said he would go to his room and think it over. I said I'd do the same. In a very few minutes, the name of the ideal man popped into my mind, and I headed for Bill's room. He and I met halfway.

His first words were, "I have the very man!"

As casually as I could manage, I said, "You mean Roy Geiger, of course."

174

Bill was flabbergasted. "Right! How did you know?"

After Roy's magnificent performance on Guadalcanal, he had gone back to Washington as Chief of Marine Aviation. We requested him at once, the request was approved, and although Archie led the troops ashore, Roy arrived to relieve him on L-plus-8.

The landing force was composed of the 3rd Marine Division, Maj. Gen. Allen Hal Turnage commanding, and the 37th Army Division, Maj. Gen. Robert S. Beightler commanding. The 37th were veterans of New Georgia, but the 3rd Marines had not yet seen action. After the beachhead was secured, they would be relieved by another Army division, and an Army officer would take over command from Roy. The Marines are trained to capture a position, but they are not equipped to hold it, as the Army is. (None the less—thank God!—they held at Guadalcanal and at other critical spots across the Pacific.)

CHERRYBLOSSOM also called for two small preliminary landings, both on October 27, L-minus-5. Transported by Rear Adm. George H. Fort, Brig. R. A. Row's 8th New Zealand Brigade Group, veterans of North Africa, Greece, and Crete, would occupy Treasury Island, midway between Torokina and Barakoma, our airstrip on Vella. Treasury was lightly defended, and we needed it both as protection for our flank and as a location for a fighter strip, a radar station, and a small-boat base.

The other landing would be made on Choiseul Island by the 2d Marine Parachute Battalion, Lt. Col. Victor A. Krulak commanding. (Krulak is small and light—he had coxed the Naval Academy crew—but his nickname, "Brute," was not bestowed in irony; he has guts and muscle enough for half a dozen men.) In Roy Geiger's description, this was to be "a series of short right jabs to throw the enemy off balance and to conceal the real power of our left hook to his belly at Empress Augusta Bay." We expected it to deceive him into rushing reinforcements across to an area which we would abandon as soon as they arrived.

A more elaborate deception was staged at the Shortlands. Our combat patrols deliberately left evidence of their visit, and almost every day our photo planes made leisurely, low-level flights across the area, followed by or following our bombers. The Japs fell for it.

175

They began to move troops, artillery, and heavy equipment over from Bougainville, as we were hoping, and we learned from their officers after the war that they firmly believed this would be the scene of our landing.

At the same time, beginning on October 15, we started softening up the enemy's airfields. General Kenney's Fifth Air Force was making helpful attacks on Rabaul every now and then, and although SOPAC planes took part in them, we reserved our major efforts for the fields on Bougainville. The Kieta seaplane base was little more than a nuisance, and the Kieta fighter strip was not yet operational. The fields that counted were Buka, Bonis, Kahili, Kara, and Ballale.

Buka and Bonis were near the northern end of the island; they were twin fields, a mile apart, separated by Buka Passage. The others were in the south; Kahili, the strongest of all, was on the coast, with Kara 7 miles inland, and Ballale 13 miles offshore. These three lay between Barakoma and Torokina, so we hit them hardest and oftenest. During the two weeks before the landing, we sent against them an average of four strikes a day. On L-minus-1, we dropped 148 tons of bombs on Kara alone.

I flew up to Espiritu on L-minus-8 and spent the night on the flagship of the Commander of the Transport Group, Commo. Lawrence F. Reifsnider. I have said that our charts of the northern Solomons were sketchy and far from reliable; hundreds of square miles of the interior were dismissed with "Unexplored." But my worries were nothing to those of Reif, on whose pin-point navigation the success of the landing depended. Long stretches of coast line around Torokina were dotted, indicating mere guesses at the contour; southern Bougainville was marked "Abnormal magnetic variation reported here"; and an aerial survey showed the whole island to be 8 to 10 miles northeast of its charted position. Moreover, a last-minute reconnaissance by the submarine *Guardfish* discovered two uncharted shoals of less than 4 fathoms, close to Reif's run-in point, and he was afraid that other shoals even shallower might exist. (They did, too.)

Reif is usually cool, but he admitted that his aplomb was being gnawed by the prospect of taking an invasion force through such waters, in total darkness, toward a beach that might be 10 miles off base.

176

I laughed and told him, "You won't have any trouble, Reif. You're too good a sailorman. Besides, it's a simple job!"

He didn't believe a word I said, and I didn't either. Fortunately we were able to supply him with accurate air maps just before he sailed.

Our landing on Treasury was opposed from the beach and attacked from the air, but was completed without undue casualties. That night Krulak's 800 Marines plunged into Choiseul at Voza and began their twelve-day raid, during which they lost twelve men but killed 143 and prevented the enemy from giving his whole attention to Torokina. The Marines not only planted the usual booby traps along their trail, but whenever they came to a particularly tall tree from which Jap snipers might harass their retirement, they studded its trunk with old razor blades. The rear guard told Krulak that the trick paid off in screams and curses.

When L Day came, we were hitting the enemy on five fronts, some of them 200 miles apart—Treasury, Choiseul, Torokina, Buka-Bonis, and the Shortlands. The first strike at Buka-Bonis began soon after midnight of October 31, when Tip Merrill took four light cruisers and eight destroyers close inshore and plastered the two fields with 300 rounds of 6-inch and 2,400 rounds of 5-inch. The only damage his force received was from a shell fragment that nicked his flagship, the *Montpelier*, and wrecked Tip's own typewriter. He now headed southeast at 30 knots to conduct—for the first time in the SOPAC area—a broad-daylight bombardment of enemy positions. The sun rose at 0614 that morning, and at 0631 Tip opened fire on the Shortlands and Ballale. Return fire was heavy, but again he was lucky; only five of his men were wounded, and one destroyer received minor damage.

Two bombardments in seven hours will exhaust the toughest crews, so Tip was directed to steam south for his base at Purvis Bay. His ships could have arrived that night. Before they actually arrived, two days later, they had fought a savage surface battle and had stood off an air attack.

While Tip was bombarding the Shortlands, planes from the *Saratoga* and the light carrier *Princeton* were churning up the wreckage he had left at Buka-Bonis. This was the *Sara's* first action in more than a year and only the third altogether that she had fought. She was a hard-luck ship. When war broke out, she was at

177

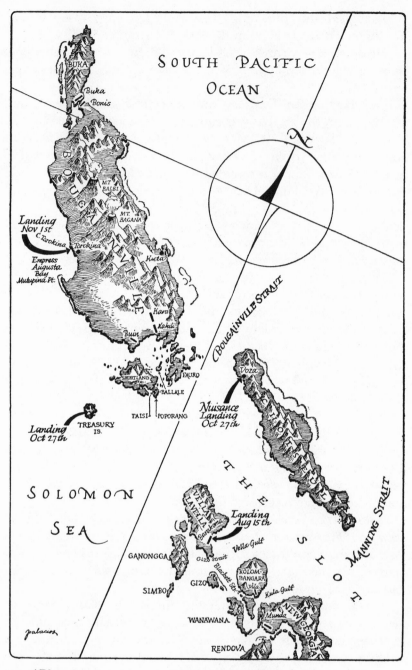

SOUTH PACIFIC
OCEAN

N

BUKA

Buka
Bonis

B O U G A I N V I L L E

MT
BALBI

MT.
BAGANA

Landing
Nov 1st
C. Torokina
Torokina

Empress
Augusta
Bay
Mutupina Pt.

Kieta

Kara

Buin   Kahili

SHORTLAND
FAURO
BALLALE
FAISI   POPORANG

Landing
Oct 27th

TREASURY
IS.

BOUGAINVILLE STRAIT

Voza

Nuisance
Landing
Oct 27th

C H O I S E U L

SOLOMON

SEA

T H E

S L O T

MANNING STRAIT

VELLA
LAVELLA
Barakoma

Landing
Aug 15th

Vella Gulf

GANONGGA

Gizo Strait

KOLOM-
BANGARA
Vila

Kula Gulf

SIMBO   GIZO

Blackett Str.

WANAWANA   Munda

NEW GEORGIA

RENDOVA

178

San Diego, and she rushed to Pearl and on toward Wake only to be called back without having fired a shot. A week later, she was torpedoed by a submarine, so she missed Midway. She came to the South Pacific that summer and was torpedoed again, and although she returned in November, she was restricted to minor operations. The fleet had already nicknamed her "the Reluctant Dragon" and "the Sara Maru" and "the Pond Lily." This recent year of swinging round the hook won her still another name, "the Model Housing Project."

Now she had a chance to prove her worth. Rear Adm. Frederick C. Sherman, commanding her task group, closed the northeast coast of Bougainville and struck Buka-Bonis twice on L Day and twice more on L-plus-1, destroying twenty-one planes and damaging ships and installations. The enemy knew the location of Ted's force and even its composition, because Radiotokyo later reported that they had sunk one large and one medium carrier; but for some reason, he was not attacked. We now withdrew him to refuel in the vicinity of Rennel Island, about 100 miles south of Guadalcanal —a position which, while reasonably safe from air attack, yet was far enough forward to permit his being rushed into the line again. This precaution proved our salvation.

The landing at Torokina began on schedule. Mine sweepers led the way to the anchorage, and after the transports and escorting destroyers had bombarded the beaches, thirty-one TBF's from Munda bombed and strafed for five minutes. At 0726, exactly as the air cover lifted its fire, the first boatloads of Marines waded ashore. The Japanese garrison in the immediate vicinity numbered about 300. Half of them were killed, and the survivors fled inland. Our loss of seventy men tells only part of the story. The beach and terrain conditions were worse than any we had previously encountered. A strong onshore wind made the surf so high that eighty-six landing craft broached and were stranded, ruining much of their cargo and overburdening the rest of the boat pool, with a consequent delay in the delivery of supporting troops. Moreover, many of the beaches bordered so closely on a vast swamp and were so narrow themselves that they became piled with tons of gear, vehicles, and machinery which should have been dispersed and put to use.

The slowness of the unloading was aggravated by two air

attacks which broke through our fighter screen, and further by a transport's grounding on an uncharted shoal. As a result, this ship and three others were unable to empty, and although they stood out with the retiring convoy at nightfall, they were ordered to return at dawn next morning. Meanwhile, they had to be protected from possible attack by a force that the enemy had concentrated at Rabaul. Tip Merrill's ships were the only ones available. These are their names—the light cruisers *Montpelier, Cleveland, Columbia,* and *Denver,* and the destroyers *Charles Ausburne, Dyson, Claxton, Spence, Thatcher, Converse, Foote,* and *Stanly.* Weary as they were, we sent them north, into the Battle of Empress Augusta Bay.

The enemy came down in three groups, totaling three heavy cruisers, one light cruiser, and six destroyers. Tip met him in darkness and rain at 0245 on November 2, about 50 miles northwest of our beachhead, in a furious torpedo- and gun-fight that lasted until 0536. Each force had three ships damaged, but whereas the enemy lost a light cruiser and a destroyer, Tip did not lose a ship. Later that morning, as he was trudging home in pace with his cripples, they were struck by sixty-five bombers from Rabaul, and shot down seventeen of them at the cheap price of two hits on the *Montpelier's* catapult. Purvis Bay welcomed them the following afternoon with the conventional signal, "What do you require?"

The captain of the *Denver* answered simply, "Sleep."

Editor's Note:
Following is Radiotokyo's account of this battle:
"Our naval surface units on the night of November 1 encountered and engaged with enemy cruiser and destroyer squadrons off Gazelle Bay, Bougainville Island. The enemy suffered these losses: one large cruiser and two large destroyers instantaneously sunk, two large cruisers and one large cruiser or destroyer sunk, while one or two large cruisers and two destroyers were heavily damaged. In addition one destroyer was set ablaze by the enemy's own shells. Our losses were one destroyer sunk and one cruiser slightly damaged."

On the fourth, our scouts reported that another enemy force was standing in to Rabaul from Truk—eight heavy cruisers, two light cruisers, and eight destroyers. Presumably they would fuel, then run down to Torokina the following night and sink our transports and bombard our precarious positions. This was the most desperate emergency that confronted me in my entire term as COMSOPAC. Even if Tip Merrill had been within reach, and fresh, he would not have had a prayer of stopping such an armada, yet CHERRY-BLOSSOM's success—perhaps the success of the South Pacific War—hung upon its being stopped.

CAPTAIN THURBER:

The Operations staff had flown up to Guadalcanal late in October, to be closer at hand for CHERRYBLOSSOM. We were all at Camp Crocodile there when we got the news of this force. Doug Moulton and I worked over the operations chart and found that it was possible for the *Sara* and *Princeton* task groups to make a high-speed run northward and get in the first blow. We wrote a dispatch ordering the strike and assigning priority of targets—cruisers first, destroyers next—checked it with "Mick" Carney, and took it into the Admiral's Quonset hut for his official approval.

Before he read it, he asked us, "You're not going to send Merrill to Rabaul, are you?"

We said, "No, sir. This is Ted Sherman again."

I sincerely expected both air groups to be cut to pieces and both carriers to be stricken, if not lost (I tried not to remember that my son Bill was aboard one of them); but we could not let the men at Torokina be wiped out while we stood by and wrung our hands.

VICE ADM. ROBERT B. CARNEY, WHO SUCCEEDED CAPTAIN BROWNING AS CHIEF OF STAFF IN JULY, 1943:

Every one of us knew what was going through the Admiral's mind. It showed in his face, which suddenly looked 150 years old. He studied the dispatch for a few seconds, then handed it back. All he said was, "Let 'er go!"

This strike of Sherman's was extraordinarily heavy—ninety-seven planes. He was able to send in that many because he did not have to withhold fighters for his own protection; his launching position, southwest of Bougainville, permitted us to furnish him Navy fighter cover from Barakoma. The weather was foul that day, the AA fire at Rabaul was intense, and the interception was determined. (The Japs had Navy pilots there, and damned good they were—far better than their Army pilots.) But the carrier planes bored through, shooting down twenty-five enemy fighters for five of their own, and damaging six cruisers and two destroyers.

181

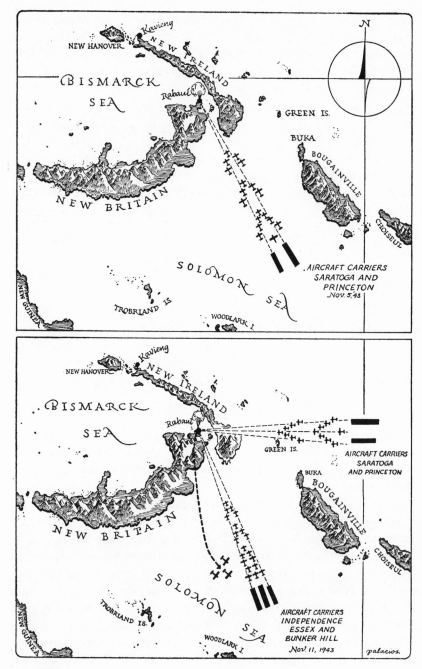

AIRCRAFT CARRIERS
SARATOGA AND
PRINCETON
Nov. 5, 43

AIRCRAFT CARRIERS
SARATOGA
AND PRINCETON

AIRCRAFT CARRIERS
INDEPENDENCE
ESSEX AND
BUNKER HILL
Nov. 11, 1943

The Japs changed their plans abruptly. The Tokyo Express canceled its run that night, and next morning only one cruiser and a few destroyers were left in Rabaul's Simpson Harbor; the rest had fled for Truk and the Empire. I took a deep breath; so did the men at Torokina; so did Ted Sherman.

Incidentally, General Kenney had promised a simultaneous attack in strength by his heavy bombers and had assured us that they could lay Rabaul flat. The last thing our pilots saw as they ducked back into the clouds—the same clouds that hid our carriers—was Kenney's bombers, eight of them. I have always resented the feebleness of his support at this critical time, and I told General MacArthur as much the next time I saw him.

EDITOR'S NOTE:
Following is an extract from Radiotokyo's account of this strike:
"In an air raid against Rabaul, the much vaunted reinforced enemy air force suffered the loss of 200 planes out of 230. . . . The shooting down of 90 per cent of the enemy total air strength represents a new world record. . . . A Japanese torpedo-plane formation took off from its base in the evening of November 5 and carried out a frontal attack against the enemy carrier striking force southeast of Bougainville Island [note that our force was actually southwest], sinking two carriers as well as four cruisers."

Now the strain relaxed. CINCPAC lent us three new light cruisers to supplement Tip Merrill's ships; and we were also lent a carrier task force built around the *Essex* and *Bunker Hill* and the light carrier *Independence*, under Rear Adm. Alfred E. Montgomery, for a warm-up operation before their appointment at Tarawa on November 21.

Five air groups, we figured, ought to change the name of Rabaul to Rubble. We threw them in on the eleventh, as an ironic memorial to Armistice Day—Sherman's group striking from northeastward of Bougainville, and Montgomery's from southwestward. Although the weather again shut down tight, screening the targets and preventing a co-ordinated attack, they sank a destroyer, damaged other ships, and destroyed twenty-four planes for seven. Sherman's group escaped detection for the second time. Montgomery's planes were trailed home by some sixty to seventy Japs, but the fighter cover we had sent from Barakoma, as on the fifth, helped them shoot

183

down more than fifty at a cost of only three, and his ships were not touched.

Simpson Harbor was empty next morning. Where had those crippled ships gone? Our guess was to Truk as before, under concealment of the heavy weather front. Truk was 700 miles due north, an easy jaunt for our carriers. If our five air groups caught all those cripples there, they might finish off enough of them to put the Imperial Fleet in acute distress, and thereby shorten the war. It looked like a God-sent opportunity, but authority to exploit it was not received.

We knew at the time of these carrier strikes that they had solved an urgent local problem, but I did not appreciate their full effect until after Japan's surrender, when I read a transcript of the interrogation of Capt. Toshikazu Ohmae, of the Japanese Naval General Staff, conducted by the United States Strategic Bombing Survey. Here, in part, is Tomae's statement:

"The specific plan to counter an American invasion of the Gilberts was as follows: . . . Aircraft from the Bismarcks would attack the invasion forces and then land at fields in the Marshalls-Gilberts area. . . . Warships at Truk would . . . move to the Gilberts. . . . Two factors radically changed these plans. The first was the serious damage received by several Second Fleet cruisers at Rabaul by carrier air attack on 5 November 1943. . . . The second was the intensified air war in the Solomons . . . which absorbed our air forces already in the western Solomons and also required employment of the short-range planes which were being held at Truk for defense of the Marshalls-Gilberts.

"Consequently, the original plans for the defense of those islands could not be carried out when American forces invaded in November, because there was insufficient surface and air strength available to make effective resistance."

On November 3 I crossed from Guadalcanal to Purvis Bay, to get a firsthand account of the Battle of Empress Augusta Bay from Tip Merrill and also to hear the personal experience of my new flag secretary, Lt. Comdr. Harold E. Stassen, who had been an eyewitness on Tip's flagship.

CAPTAIN MOULTON:
As soon as the staff saw how well Stass fitted in, we began kidding him.

184

"Of course," we said, "we all expect White House sinecures when you're elected."

Stass told us, "I wouldn't have a chance to fix you up. If I'm elected, I'll have the shortest term in history. I'll be inaugurated one day, I'll announce my cabinet the next day, I'll give a SOPAC party the third day, and on the fourth day I'll be impeached for it ."

From Purvis Bay I flew north to Bougainville. By then, November 10, our lines contained enough territory for the airstrips, and construction had begun, despite sniping and shellfire that ranged from sporadic to continual. Living was still rather primitive, but once the swamps were drained and huts were built, Bougainville became an extremely comfortable camp (except along the combat perimeter). It had the best climate of any of the Solomons, in my opinion. The soil was volcanic sand, so it absorbed even the most furious cloudburst, instead of turning to knee-deep mud as on New Georgia. The underbrush was trimmed out, but the trees were left for shade, and a pleasant breeze blew steadily. Best of all, there was a minimum of malaria, thanks to the increasing efficiency of our malaria-control squads.

I was told about a surprise inspection they made at the movies one night, to see that every man was wearing shoes and socks, as required. One man wasn't. When they hauled him into the light, they found he was a Jap. He had deserted his command, he said, and had been hiding out in a foxhole in no man's land. After dark, he would sneak through our lines and help himself to chow from the officers' galley, then attend the movies. He hadn't missed a show for a week!

The end of November produced a destroyer action, the Battle of Cape St. George, that was as smart as Moosbrugger's Battle of Vella Gulf, which it closely resembled. The opposing forces were evenly matched: five veteran ships of Capt. Arleigh A. Burke's famous DESRON 23—the *Charles F. Ausburne, Claxton, Dyson, Converse,* and *Spence*—against five Jap ships. Again they met at night, on November 24/25. Again the Japs were evacuating troops, 700 of them, to Rabaul from Buka. Again at no cost in casualties or damage, the Americans sank three enemy destroyers and damaged a fourth. Moreover, "31-Knot" Burke clinched his victory by chasing the two survivors almost into Simpson Harbor.

185

I do not detract from his courage when I say that planes from our fields on New Georgia and Vella Lavella were keeping the Japs at Rabaul not only off-balance but groggy. A few weeks later, when the fields at Treasury and Empress Augusta also became operational, we were able to redouble our blows and neutralize Rabaul completely. These strikes were commanded by Maj. Gen. Ralph J. Mitchell, of the Marines, who had succeeded Nate Twining as my COMAIRSOLS. (I had sent Nate home on leave, expecting him to return, but "Hap" Arnold had kidnaped him and ordered him to Italy in command of the Fifteenth Air Force.) Whenever I hear blather about interservice friction, I like to recall that our Army, Navy, and Marine airmen in the Solomons fought with equal enthusiasm and excellence under rear admirals, then under a major general of the Army, and finally under a major general of Marines.

In December, I received orders to proceed to Pearl for a conference with Nimitz, from there to Los Angeles, to attend a meeting of industrialists, and on to Washington for a conference with Ernie King. First I flew across to Brisbane, to take leave of General MacArthur. We were chatting along when he suddenly said, "I'll tell you something you may not know: they're going to send me a big piece of the fleet—put it absolutely at my disposal. And I'll tell you something else: the British are going to do the same."

He paused a moment. "I want my naval operations to be in charge of an American. Whoever he is, he'll have to be senior enough to outrank the Britisher, or at least equal him."

He paused again, then shot at me, "How about *you*, Bill? If you come with me, I'll make you a greater man than Nelson ever dreamed of being!"

I said that I was flattered, but in no position to commit myself; however, I'd certainly tell King and Nimitz about his offer. I did, and that's the last I heard of it.

Bill Riley, Doug Moulton, and Bill Kitchell went with me on my Stateside trip. We reached Pearl on December 26, and I spent 4 days with Nimitz, reviewing the South Pacific campaigns and discussing future moves. San Francisco showed me two brand-new sights—an East-West football game, and a lady Marine; and two other sights that I hadn't seen in much too long—my wife Fan, who

186

flew out from Wilmington to meet me, and young Bill, whose ship happened to be in port. It was my first meeting with Fan in sixteen months and my first with Bill since he had been a castaway.

Next morning my staff came up to our hotel room. I broke in on some story that Fan was telling them and got from her a firm "Shut up!" for my interruption.

Bill Riley laughed until he cried. "I never would have believed it," he said, "but there *is* somebody who dares tell him to shut up!" (Little did he know!)

After the meeting at Los Angeles, I reported to Washington for temporary duty.

EDITOR'S NOTE:

On January 12, Secretary Knox awarded Admiral Halsey a Gold Star in lieu of a second Distinguished Service Medal, with the following citation:

"For exceptionally meritorious and distinguished service to the Government of the United States in a position of great responsibility as Commander South Pacific Force and South Pacific Area from October 19, 1942, to December 7, 1943. In command of Naval Forces and certain Army ground and air forces during this critical period, Admiral Halsey conducted a brilliantly planned and consistently sustained offensive, driving the enemy steadily northward and occupying strategic positions through the Solomons, thereby securing the South Pacific Area for the United Nations. A forceful and inspiring leader, Admiral Halsey indoctrinated his command with his own fighting spirit and an invincible determination to destroy the enemy. His daring initiative and superb tactical skill have been responsible for the continued success of the South Pacific Campaign and have contributed vitally toward breaking down Japanese resistance."

I had several long talks with Ernie King. Since we were about ready to ring down the curtain in the South Pacific theater, the chief question was where we should play the final scenes. I said that I saw no need to storm Rabaul or the secondary base of Kavieng, on the northwestern end of New Ireland. Both of them had been hit repeatedly from the air in December and early January (we had celebrated the holidays by striking Kavieng on Christmas and again on New Year's), but although their offensive value was nearing zero, they could still put up a strong defense. Further, the geography of the area begged for another by-pass. Commanding the eastern approach to Rabaul was Green Island, 120 miles away; commanding the northern approach to Kavieng was Emirau, 90 miles away; and commanding the western approaches to both Rabaul and Kavieng was Manus, 220 miles from Kavieng. All three islands were push-overs, and when they fell, Japan's South Pacific campaign would fall with them.

By the time I left Washington, toward the end of January, I think I had carried my point with Ernie. Now I had to convince MacArthur and Nimitz. A conference had already been arranged at Pearl. MacArthur could not attend, but he was sending his Chief of Staff, Lt. Gen. Richard K. Sutherland, with authority to make decisions in his name. The others present would be General Kenney, Nimitz and key members of his staff, myself and Mick Carney.

My plane was grounded at Fort Worth and again at San Francisco, and the conference had adjourned when I finally arrived, but Mick briefed me on what had happened. MacArthur had accepted our programs for the occupation of Green and Manus and had set the respective L Days for February 15 and 29. On the other hand, he had rejected the program for Emirau and still stood by his determination to storm Kavieng, not on May 1, as he had originally proposed, but on April 1.

Mick had already sent dispatches to start the wheels turning, and they were gathering speed when we reached Nouméa, early in February. The Green operation went through as planned, against only cursory resistance. So did the Manus operation. Elements of the 1st Cavalry Division, under Brig. Gen. William C. Chase, soon occupied the entire island, except for a small corner. This, I am told, the Army deliberately did not clear, but kept as a sort of game preserve, an area where new troops could practise scouting and patrolling. Food was left where the Japs would find it, so that they would stay in good physical condition, and each patrol was given a bag limit of two. I don't know how long the supply lasted; I imagine the game wardens weren't too harsh on an overenthusiastic sportsman.

Fighter strips were built on both Manus and Green, and work was started to make Manus an advanced naval base as well, with full facilities for repairing and supplying the fleet. This work had hardly begun when I received a dispatch from my representative on MacArthur's staff, Capt. Felix L. Johnson, urgently requesting me to come to Brisbane at once. Mick, Bill Riley, Doug Moulton, and Ham Dow flew over with me. We went from the plane straight to MacArthur's office, where Felix met us. MacArthur was waiting for us, with his top staff officers and Vice Adm. Tom Kinkaid, commanding the Seventh Fleet. (Incidentally, there was an unusual bond between our two staffs: my Chief of Staff's son, Capt. Robert B. Carney, Jr., of the Marines, had married MacArthur's Chief of Staff's daughter, Miss Natalie Sutherland.)

Before even a word of greeting was spoken, I saw that MacArthur was fighting to keep his temper. What galled him, it soon appeared, was this: Nimitz, knowing that I not only had planned the layout for the base at Manus but had furnished naval forces to construct it, had sent a dispatch to COMINCH, with a copy to MacArthur, suggesting that the boundary of my area be extended to include Manus. I had had no hand in originating the dispatch; I did not even hear of it until after it had been sent; but MacArthur lumped me, Nimitz, King, and the whole Navy in a vicious conspiracy to pare away his authority.

Unlike myself, strong emotion did not make him profane. He did not need to be; profanity would have merely discolored his eloquence. It continued for about a quarter of an hour, illuminating two main themes: he had no intention of tamely submitting to such interference; and he had given orders that, until the jurisdiction of Manus was established, work should be restricted to facilities for ships under his direct command—the Seventh Fleet and British units.

When he had finished, he pointed his pipestem at me and demanded, "Am I not right, Bill?"

Tom Kinkaid, Mick, Felix, and I answered with one voice, "No, sir!"

MacArthur smiled and said pleasantly, "Well, if so many fine gentlemen disagree with me, we'd better examine the proposition once more. Bill, what's your opinion?"

"General," I said, "I disagree with you entirely. Not only that, but I'm going one step further and tell you that if you stick to this order of yours, you'll be hampering the war effort!"

189

His staff gasped. I imagine they never expected to hear anyone address him in those terms this side of the Judgment Throne, if then. I told him that the command of Manus didn't matter a whit to me. What did matter was the quick construction of the base. Kenney or an Australian or an enlisted cavalryman could boss it for all I cared, as long as it was ready to handle the fleet when we moved up New Guinea and on toward the Philippines.

The argument had begun at 1700. By 1800, when we broke up, I thought I had won him around, but next morning at 1000 he asked us to come back to his office. (He kept unusual hours—from 1000 until 1400, and from 1600 until 2100 or later.) It seemed that during the night he had become mad all over again, and again was dead set on restricting the work. We went through the same arguments as the afternoon before, almost word for word, and at the end of an hour we reached the same conclusion: the work would proceed. I was about to tell him good-by and fly back to Nouméa when he suddenly asked if we would return at 1700. I'll be damned if we didn't run the course a third time! This time, though, it was really final. He gave me a charming smile and said, "You win, Bill!" and to General Sutherland, "Dick, go ahead with the job."

We returned to Nouméa on March 11. On the fourteenth, another surprise exploded in my face: a dispatch from the Joint Chiefs of Staff to MacArthur and myself directed that the seizure of Emirau be substituted for the seizure of Kavieng. MacArthur must have been as astonished as I was. When we parted in Brisbane, both of us understood that the Kavieng operation was still on the cards. The new directive did not set a date for L Day, but ordered us to make it as soon as possible. This entailed no more than dusting off our original plan, picking the landing force, and notifying Ping Wilkinson and Roy Geiger to load them in. The best troops available on such short notice were the 4th Regiment of the 3rd Marine Division, then at Guadalcanal. They began embarking at once, despite screams of rage from my old friend Lt. Gen. Holland M. Smith, commanding the Fleet Marine Force. "Howling Mad" was knee-deep in plans for the occupation of Guam in July and had earmarked this regiment for part of his forces. When he quieted down, I explained that (1) I had no other troops at the moment; (2) I couldn't wait for them to arrive, because this was a rush job;

190

(3) Intelligence had informed us that Emirau was held very lightly, if at all; and (4) I would relieve his precious regiment promptly and hand it back to him. Howling Mad subsided to a grumble, and the occupation went forward.

Commanded by Brig. Gen. Alfred H. Noble, the landing force left Guadalcanal on March 18 and took over Emirau on the twentieth, thereby establishing a record of six days between "Stand by to shove off!" and "Well done!" Although the convoy sailed more than 800 miles through waters recently dominated by enemy sea and air power, not a plane rose from Rabaul, Kavieng, or Truk to intercept it, and not a destroyer or even a submarine appeared. Further, the island was ours at the price of one casualty: a Seabee fell off a bulldozer and broke his leg. The 1st Marine Division, meanwhile, and units of the Sixth Army had landed on New Britain under MacArthur's direction and had cut off the only overland escape from Rabaul. The encirclement was complete. Some 50,000 Japs were sealed into New Britain and New Ireland, and some 30,000 more into Bougainville and Choiseul. Control of the land, the sea, and the air was ours. The South Pacific campaign was finished.

Correction: It was not quite finished. At the beginning of this chapter, I said that we estimated the Japs would need four months to supply and reinforce the troops we had pushed back from Torokina on November 1. On March 7 they began their expected counterattack. They had brought up heavy artillery by tractors and man power, and shells by man power alone. Prisoners told us later that every 100-pound shell required two men to make a four-day trip.

I had flown up to Guadalcanal to discuss the Emirau operation with Ping and Roy, so I continued on to Bougainville to watch the fighting. I particularly wanted to visit the western sector of our perimeter, where the 37th Division had beat off a heavy assault the day before I arrived, and the sector where the Americal Division had just retaken a critical area overlooking the Piva air strip. I was striding along the lines, as usual paying no attention to where I stepped, when I tripped and fell flat. I thought it was a root, but it wasn't. It was a foot, in a split-toed shoe, sticking up from the ground. Private Watanabe or Corporal Yamatoya, or whoever he

191

had been, had a rare distinction: he was the only Jap who brought me to my knees.

That afternoon, Bill Kitchell and I went down to the Torokina River for a swim. A lot of troops were there, splashing and scrubbing, when we got out of our jeep. A Negro soldier was the first to spot my insignia. He shouted, "Fo' Gawd! Fo' stars!" and stood up, mother-naked, and gave me a smart salute.

The counterattack lasted eighteen days. It cost the enemy about 10,000 dead and ourselves fewer than 1,000. On March 25, organized resistance in the Solomons ended forever.

April passed quietly. Early in May I was directed to proceed to San Francisco for a conference with King and Nimitz, who told me that my present dual command—of the South Pacific and the Third Fleet—would be split up in June; I would be relieved as COMSOPAC and would go to sea as COMTHIRDFLEET. I returned to Nouméa in time to make a farewell swing around my old territory. My first stop was New Zealand. In the middle of a luncheon given for me by the Prime Minister, Peter Fraser, I received a note from the Governor General, Sir Cyril Newall, informing me that the King had appointed me an Honorary Knight Commander of the Order of the British Empire. I wasn't quite sure what this meant, but I could hardly believe that it entitled my impertinent staff to begin addressing me as "Sir Butch."

From New Zealand I flew north to Espiritu, and on up the chain to Emirau, stopping at each of our bases to take leave of my friends. The old battlefields were already disappearing into the jungle or under neat, new buildings. Where 500 men had lost their lives in a night attack a few months before, eighteen men were now playing baseball. Where a Jap pillbox had crouched, a movie projector stood. Where a hand grenade had wiped out a foxhole, a storekeeper was serving cokes. Only the cemeteries were left.

Back in Nouméa, Miff Harmon generously gave me the Army's Distinguished Service Medal.

EDITOR'S NOTE:
General Harmon prefaced the award by saying, "The esteem and respect in which Halsey is held by the Army, and particularly by the Army of the SOPAC forces, can hardly be expressed by me here and now, or by the phraseology of a citation. . . ."

The citation follows:

"For exceptionally meritorious and distinguished service in a position of great responsibility from December 8, 1943, to May 1, 1944. Having created and integrated a well-knit combat force through his superior leadership, personal guidance, and strict adherence to the sound principles of unity of command, Admiral Halsey used this powerful striking force with such vigor and determination as to crush the Japanese garrison on certain South Pacific island groups and isolate enemy forces in others. As a result of Admiral Halsey's conduct of command, the Army forces in the South Pacific area were splendidly cared for and were able to accomplish the combat and logistic missions assigned in the most effective manner."

On the morning of June 15, I turned over my command to Vice Adm. John Henry Newton, who had been Deputy COM-SOPAC for eight months. Next morning I took off for Pearl. Troops lined the way to the fleet landing. Their cheers and the bands and the flags stung my eyes. I never saw Nouméa again.

☆
☆ 12 ☆
☆ ☆

BETWEEN the first and second phases of my war career, I spent two months in hospitals and a month in idleness. Between the second and third phases, there was no such restful interlude, as is shown by successive entries in my war diary for 1944:

15 JUNE E.L.D. [East Longitude Date.] On this date Adm. William F. Halsey, Jr., relinquished command of the South Pacific Force and Area to Vice Adm. John Henry Newton at headquarters at Nouméa, New Caledonia.

16 JUNE E.L.D. Admiral Halsey, accompanied by senior members of his staff, departed Nouméa at 0900, with the au revoirs and well-wishes of a crowd of SOPACers.

17 JUNE W.L.D. Upon arrival at Pearl at 0800, Admiral Halsey and Rear Admiral Carney proceeded to new offices in the JICPOA building [Joint Intelligence Center Pacific Ocean Areas].

18 JUNE W.L.D. Commander Third Fleet and Staff, at headquarters preparing preliminary plans for occupation of western Carolines, . . . received copy of Joint Chiefs of Staff dispatch to CINCPOA [Nimitz] and CINCSOWESPAC [MacArthur] requesting views and recommendations as to by-passing present selected objectives and proceeding at earlier date to Japan or Formosa. Admiral Halsey expressed the view that part or all of the immediate objectives in the western Carolines could be by-passed, and the operations against the Philippines could be accelerated.

These "immediate objectives" were three islands in the Palau group—Peleliu, Angaur, and Babelthuap; the island of Yap, about 280 miles northeast; and Ulithi atoll, 120 miles further. I had been

194

weighing this operation ever since it had been broached to me. early in May, at the conference with King and Nimitz in San Francisco, and the more I weighed it, the less I liked it. Ulithi had a useful anchorage, but I saw no need for any of the other islands Yap's only value was as a minor staging point for aircraft. The Palaus threatened the route between New Guinea and the Philippines, but although they also offered an anchorage—Kossol Roads—and several sites for airfields, I felt that they would have to be bought at a prohibitive price in casualties. In short, I feared another Tarawa—and I was right.

Chester Nimitz and Mick Carney both disagreed with me about the western Carolines, but we agreed completely on long-range strategy. Almost alone among senior admirals, Chester and I advocated invading the central Philippines, building a major base, and jumping from there to the home islands of Japan, via Iwo Jima and Okinawa. Ernie King, on the other hand, strongly recommended by-passing the Philippines and occupying Formosa, which I considered more redoubtable and more useless than the Palaus. When Mick Carney protested that the Philippines were indispensable, Ernie asked, "Do you want to make a London out of Manila?"

Mick said, "No, sir. I want to make an England out of Luzon!"

Ray Spruance favored a base at Nimrod Sound, south of Shanghai. Still others argued for landings on the Shantung Peninsula, or on Quelpart Island, at the southern end of Korea Strait, or on Korea itself. They defended their inch-by-inch policy right up to the spring of 1945, when they received a directive flatly ordering the invasion of Kyushu. (This was scheduled for November 1 and would have been followed by an invasion of Honshu, the main island, in February, 1946.) The arguments sometimes became heated. I remember that when I had advanced my objections to Ray Spruance's plan, he said, "Then I guess I'd better handle this one!"

"Go ahead," I told him. "I don't want any part of it!"

The western Carolines operation was slightly simplified by the eventual decision not to invade Babelthuap, but it was still complex enough to require six solid weeks of work by Ping Wilkinson, Roy Geiger, myself, and our three staffs. The final plan called for the "capture of Angaur and Peleliu as Phase ONE, with capture of

195

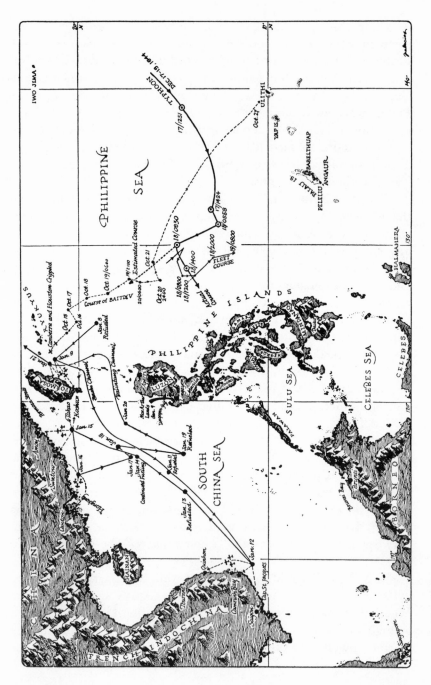

Yap and Ulithi as Phase TWO. Target date for the first phase 15 September and for second phase 5 October. Operation to be commanded by Commander THIRD Fleet, with Commander THIRD Amphibious Force [Ping Wilkinson] commanding joint expeditionary force, and Maj. Gen. Julian C. Smith, USMC, commanding all expeditionary troops." Roy Geiger, commanding the III Marine Amphibious Corps, was in charge of the first phase, and Maj. Gen. John R. Hodge, commanding the XXIV Army Corps, was in charge of the second. Although I was over-all commander, I would not see the landings, since the fleet would be far to the westward, blanketing enemy airfields in the central Philippines.

My flagship, the battleship *New Jersey*, sortied from Pearl on August 24, escorted by three destroyers. Consideration of a suitable Third Fleet flagship had begun months before in the South Pacific. My first inclination had been to pick a carrier. I had spent so many years in them that I would have felt more at home there than in anything but a destroyer, which was now too rough for my old age; but carriers are vulnerable, and we could not afford to risk having flag functions interrupted by battle damage. My only alternative, therefore—the only other ships that could keep pace with the 32-knot carriers—was the new 45,000-ton *Iowa* class, so I requested one and drew the *New Jersey*. Meanwhile, we had sent observers to the Marianas campaign and had placed them with Spruance on a heavy cruiser, with Mitscher on a fast carrier, and on two battleships, to determine the deficiencies, if any, of the different flag plots. On the basis of their recommendations, the *New Jersey's* flag plot was extensively altered, and when we put to sea, it was the best in the fleet. In fact, it was used as a model for the flag plot in her younger sister ship, the *Missouri*.

My grandiose title, "Commander Third Fleet," may seem top-heavy for three destroyers and one battleship. The explanation is, of course, that the Third Fleet was almost identical with the powerful Fifth Fleet, which comprised well over 500 warships. When Ray Spruance commanded them, they were designated the Fifth Fleet; when I commanded them, they were the Third. Instead of the stagecoach system of keeping the drivers and changing the horses, we changed drivers and kept the horses. It was hard on the horses, but it was effective. Moreover, it consistently misled the Japs into an exaggerated conception of our seagoing strength.

197

While I was working at Pearl, Ray had been scourging the western Pacific. He had covered four landings; he had fought the crucial Battle of the Philippine Sea on June 19; and he had struck at Guam and Saipan, at the Bonins, the Volcanoes, and the Ryukyus. Now it was his turn to rest. We changed drivers in mid-ocean on August 26. The Fifth Fleet vanished, and the Third Fleet appeared in its place. This place, at the moment, was off Iwo Jima, 3,000 miles from my flagship, so the usual ceremony of taking over had to be a matter of bookkeeping. I never saw Ray at all, and I did not see the heart of the fleet, Pete Mitscher's Fast Carrier Task Force, TF 38, until we rendezvoused two weeks later. None the less, as of August 26, I was in strategic command.

Pete had not been waiting idly for our arrival. As soon as his planes had finished with Iwo Jima, he stood south and sent three of his task groups to bludgeon the Palaus on September 6, 7, and 8, while the fourth group hit Yap. On the ninth and tenth, he made two heavy strikes against Mindanao, the southernmost of the big Philippine islands. These had been intended as the first of a series, but when he reported that the Fifth Air Force had already flattened the enemy's installations and that only a feeble few planes rose to meet him, I decided to switch the rest of his strikes to the central Philippines, since here were the last air bases that endangered the Palau landings.

Pete's force and mine joined up on the eleventh. Normally he would have come aboard the *New Jersey* for a visit. I told him to stay put; I would visit him instead. I hadn't been with the fleet for more than two years; I wanted to see what the new carriers and planes looked like. Transfers of personnel between ships at sea used to be done by breeches buoy, but I found that fancy chairs had replaced them. In fact, there was hot competition to see which ship could furnish the fanciest. If I remember correctly, the chair that swung me aboard Pete's flagship, the carrier *Lexington*, was equipped with an ash tray and a surrey top. (When Slew McCain relieved Pete and objected to the slowness of the *New Jersey's* chair, we handed him a buggy whip and suggested that he flog the air on the way across.)

We opened our attack on the central Philippines on September 12, from a position within sight of the mountains of Samar. That

198

day we flew 1,200 sorties; on the thirteenth, another 1,200; and when the last plane had returned aboard on the fourteenth, our Air Combat Intelligence officers showed me a box score that made me whistle. We had shot down 173 planes, destroyed 305 more on the ground, sunk fifty-nine ships, and probably sunk another fifty-eight, besides tremendous damage to installations. Our losses? Eight planes in combat, one operationally, and ten men!

These figures were so dazzling that I sent a blanket dispatch to all the carriers: BECAUSE OF THE BRILLIANT PERFORMANCE MY GROUP OF STARS HAS JUST GIVEN, I AM BOOKING YOU TO APPEAR BEFORE THE BEST AUDIENCE IN THE ASIATIC THEATER.

The audience was Manila, which had the largest concentration of enemy planes in the Philippines. My decision to poke a strike into this hornet's nest was not made hotly, without forethought. The South Pacific campaign had impressed us all with the necessity of being alert for symptoms of enemy weakness and of being ready to exploit them—if a stuck door yields unexpectedly, you may fall on your face. I intended probing just as an infantry patrol probes—finding a soft spot and pressing it until I met resistance that I could not overcome. (Back in Pearl, we had approached our planning for the Third Fleet in the spirit that a sudden development might extend its scope to Formosa, China, the Ryukyus, and even the Empire itself. Pearl considered these targets so far afield that it was reluctant to prepare intelligence data for them. It laughed at us and accused us of delusions of grandeur.)

Here was a case in point. We had just dealt a crippling blow to Jap air power, and we had found the central Philippines a hollow shell with weak defenses and skimpy facilities. In my opinion, this was the vulnerable belly of the Imperial dragon. The time might be ripe not only to strike Manila, but perhaps to mount a far larger offensive. Specifically, I began to wonder whether I dared recommend that MacArthur shift to Leyte the invasion which he had planned for Mindanao, and advance the date well ahead of the scheduled November 15. . . .

I consulted my staff. They evaluated our combat reports, our intelligence data, and the availability of Nimitz' and MacArthur's forces. Finally they said, "Yes."

I sat in a corner of the bridge and thought it over. Such a

199

recommendation, in addition to being none of my business, would upset a great many applecarts, possibly all the way up to Mr. Roosevelt and Mr. Churchill. On the other hand, it looked sound, it ought to save thousands of lives, and it might cut months off the war by hurrying the Nips and keeping them off-balance.

I sent for Mick Carney and Harold Stassen and told them, "I'm going to stick my neck out. Send an urgent dispatch to CINCPAC—"

This dispatch, sent on September 13, recommended (1) that seizure of Yap and the Palaus be abandoned; (2) that the ground forces thereby released be put at General MacArthur's disposal; and (3) that an invasion of Leyte be undertaken at the earliest possible date.

CINCPAC replied promptly. The first phase of the western Carolines operations was to be carried out as planned, but he would give fresh study to Yap, and was informing COMINCH and CINCSOWESPAC of my suggestions. Providentially, at this very moment Mr. Roosevelt and Mr. Churchill were in session with the Joint Chiefs of Staff at Quebec. Ernie King presented my dispatch, and after a quick exchange of messages, to get MacArthur's opinion, they approved the new plan and instructed him to cancel the invasion of Mindanao and to invade Leyte instead, on October 20.

If he had used Mindanao as a steppingstone, he would not have reached Leyte until December 20. The new plan advanced the war two months or more.

EDITOR'S NOTES:

1) Following is an extract from General Marshall's "Biennial Report of the Chief of Staff of the United States Army to the Secretary of War, July 1, 1943, to June 30, 1945:"

"The OCTAGON conference was then in progress at Quebec. The Joint Chiefs of Staff received a copy of a communication from Admiral Halsey to Admiral Nimitz on 13 September. He recommended that three projected intermediate operations against Yap, Mindanao, and Talaud and Sangihe Islands to the southwest be canceled, and that our forces attack Leyte in the central Philippines as soon as possible. . . . General MacArthur's views were requested and 2 days later he advised us that he was already prepared to shift his plans to land on Leyte 20 October, instead of 20 December as previously intended. It was a remarkable administrative achievement.

"The message from MacArthur arrived at Quebec at night and Admiral Leahy (Chief of Staff to the President), Admiral King, General Arnold, and I were being entertained at a formal dinner by Canadian officers. It was read by the appropriate staff officers who suggested an immediate affirmative answer. The message, with their recommendations, was rushed to us and we left the table for a conference. Having the utmost confidence in General MacArthur, Admiral Nimitz, and Admiral Halsey, it was not a difficult decision to make. Within 90 minutes after the signal had been received in Quebec, General MacArthur and Admiral Nimitz had received their instructions to execute the Leyte operation on 20 October, abandoning the three previously approved intermediary landings."

2) Following is an extract from President Roosevelt's "Message on the State of the Union," delivered to Congress on January 6, 1945:

"Last September . . . it was our plan to approach the Philippines by further stages, taking islands which we may call A, C, and E. However, Admiral Halsey reported that a direct attack on Leyte appeared feasible. . . . Within the space of 24 hours, a major change of plans was accomplished which involved Army and Navy forces from two different theaters of operations—a change which hastened the liberation of the Philippines and the final day of victory—a change which saved lives which would have been expended in the capture of islands which are now neutralized far behind our lines."

The western Carolines landings represented the extremes of amphibious warfare. Peleliu, where Maj. Gen. William H. Rupertus' 1st Marine Division landed on September 15, was as tough as they come; its pillboxes and caves were so heavily fortified that the island was not secured for a month. Angaur was much softer; Maj. Gen. Paul J. Mueller's 81st Infantry Division landed there on the seventeenth, crushed its flimsy defenses in three days, and by the twenty-second was able to send detachments to reinforce the Marines on Peleliu. Softest of all was Ulithi; on the twenty-third, a regimental combat team occupied it against no opposition whatsoever. We had gained two harbors, one airstrip, and the sites for two future strips, but the cost was 8,000 men killed, wounded, or missing. The enemy lost about 12,000 killed.

Now we stood northwestward for the attack on Manila which

we had promised ourselves—our first since we had been driven from the islands over two years before. The night before we struck, I called in our Filipino stewards and pointed out our targets on a chart of the city. I told them, "I want you to know what we're going to do, because many of you have relatives in Manila. All of us pray that none of them are injured."

Benedicto Tulao, a chief steward who had been with me for years, asked me, "Those are Japanese installations there, sir?"

"Yes."

He said firmly, "Bomb them!"

As we hoped, our attack caught the Japs with their flaps down, and we bombed and strafed Clark and Nichols Fields for ten minutes before a single fighter took the air against us. When I visited Manila nine months later, I was told that when our planes appeared, the Jap officers pointed at them and bragged, "See our splendid war eagles! How swiftly they fly! How smoothly they maneuver!" About then the bombs began to fall.

We hit them four times on the twenty-first and expected to hit them four times more next day, but the approach of foul weather and the dearth of suitable targets influenced Pete Mitscher to recommend that I cancel the last two strikes. I did. His score for the six was 405 planes destroyed or damaged, 103 ships sunk or damaged, both airfields gutted, and the harbor littered with wrecks. Our losses were fifteen planes and about a dozen men. None of our ships was touched, although we had launched from only 40 miles off the east coast of Luzon, less than 150 miles from Manila itself.

The twenty-third was fueling day. We sent for Pete's Chief of Staff, "31-Knot" Burke of the destroyer actions in the South Pacific, to discuss the possibility of striking Coron Bay on the twenty-fourth. This was an excellent anchorage which the Japs were believed to favor because of the unlikelihood that any air attack would dare reach so far, across the Philippines and out to their western rim. Now, we agreed, was the perfect time to hit it; every ship able to flee the shambles of Manila Harbor had certainly done so, and Coron Bay was their best available refuge.

As soon as fueling was completed, we started a high-speed run-in which brought us to San Bernardino Strait at dawn. The target was still 350 miles away, but we could get no closer; we launched the

202

first of our strikes at 0550. My war diary tells the story of the day with a conciseness that I cannot improve:

Two large AO [tankers] were exploded. One large AP [transport], 3 large AO, 2 large AK [cargo ships], 6 medium AK, 5 small AK, 1 DD, 3 DE [destroyer escorts], and 11 small craft were sunk. Damaged and probably sunk were 1 large AP, 2 large AO, 1 medium AO, 1 large AK, 15 medium AK, 21 small AK, 10 smaller ships, and 2 DE. Air opposition was negligible and was quickly disposed of, 36 planes being destroyed. When the reports of the past three weeks' operations had been totaled, 1,005 enemy planes had been destroyed and 153 ships sunk, excluding small craft.

Whenever the occasion permitted, my staff tried to counteract the grimness of war with a lighthearted dispatch to our forces. The one that Mick Carney now sent in my name was among his most successful compositions: THE RECENT EXCEPTIONAL PERFORMANCE YIELDED GRATIFYING GATE RECEIPTS, AND ALTHOUGH THE CAPACITY AUDIENCE HISSED VERY LOUDLY, LITTLE WAS THROWN AT THE PLAYERS X AS LONG AS THE AUDIENCE HAS A SPOT TO HISS IN, WE WILL STAY ON THE ROAD.

First we gave ourselves a little rest and a chance to rearm, re-fuel, and reprovision in peace. One task group stayed to cover the Palaus while the other three retired to Manus, Saipan, and Kossol Roads. Our group's arrival at Saipan on the twenty-eighth allowed me leisure for something I had been wanting to do for a long time: I presented Mick with a Gold Star in lieu of a second Distinguished Service Medal—not for his jocular dispatches, I hasten to say, but for his brilliant staff work in the South Pacific. He had won his first DSM in the Atlantic, early in the war.

My leisure lasted only a few hours. At dusk that evening, a Thursday, my PB2Y3 took off on the 1,100-mile flight to Hollandia, New Guinea, where we spent Friday conferring with MacArthur's staff about the Leyte invasion. On Saturday we flew up to the Palaus, for a tour of Peleliu and Angaur and for more conferences. And on Sunday, October 1, we flew across to Ulithi, where the fleet was assembling.

Harold Stassen eame out to our moorings in my barge. He was still 100 yards away when he yelled at Bill Kitchell, who was with me, "Hey, Bill! The fifth one has arrived and it's a girl!"

She was already three weeks old, but this was Bill's first news of her. His delight snapped me out of a sour mood that I had been in ever since Hollandia, where I had received a dispatch from CINCPAC suggesting that we had missed an opportunity by not mining Manila Bay during our recent strikes. I disagreed vigorously. Aerial mining proved valuable on many occasions during the war, but it should be undertaken by shore-based planes, in my opinion, and not by carrier planes. Moreover, carrier planes are not equipped to mine at night; if they mine in daylight, the enemy not only can see where the mines are laid but has a sitting-duck shot at the planes, since the operation requires a low-speed, low-altitude approach on a steady course. Lastly, mines take up space on a carrier that could be better devoted to bombs and torpedoes.

The trip to the Palaus was a triple milestone for me. It was my first experience with an area sprayed with DDT, and despite the fact that this was a battlefield, I did not see a fly or a mosquito or an insect of any sort. (I remembered Guadalcanal, where our casualties from malaria were twice our casualties from the enemy.) Again, the Palaus was the last time I commanded amphibious troops, and the last time I was under fire ashore.

After a month at sea, we had hoped for at least a week at anchor, but forty-eight hours was the most that we could manage. A typhoon drove us out of Ulithi on October 3, and although we returned next day, we had to sortie on the sixth to begin running interference for MacArthur's landing on Leyte. We had already smashed Japan's air strength in the Philippines (General Kenney later counted nearly 3,000 wrecked planes on the various fields); now we had to knock out the bases from which this strength could be renewed. Many of the largest bases were on Formosa; others were in the Nansei Shoto chain, between Formosa and Japan proper. Our plan was to send a cruiser-destroyer task group against Marcus Island to simulate the overtures to a landing, with bombardments, smoke screens, floating lights, and other pyrotechnics; and while the Nips watched Marcus, and jumped and chattered, we would hit the Nansei Shotos, 1,500 miles away.

Our approach was helped by two agents new to the Third Fleet: Navy scout planes from Saipan, and the typhoon, now known as "Task Force Zero" because it had curved northward and was

204

grounding potential opposition ahead of us. (In our Night Order Book for October 8, I find that Mick Carney made this entry: "TF 0 arrives Tokyo and RON"—remains overnight.) Our long-range scouts, Liberators, sank the enemy's picket boats and interdicted his search planes, so we ran in unobserved on the night of the ninth, launched early the next morning, and struck along a 300-mile arc, from Amami O Shima on the north to Myako Jima on the south.

The Japs were sound asleep. We destroyed ninety-three of their planes, sank eighty-seven ships, and spread havoc on the ground. Here is a short sample from the final report: "Ammunition and fuel storages at Naha were left blazing and exploding. Tukuna air facilities were demolished. Barracks were destroyed at Yontan. Four warehouses at Ie Shima were strafed and burned." And so on. None of our ships was damaged, nor were any in the Marcus force.

While we were fueling next day, we sent a fighter sweep over the fields on Luzon, and as soon as fueling was completed, we headed for Luzon ourselves. This was another piece of trickery; at nightfall, we swung 60 degrees to starboard and shaped a course for Formosa, a virgin target. The trick didn't work. The Japs on Formosa were ready for us, and if they hadn't made the mistakes of staying on the defensive and underestimating our power, we might have had a rugged time. (On the other hand, the fundamental mistake was mine: I should have struck Formosa first; not only was it stronger, but it had been alerted by the Nansei Shoto strikes.) The first day of our attack, we concentrated on aircraft; the second day, we gave shipping the priority. The totals for the two days were 520 planes destroyed, thirty-seven ships sunk, and seventy-four probably sunk; our losses were fifty-two planes.

I was vaguely aware that this second day, October 13, was a Friday, but I had been contemptuous of my old jinx since young Bill's rescue. We landed the last strike by 1800 and came to our retirement course. At 1842 I was informed that the heavy cruiser Canberra, Capt. Alexander R. Early, had been torpedoed in a dusk air attack and was dead in the water. I looked at the chart: she was 90 miles from Formosa, 300 from Aparri Field on Luzon, 400 from Naha Field on Okinawa—and 1,300 from our nearest base, Ulithi. We were squarely in the Jap dragon's jaws, and the dragon knew it.

Should we abandon the Canberra and sink her, and withdraw

the rest of the fleet? Or should we try to tow her home, at the price of a running fight throughout most of those 1,300 miles? We decided to fight our way out.

The *Wichita*, another heavy cruiser, took her in tow at a heart-breaking 4 knots. (Thirteen hundred miles at 4 knots is more than thirteen days). I sent all available ships to strengthen the screen of their task group and I ordered a cruiser-destroyer force out from Saipan to meet them. It was obvious that the Japs would try a *coup de grâce* next morning, so we struck first, with fighter sweeps over Luzon and Formosa. Here is part of the story, from my war diary: "This day's total aircraft shot down at target, 11; destroyed on ground, 55." Here is another part: "Shot down near force by search and CAP, 75; shot down by ships' AA, 21." The Japs were pouncing, as we had expected. And here is the rest: "At 2100, message was received that heavy cruiser *Houston*, Capt. William W. Behrens, had been torpedoed; her engine room flooded; and task group was under continuous attack."

The *Houston* and the *Canberra* were both namesakes of ships already sunk. The original *Canberra*, an Australian cruiser, had been lost in the Battle of Savo Island, and the original *Houston* off Java, early in 1942. My jinx had a savage sense of humor!

This second torpedoing was echoed by an explosion at Radio-tokyo, which screeched that their intrepid fliers had almost anni-hilated my fleet, and that their own fleet was sprinting down from the Empire to complete the job. Congratulatory messages from Hitler and Mussolini were sprayed over the air, and local digni-taries ranging from cabinet ministers to a keeper in the Tokyo zoo united in praise of the glorious victory. The keeper had evidently been ruffled by a remark of mine, that "the Japs are losing their grip, even with their tails," because he hoped that "we get that man Halsey alive. I have already reserved a special cage for him in the monkey house." (When we went ashore at Tokyo, I wanted to call on him and invite him to show me the cage, but I never got around to it.)

At first I thought that this jubilation was merely more of the Japs' familiar self-hypnosis, but its extreme hysteria convinced me that they really believed we had been crushed. In fact, I found a possible basis for the belief. All through the nights of the twelfth and

206

thirteenth, Jap planes burned on the water around our fleet, and when one of our ships was momentarily silhouetted against the blaze, it was hard to realize that she herself was not afire. No doubt the Jap pilots who escaped had the same illusion and reported our "annihilation" in all sincerity.

The torpedoing of the *Houston* reawakened my fears that an attempt at salvage would mean throwing good ships after bad. Every fifteen minutes I glanced at the pin that represented the two cripples on my chart and cursed because it had inched no closer to safety. They couldn't maneuver to protect themselves, they immobilized the two other cruisers that were towing them, and they were a drag on the whole fleet, which was committed to supporting MacArthur's landing on the twentieth, only six days off. Frankly, I wanted to sink them and run beyond the range of the Japs' shore-based air before a worse disaster struck us.

Mick Carney and Rollo Wilson, who had succeeded Ray Thurber as my Operations officer, talked me out of it. They even persuaded me that we had a chance to make capital of our handicap. Our basic orders, they pointed out, stated that "in case opportunity for the destruction of a major portion of the enemy fleet offers or can be created, such destruction will become the primary task." Here was that opportunity, right in our laps. The enemy already believed that he had cut our fleet to pieces, and had announced that he was pursuing its remnants. Why not hide our real strength, lure him into attacking the task group around the cripples, in the supposition that these were the remnants, and then spring the trap and blow him out of the water?

Why not, indeed?

I notified MacArthur that I was disposing the fleet for possible surface action and temporarily would have to suspend my promised support. We reinforced "Crippled Division 1," rechristened it with a name even more to its distaste, "the Bait Division," and told COMBAITDIV, Rear Adm. Lloyd J. Wiltse, to have the air kept busy with urgent "distress" messages. Two of my carrier task groups I ordered to an intercepting position east of the BAITDIV, beyond range of enemy patrol planes, and the other two I ordered to strike Luzon, since this was the probable source of further air attacks. Finally I sent a dispatch to Nimitz: THE THIRD FLEET'S SUNKEN AND

207

DAMAGED SHIPS HAVE BEEN SALVAGED AND ARE RETIRING AT HIGH
SPEED TOWARD THE ENEMY.

As the fifteenth wore on, our trap looked better and better. At
0800, a submarine reported three heavy cruisers and a light cruiser
standing south from Bungo Suido, between Kyushu and Shikoku;
and early in the afternoon, a B-29 reported sighting two battleships
at Takao, Formosa, and another leaving Swatow on a course of
130 degrees, which was aimed right at us. Air attacks continued
through the day and intensified on the sixteenth, when sixty planes
struck at the BAITDIV. Fifty were shot down, but the *Houston* took
another torpedo, which gave her a list of 10 degrees and made her
bow crab 30 degrees to port. She and the *Canberra* had been taken
over by ocean-going tugs, but her yawing restricted their speed of
advance to only 3½ knots.

Meanwhile, the two task groups to eastward still lay in ambush.
Although their patrols shot down every plane that approached,
they were apprehensive that one, which had suddenly popped out
of the low clouds, might have had time to broadcast an alarm before
it was destroyed. My war diary for that night tells the developments:

At 2013, searches were launched to the north and northwest to a
distance of 300 miles. At 2030, the submarine *Skate* sighted 1 DD and 2 DE
on course 010 to the east of Amami O Shima. Night searches were negative. It was evident that the enemy had received a sighting report and had
retired just before the trap could be sprung.

So the plot fell through, but it had a happy ending. The
BAITDIV reached Ulithi safely on the twenty-seventh, and the *Canberra* and *Houston* lived to fight again. Watching them limp across
the ocean took years off my life, but every time I commiserate with
myself, I realize how infinitely more agonizing was the strain on the
men aboard the cripples. It took guts to spend day after day in the
center of a bull's-eye, and it took seamanship to fuel and to ride out
a typhoon under tow.

Pete Mitscher once said, "I'm proud to be an American. Only
the finest country on earth could produce boys like these." That is
my feeling exactly.

With the BAITDIV on its way home, we were able to renew our
strikes on Luzon and to cover General MacArthur's landing on

208

Leyte. In the thirteen days between our first strike on Okinawa and our last in support of the landing, we had sunk 140 ships and damaged 248, and we had shot down 685 planes and destroyed 540 on the ground. Our own losses were ninety-five planes, but many of the pilots and crewmen were recovered. No ships were lost; and excepting the *Canberra* and *Houston*, none suffered serious damage.

President Roosevelt sent us a personal message which was broadcast to all hands: IT IS WITH PRIDE THAT THE COUNTRY HAS FOLLOWED YOUR FLEET'S MAGNIFICENT SWEEP INTO ENEMY WATERS X IN ADDITION TO THE GALLANT FIGHTING OF YOUR FLIERS, WE APPRECIATE THE ENDURANCE AND SUPERSEAMANSHIP OF YOUR FORCES.

We would have liked to rest for awhile, but we had no time. There was a battle over the horizon, and we went to meet it.

☆

☆ 13 ☆

☆ ☆

SHORTLY before dawn on October 23, I received a dispatch from a Seventh Fleet picket submarine, the *Darter:* MANY SHIPS INCLUDING 3 PROBABLE BBS [battleships] 08-28 N 116-30 E COURSE 040 SPEED 18 X CHASING. This position is near the southwestern tip of the Philippine group, and the course is toward Coron Bay and Manila. The main strength of the Japanese Fleet was based, we knew, at Singapore and at Brunei, in Borneo. If it stayed holed up there, we planned to go down and dig it out. On the twenty-second, however, our submarines and patrol planes had reported that enemy units were restless, and the *Darter's* dispatch was proof that a major movement was afoot.

Certain details of fleet organization are essential to an understanding of the tremendous battle that now loomed. The key point is that we had two fleets in Philippine waters under separate commands: my Third Fleet was under command of Admiral Nimitz; Tom Kinkaid's Seventh Fleet was under command of General MacArthur. If we had been under the same command, with a single system of operational control and intelligence, the Battle for Leyte Gulf might have been fought differently to a different result. It is folly to cry over spilled milk, but it is wisdom to observe the cause, for future avoidance. When blood has been spilled, the obligation becomes vital. In my opinion, it is vital for the Navy never to expose itself again to the perils of a divided command in the same area.

The Third and Seventh Fleets also differed in functions and weapons. The Seventh Fleet was defensive; having convoyed Mac-

Arthur's transports to Leyte, it stood by to protect them with its cruisers, destroyers, old battleships, and little escort carriers. The Third Fleet was offensive; it prowled the ocean, striking at will with its new battleships and fast carriers. These powerful units were concentrated in Pete Mitscher's Task Force 38, which was made up of four task groups, commanded by Vice Adm. Slew McCain and Rear Adms. Gerald F. Bogan, Ted Sherman, and Ralph E. Davison. The task groups were not uniform, but they averaged a total of twenty-three ships, divided approximately as follows—two large carriers, two light carriers, and two new battleships, with a screen of three cruisers and fourteen destroyers. My flagship, the *New Jersey*, was in Bogan's group; Mitscher's flagship, the *Lexington*, was in Sherman's.

The morning of October 23 found McCain's group on its way to Ulithi for rest and replenishment. The other three were standing eastward of the Philippines, awaiting their turn to retire, and meanwhile preparing further strikes in support of MacArthur. On the basis of the *Darter's* report, I ordered them to close the islands and to launch search teams next morning in a fan that would cover the western sea approaches for the entire length of the chain. Experience had taught us that if we interfered with a Jap plan before it matured, we stood a good chance of disrupting it. The Jap mind is inelastic; it cannot adapt itself to an altered situation.

The three task groups reached their stations that night—Sherman, off the Polillo Islands; 140 miles southeast of him, Bogan, off San Bernardino Strait; 120 miles southeast of Bogan, Davison, off Surigao Strait. Their search teams flew out at daybreak on the twenty-fourth. At 0820, one of Bogan's teams reported contact with five battleships, nine cruisers, and thirteen destroyers south of Mindoro Island, course 050, speed 10 to 12 knots. (This force, the Central Force, was the same that had been dimly sighted by the *Darter;* she and a sister sub, the *Dace*, had already sunk two of its heavy cruisers and damaged a third.)

My log summarizes the events of the next few minutes:

At 0822, I rebroadcast Bogan's report at the top of my radio voice.

At 0827, I ordered Sherman and Davison to close on Bogan at their best speed.

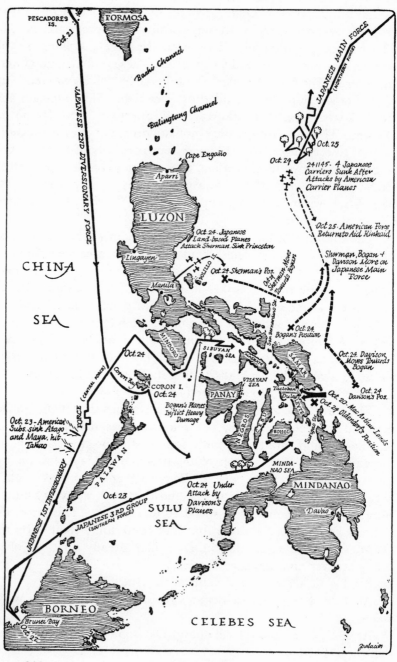

PESCADORES IS.
Oct. 21

FORMOSA

Bashi Channel

Balingtang Channel

Cape Engaño

Aparri

LUZON

JAPANESE 2ND DIVERSIONARY FORCE

CHINA

SEA

Lingayen

Manila

Oct. 24. Japanese Land-based Planes Attack Sherman. Sink Princeton

POLILLO IS.

Oct. 24. Sherman's Pos.

MINDORO

Oct. 24

Coron Bay

CORON I.
Oct. 24

SIBUYAN SEA

Bogan's Planes Inflict Heavy Damage

MASBATE

PANAY

VISAYAN SEA

NEGROS

JAPANESE 1ST DIVERSIONARY FORCE (CENTRAL FORCE)

Oct. 23 - American Subs. Sink Atago and Maya. hit Takao

PALAWAN

Oct. 23

JAPANESE 3RD GROUP (SOUTHERN FORCE)

SULU

SEA

Oct. 24 Under Attack by Davison's Planes

MINDANAO SEA

BOHOL

Surigao Str.

MINDANAO

Davao

BORNEO

Brunei Bay

Ist Oct. 22

CELEBES SEA

JAPANESE MAIN FORCE (NORTHERN FORCE)

Oct. 25

Oct. 24

241145- 4 Japanese Carriers Sunk After Attacks by American Carrier Planes

Oct. 25. American Force Returns to Aid Kinkaid

Sherman, Bogan + Davison Move on Japanese Main Force

Oct. 24 Sherman Moves Towards Bogan

San Bernardino Str.

Oct. 24. Bogan's Position

Oct. 24. Davison Moves Towards Bogan

SAMAR

Tacloban
Dulag

LEYTE

Oct. 24. Davison's Pos.

Oct. 20. MacArthur Lands

Oct. 24 Oldendorf's Position

palacio

212

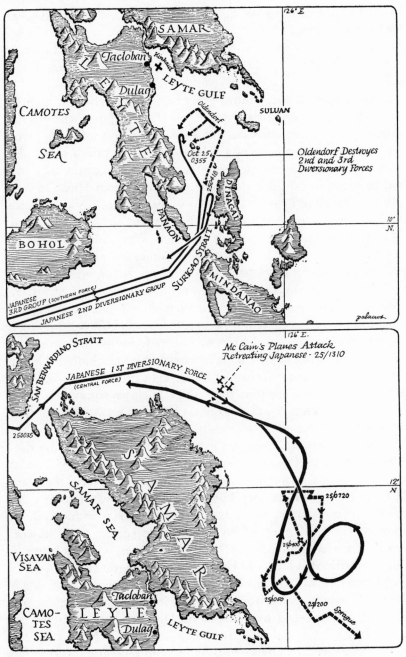

SAMAR

Tacloban

Kinkaid

LEYTE GULF

Dulag

SULUAN

CAMOTES

SEA

Oldendorf

Oct 25
0355

Oldendorf Destroyes
2nd and 3rd
Diversionary Forces

DINAGAT

260418

PANAON

SURIGAO STRAIT

BOHOL

MINDANAO

JAPANESE
3RD GROUP (SOUTHERN FORCE)

JAPANESE 2ND DIVERSIONARY GROUP

palacios

SAN BERNARDINO STRAIT

Mc Cain's Planes Attack
Retreating Japanese - 25/1310

JAPANESE 1ST DIVERSIONARY FORCE
(CENTRAL FORCE)

250035

SAMAR

12°
N.

250720

VISAYAN
SEA

250400

CAMO-
TES
SEA

Tacloban

250050

250200

LEYTE

Dulag

LEYTE GULF

213

At 0837, I ordered all task groups by TBS, "Strike! Repeat: Strike! Good luck!"

And at 0846, I ordered McCain to reverse course and prepare to fuel at sea. If the battle developed as I expected, we would need him.

Our planes hit the Central Force again and again through the day and reported sinking the battleship *Musashi* (Japan's newest and largest), three more cruisers, and a destroyer, and inflicting severe damage on many other units. These seemed to mill around aimlessly, then withdrew to the west, then turned east again, as if they had suddenly received a do-or-die command from Hirohito himself. (A year later I learned that our guess was close. Vice Admiral Kurita, commanding the Central Force, had strongly considered retiring, but had received this dispatch from Admiral Toyoda, Commander in Chief of the Japanese Combined Fleet: WITH CONFIDENCE IN HEAVENLY GUIDANCE, THE ENTIRE FORCE WILL ATTACK.)

That they might attempt to transit San Bernardino Strait, despite their fearful mauling, was a possibility I had to recognize. Accordingly, at 1512 I sent a preparatory dispatch to all task-force commanders in the Third Fleet and all task-group commanders in TF 38, designating four of their fast battleships (including the *New Jersey*), with two heavy cruisers, three light cruisers, and fourteen destroyers, and stating that these ships WILL BE FORMED AS TF 34 UNDER VADM [Willis A.] LEE, COMMANDER BATTLE LINE X TF 34 WILL ENGAGE DECISIVELY AT LONG RANGES.

This dispatch, which played a critical part in next day's battle, I intended merely as warning to the ships concerned that *if a surface engagement offered*, I would detach them from TF 38, form them into TF 34, and send them ahead as a battle line. It was definitely *not* an executive dispatch, but a battle plan, and was so marked. To make certain that none of my subordinate commanders misconstrued it, I told them later by TBS, "If the enemy sorties [through San Bernardino], TF 34 will be formed *when directed by me*."

Meanwhile, at 0943, we had intercepted a message from one of Davison's search teams, reporting that it had sighted the enemy's Southern Force—two old battleships, three heavy cruisers, one light cruiser, and eight destroyers, southwest of Negros Island, course 060, speed 15 knots—and had scored several damaging hits with bombs and rockets. We did not send a strike against this comparatively weak force for two reasons: it was headed for Surigao Strait, where Kinkaid was waiting with approximately three times its weight of metal—six old battleships, four heavy cruisers, four light cruisers, and twenty-six destroyers, plus thirty PT's; second, Davison's planes, the only ones able to reach it, were more urgently needed at the Central Force, now that Sherman's group was under violent attack by shore-based planes from Luzon. He shot down 110 of them, but they succeeded in bombing the light carrier *Princeton*. The fires reached her magazines and fuel tanks, and late that afternoon he had to order her abandoned and sunk—the first fast carrier that the Navy had lost since the *Hornet* was torpedoed at the Battle of Santa Cruz two years before, almost to the day.

(The captain of the *Princeton* was Capt. William H. Buracker, who had been my Operations officer at the beginning of the war. He would have been detached in a few days, and his relief was already aboard—Capt. John M. Hoskins. The bomb that gave the *Princeton* her deathblow nearly gave Hoskins his; it mangled one foot so badly that the ship's medical officer, himself wounded, cut it off with a sheath knife. Hoskins was then put into a stretcher and carried through the flames to the fo'c'sle, but before letting himself be lowered to a whaleboat standing by, he smiled, saluted Bill Buracker, and asked, "Have I your permission to leave the ship, sir?"

(Later, fitted with an artificial foot, he requested command of the new *Princeton* and recommended himself as being "one foot ahead of the other applicants"; further, he said, he could beat them all turning out for general quarters, because he was already wearing a sock and a shoe. I am happy to say that Hoskins put the new *Princeton* in commission and is now a rear admiral.)

The discovery of the Southern Force buttressed my conviction that the Japs were committed to a supreme effort, but the final proof was still lacking—their carriers. Neither our submarines nor search planes had found them yet, but we were dead certain that they would appear; our only doubt was from what direction. Mitscher thought from the China Sea. My staff thought from Empire waters. I agreed with my staff and ordered a thorough search northward. While we waited for a report, Doug Moulton must have

215

pounded the chart fifty times, demanding, "Where the hell *are* they, those goddam carriers?" At 1730 our guess was proved correct. Sherman informed me, 3 CARRIERS 2 LIGHT CRUISERS 3 DESTROYERS 18-32 N 125-28 E COURSE 270 SPEED 15.

This position, 200 miles east of Cape Engaño, the northeastern tip of Luzon, was too far for us to reach, even if dusk had not already fallen. But now we had all the pieces of the puzzle. When we put them together, we noticed that the three forces had a common factor: a speed of advance so leisurely—never more than 15 knots—that it implied a focus of time and place. The crippled Central Force's dogged second approach to San Bernardino, and the weak Southern Force's simultaneous approach to Surigao against overwhelming strength, were comprehensible only if they were under adamant orders to rendezvous with the carriers—the Northern Force—off Samar next day, the twenty-fifth, for a combined attack on the transports at Leyte.

We had no intention of standing by for a test of our theory. Our intention was to join battle as quickly as possible. Three battles offered. The Southern Force I could afford to ignore; it was well within Kinkaid's compass. The Central Force, according to our pilots, had suffered so much topside damage, especially to its guns and fire-control instruments, that it could not win a decision; it, too, could be left to Kinkaid. (The pilots' reports proved dangerously optimistic, but we had no reason to discredit them at the time.) On the other hand, not only was the Northern Force fresh and undamaged, but its carriers gave it a scope several hundred miles wider than the others. Moreover, if we destroyed those carriers, our future operations need fear no threat from the sea.

We had chosen our antagonist. It remained only to choose the best way to meet him. Again I had three alternatives:

1. *I could guard San Bernardino with my whole fleet and wait for the Northern Force to strike me.* Rejected. It yielded to the enemy the double initiative of his carriers and his fields on Luzon and would allow him to use them unmolested.

2. *I could guard San Bernardino with TF 34 while I struck the Northern Force with my carriers.* Rejected. The enemy's potential surface and air strength forbade half-measures; if his shore-based planes joined his carrier planes, together they might inflict far more damage on my half-fleets separately than they could inflict on the fleet intact.

216

3. *I could leave San Bernardino unguarded and strike the Northern Force with my whole fleet.* Accepted. It preserved my fleet's integrity, it left the initiative with me, and it promised the greatest possibility of surprise. Even if the Central Force meanwhile penetrated San Bernardino and headed for Leyte Gulf, it could hope only to harry the landing operation. It could not consolidate any advantage, because no transports accompanied it and no supply ships. It could merely hit and run.

My decision to strike the Northern Force was a hard one to make, but given the same circumstances and the same information as I had then, I would make it again.

I went into flag plot, put my finger on the Northern Force's charted position, 300 miles away, and said, "Here's where we're going. Mick, start them north."

The time was about 1950. Mick began to scribble a sheaf of dispatches: McCain to close us at his best speed; for Bogan and Davison, COURSE 000 [due north] SPEED 25; Sherman to join us as we dashed by; for Kinkaid, CENTRAL FORCE HEAVILY DAMAGED ACCORDING TO STRIKE REPORTS X AM PROCEEDING NORTH WITH 3 GROUPS TO ATTACK CARRIER FORCE AT DAWN; for the light carrier *Independence*, which was equipped with night fighters, AT 2400 LAUNCH 5 PLANES TO SEARCH SECTORS 320-010 [roughly, from northwest to north-by-east] TO 350 MILES; finally, at 2330, for Mitscher, SLOW DOWN TO 16 KNOTS X HOLD PRESENT COURSE UNTIL 2400, THEN PROCEED TOWARD LAT 16 LONG 127 [northeastward].

The purpose of this was to avoid overrunning the Northern Force's "daylight circle," the limit which it could reach by dawn from its last known position. If the enemy slipped past my left flank, between me and Luzon, he would have a free crack at the transports. If he slipped past my right flank, he would be able to shuttle-bomb me—fly from his carriers, attack me, continue on to his fields on Luzon for more bombs and fuel, and attack me again on the way back. I had to meet him head-on, and I was trusting the *Independence*'s snoopers to set my course.

They began to report at 0208: CONTACT POSIT 17-10 N 125-31 E X 5 SHIPS 2 LARGE 2 SMALL 1 SIZE UNREPORTED.

At 0214: CORRECTION X 6 SHIPS 3 LARGE 3 SMALL COURSE 110 SPEED 15.

At 0220: ANOTHER GROUP 40 MILES ASTERN OF FIRST.

217

At 0235: SECOND GROUP 6 LARGE SHIPS.

We had them!

Later sightings, in daylight, established the composition of the Northern Force as one large carrier, three light carriers, two hermaphrodite battleships with flight decks aft (a typical gimcrack Jap makeshift), three light cruisers, and at least eight destroyers.

I ordered TF 34 to form and take station 10 miles in advance, and my task-group commanders to arm their first deckload strike at once, launch it at earliest dawn, and launch a second strike as soon afterward as possible. Our next few hours were the most anxious of all. The pilots and aircrewmen knew that a terrific carrier duel was facing them, and the ships' companies were sure that a big-gun action would follow.

The first strike took off at 0630. An hour and a half passed without a word of news. . . . Two hours. . . . Two hours and a quarter. . . . God, what a wait it was! (Mick admitted later, "I chewed my fingernails down to my elbows.") Then, at 0850, a flash report reached me: ONE CARRIER SUNK AFTER TREMENDOUS EXPLOSION X 2 CARRIERS 1 CL [light cruiser] HIT BADLY OTHER CARRIER UNTOUCHED X FORCE COURSE 150 SPEED 17.

We had already increased our speed to 25 knots. If the enemy held his course and speed, he would be under our guns before noon. I rubbed my hands at the prospect of blasting the cripples that our planes were setting up for us.

Now I come to the part of this narrative that I can hardly bring myself to write, so painfully does it rankle still. I can reconstruct it best from a sequence of dispatches in my war diary:

At 0648, I had received a dispatch from Kinkaid: AM NOW ENGAGING ENEMY SURFACE FORCES SURIGAO STRAIT X QUESTION IS TF 34 GUARDING SAN BERNARDINO STRAIT. To this I replied in some bewilderment, NEGATIVE X IT IS WITH OUR CARRIERS NOW ENGAGING ENEMY CARRIERS. Here was my first intimation that Kinkaid had intercepted and misconstrued the preparatory dispatch I had sent at 1512 the preceding day. I say "intercepted" because it was not addressed to him, which fact alone should have prevented his confusion. I was not alarmed, because at 0802 I learned from him, ENEMY VESSELS RETIRING SURIGAO STRAIT X OUR LIGHT FORCES IN PURSUIT.

When the Southern Force pushed into Surigao soon after midnight of the twenty-fourth, it pushed into one of the prettiest ambushes in naval history. Rear Adm. Jesse B. Oldendorf, Kinkaid's tactical commander, waited until the enemy line was well committed to the narrow waters, then struck from both flanks with his PT's and destroyers, and from dead ahead with his battleships and cruisers. He not only "crossed the T," which is every naval officer's dearest ambition; he dotted several thousand slant eyes. Almost before the Japs could open fire, they lost both their battleships and three destroyers. The rest fled, but Kinkaid's planes caught and sank a heavy cruiser later in the morning, and Army B-24's sank the light cruiser the following noon. One of Oldendorf's PT's was sunk, and one destroyer was damaged.

At 0822, twenty minutes after Kinkaid's second dispatch, I received his third: ENEMY BBS AND CRUISER REPORTED FIRING ON TU 77.4.3 FROM 15 MILES ASTERN. Task unit 77.4.3, commanded by Rear Adm. Clifton A. F. Sprague and comprising six escort carriers, three destroyers, and four destroyer escorts, was the northernmost of three similar task units in the Seventh Fleet's TG 77.4, assigned to guard the eastern approaches to Leyte. The enemy ships were evidently part of the Central Force, which had steamed through San Bernardino during the night. I wondered how Kinkaid had let "Ziggy" Sprague get caught like this, and why Ziggy's search planes had not given him warning, but I still was not alarmed. I figured that the eighteen little carriers had enough planes to protect themselves until Oldendorf could bring up his heavy ships.

Eight minutes later, at 0830, Kinkaid's fourth dispatch reached me: URGENTLY NEED FAST BBS LEYTE GULF AT ONCE. That surprised me. It was not my job to protect the Seventh Fleet. My job was offensive, to strike with the Third Fleet, and we were even then rushing to intercept a force which gravely threatened not only Kinkaid and myself, but the whole Pacific strategy. However, I ordered McCain, who was fueling to the east, STRIKE ENEMY VICINITY 11-20 N 127-00 E AT BEST POSSIBLE SPEED, and so notified Kinkaid.

At 0900 I received his fifth dispatch: OUR CVES [escort carriers] BEING ATTACKED BY 4 BBS 8 CRUISERS PLUS OTHERS X REQUEST LEE [commanding TF 34, the battle line] COVER LEYTE AT TOP SPEED

219

X REQUEST FAST CARRIERS MAKE IMMEDIATE STRIKE. I had already sent McCain. There was nothing else I could do, except become angrier.

Then came the sixth dispatch, at 0922: CTU 77.4.3 UNDER ATTACK BY CRUISERS AND BBS 0700 11-40 N 126-25 E X REQUEST IMMEDIATE AIR STRIKE X ALSO REQUEST SUPPORT BY HEAVY SHIPS X MY OBBS [old battleships] LOW IN AMMUNITION.

Low in ammunition! Here was a new factor, so astonishing that I could hardly accept it. Why hadn't Kinkaid let me know before? I looked at the date-time group of his dispatch, which told when it was filed. It was "242225," or 0725 local time, an hour and fifty-seven minutes ago! And when I compared it with the date-time groups of the others, I realized that this was actually his *third* dispatch, sent eighteen minutes after he had first informed me that TU 77.4.3 was under attack. What had delayed it I have never learned.

My message was on its way to him in five minutes: I AM STILL ENGAGING ENEMY CARRIERS X MCCAIN WITH 5 CARRIERS 4 HEAVY CRUISERS HAS BEEN ORDERED ASSIST YOU IMMEDIATELY, and I gave my position, to show him the impossibility of the fast battleships reaching him.

The next two dispatches arrived close to 1000, almost simultaneously. The first was from Kinkaid again: WHERE IS LEE X SEND LEE. I was impressed less by its desperation than by the fact that it had been put on the air "clear," not in code. I was certain that the enemy had intercepted it, and I was speculating on its effect, when the second dispatch drove all other thoughts out of my mind. I can close my eyes and see it today:

From: CINCPAC
To: COM THIRD FLEET
THE WHOLE WORLD WANTS TO KNOW WHERE IS TASK FORCE 34.

I was as stunned as if I had been struck in the face. The paper rattled in my hands. I snatched off my cap, threw it on the deck, and shouted something that I am ashamed to remember. Mick Carney rushed over and grabbed my arm: "Stop it! What the hell's the matter with you? Pull yourself together!"

I gave him the dispatch and turned my back. I was so mad I

220

couldn't talk. It was utterly impossible for me to believe that Chester Nimitz would send me such an insult. He hadn't, of course, but I didn't know the truth for several weeks. It requires an explanation of Navy procedure. To increase the difficulty of breaking our codes, most dispatches are padded with gibberish. The decoding officers almost always recognize it as such and delete it from the transcription, but CINCPAC's encoder was either drowsy or smart-alecky, and his padding—"The whole world wants to know"—sounded so infernally plausible that my decoders read it as a valid part of the message. Chester blew up when I told him about it; he tracked down the little squirt and chewed him to bits, but it was too late then; the damage had been done.

The orders I now gave, I gave in rage, and although Ernie King later assured me that they were the right ones, I am convinced that they were not. My flag log for the forenoon watch that day, October 25, gives the bare bones of the story: "At 0835 c/s [changed speed] to 25k to close enemy. At 0919 c/c [changed course] to 000. At 1115 c/c to 180"—or from due north to due south. At that moment the Northern Force, with its two remaining carriers crippled and dead in the water, was exactly 42 miles from the muzzles of my 16-inch guns, but—I quote from my war diary—

In view of the urgent request for assistance from Commander Seventh Fleet, Commander Third Fleet directed Task Force 34 [Lee] and Task Group 38.2 [Bogan] to proceed south toward San Bernardino Strait, and directed Commander Task Force 38 [Mitscher] with Task Groups 38.3 [Sherman] and 38.4 [Davison], to continue attacks against the enemy carrier force.

(The period between 1000, when I received CINCPAC's dispatch, and 1115, when we changed course, was spent in reshuffling the task force and refueling Bogan's nearly empty destroyers for our high-speed run.)

I turned my back on the opportunity I had dreamed of since my days as a cadet. For me, one of the biggest battles of the war was off, and what has been called "the Battle of Bull's Run" was on. I notified Kinkaid, TG 38.2 PLUS 6 FAST BBS PROCEEDING LEYTE BUT UNABLE ARRIVE BEFORE 0800 TOMORROW.

While I rushed south, Sherman and Davison struck the Northern

221

Force again and again, and late that afternoon it retired in straggling disorder, with four of our fast light cruisers in pursuit and two wolf packs of our submarines waiting across its course. When the butchery was done, the score for the Northern Force was

Sunk............. 4 carriers, 1 light cruiser, 2 destroyers.
Damaged......... 2 battleships, 2 light cruisers, 4 destroyers.

A curious feature of this engagement is that the air duel never came off. Our strikes found scarcely a handful of planes on the enemy carriers' decks and only fifteen on the wing. We assume that the rest had ferried into Luzon and that our attack had caught them by surprise, because during the morning our radars picked up large groups of bogeys—unidentified planes—approaching from the westward, but they presently reversed course and disappeared. They must have been unarmed, expecting to arm aboard, and when they saw that their mother ships were afire, they could do nothing but fly back to Luzon again.

Meanwhile, Kinkaid had been sending me another series of dispatches: ENEMY RETIRING TO NORTHEASTWARD. Later, CVES AGAIN THREATENED BY ENEMY SURFACE FORCES. Still later, SITUATION AGAIN VERY SERIOUS X YOUR ASSISTANCE BADLY NEEDED X CVES RETIRING LEYTE GULF. Finally, at 1145, ENEMY FORCE OF 3 BB 2 CA 9 DD 11-43 N 126-12 E COURSE 225 SPEED 20.

This position was 55 miles northeast of Leyte Gulf, but the course was not toward the entrance. Moreover, the dispatch had been filed two hours before I received it, and I had no clue as to what had happened since then. The strongest probability was that the enemy would eventually retrace his course through San Bernardino Strait, and my best hope of intercepting him was to send my fastest ships in advance. The only two battleships I had that could sustain high speeds were the *New Jersey* and *Iowa*. I threw a screen of light cruisers and destroyers around them, as TG 34.5, and told them on TBS, "Proceed at 28 knots on course 195. Prepare for 30 knots. Be ready for night action," and I notified Kinkaid that we would arrive off San Bernardino at 0100 next morning, seven hours earlier than my original schedule.

I was puzzled by the Central Force's hit-and-run tactics and still more puzzled when I learned the complete story. Four battleships, six heavy cruisers, two light cruisers, and eleven destroyers had survived our air attacks on October 24 and had transited San Bernardino that night. When they were sighted next, at 0631 on the twenty-fifth, they were only 20 miles northwest of Sprague's task unit. His 17-knot escort carriers were no match for the enemy in either speed or gun power, and at 0658 he was taken under fire at a range of 30,000 yards.

Sprague immediately turned east, into the wind, launched his available planes, and ordered all ships to make smoke. The enemy formation now divided, the heavy ships advancing to his port and the light to starboard, thereby forcing him around to the southwest, in the direction of Leyte Gulf. When the cruisers had closed to 14,000 yards, Sprague ordered his screen to fall back and deliver a torpedo attack. Two destroyers, the *Hoel* and *Johnston*, and the destroyer escort *Samuel S. Roberts* reversed course, ran within 10,000 yards of the battleships, and fired a half-salvo, then fired the other half within 7,000 yards of the cruisers. Smoke concealed the effect of their torpedoes, but it lifted to show that all three of these heroic little ships had been sunk.

The enemy continued to close, and presently his fire began to take toll. If he had had the elementary intelligence not to use armor-piercing projectiles, many of which ripped through our ships' thin skins as if through a wet shoebox, without detonating, he might have annihilated Sprague's unit, since every ship in it suffered hits. As it was, except for the three ships from the screen, Sprague's only loss to the guns was the carrier *Gambier Bay*. At 0820 she dropped astern under continuous fire, and after being riddled with 8-inch shells from the murderous range of 2,000 yards, she blew up at 0900.

For these first two hours, Sprague's gallant men fought entirely alone, at such close quarters that his CVE's' single 5-inchers were registering hits on the cruisers, and with such valor that his Avengers, their bombs and torpedoes expended, were making dummy runs to distract the battleships. Oldendorf's force not only was 100 miles away, deep in Surigao Strait, but was practically impotent. Its action early that morning, following five days of shore bombardments, had severely reduced its fuel and ammunition. The other two carrier task units that made up TG 77.4 were obligated to flying support missions for the troops on Leyte. In addition, the southern unit had been shelled, and the central unit's carriers had been subjected to a violent shore-based air attack—the *Sanga-mon* had been damaged by a bomb, the *Suwannee* and *Santee* by suicide planes, and the *Santee* had been further damaged by a torpedo. However, planes from both these task units were able to reinforce Sprague's by 0900. One of his destroyers had already crippled a heavy cruiser; and when the combined air attacks suc-ceeded in sinking three others, the enemy was panicked into break-ing off the engagement. I opened my hand and let the bird fly away off Luzon. So did the enemy off Samar.

Now came an intermission during which the offensive passed to us, but at 1050 the enemy's shore-based air struck again, this time on Sprague's wounded, exhausted carriers. One plane plunged into the *Kalinin Bay's* flight deck, causing a small blaze; another crashed through the *Kitkun Bay's* catwalk; a third dropped a bomb on the *Saint Lo* and itself crashed close aboard. The *Saint Lo's* fires could not be controlled; she was abandoned with heavy losses. The enemy still did not exploit his overwhelming advantage, and soon it was gone forever. At 1310 McCain's planes arrived. In the emergency, he had launched them from far outside their range of return; after their attacks, they had to land and rearm at Tacloban and Dulag Fields on Leyte, which had fallen to MacArthur only a few days before. Together with planes from TG 77.4, they sank a light cruiser and a destroyer and damaged most of the other ships. Sprague had lost five of his thirteen ships. TG 77.4 had lost 105 planes.

The Central Force was in full retreat by late afternoon, and by 2200 it was reentering San Bernardino, with my force still two hours away. However, shortly after midnight one of my van de-stroyers made contact with a straggler. I was able to watch the action from the *New Jersey's* bridge—the first and only surface action I saw during my entire career. The cruisers poured in their 6-inch shells, then a destroyer delivered the knockout with tor-pedoes. They must have touched off her magazines, because I felt the explosion distinctly, 15 miles away.

At that distance, none of us on the *New Jersey* could tell what type of ship had been sunk, so we put the query on the TBS. The roundup is a commentary on the accuracy of observation during a night engagement.

The light cruiser *Vincennes* reported, "She was a heavy cruiser of the *Aoba* or *Atago* class."

The light cruiser *Miami*, "A destroyer of the *Fubuki* or *Asashio* class."

The light cruiser *Biloxi* said cautiously, "A cruiser."

The destroyer *Miller*, which had fired the torpedoes, "A *Terutsuki*-class destroyer."

The destroyer *Owen*, "A *Fuso*-class battleship."

The commander of our destroyer squadron, "A *Yubari*-class light cruiser."

The commander of our cruiser division, "I have an open mind. I'll settle for a cruiser of any sort."

And that's as close to the truth as we ever came.

This was our last surface action. The air phase resumed at dawn next morning, the twenty-sixth, with McCain's and Bogan's planes harrying the Central Force's scattered remnants, still fleeing westward, while our ships searched east of Samar for other stragglers and for our airmen who had ditched the day before. We found no Jap ships, but Jap swimmers were as thick as water bugs. I was having breakfast when Bill Kitchell burst in and cried, "My God Almighty, Admiral, the little bastards are all over the place! Are we going to stop and pick 'em up?"

I told him, "Not until we've picked up our own boys."

We charted their position, along with wind and tide data, and when we had recovered all the Americans, I ordered our destroyers, "Bring in cooperative Nip flotsam for an intelligence sample. Noncooperators would probably like to join their ancestors and should be accommodated." (I didn't want to risk their getting ashore, where they could reinforce the garrison.) The destroyers brought in six.

Foul weather hampered McCain and Bogan, but that night they reported, 1 NAGATO-CLASS BB HIT WITH 2 TORPEDOES MANY BOMBS, LAST SEEN STOPPED AND BLAZING OFF SOUTH TIP MINDORO X 10 MILES SOUTH OF HER, 1 HOSHIRO-CLASS CL HIT WITH 1 TORPEDO 2 BOMBS X NORTHWEST OF PANAY ARE 2 BBS YAMATO- AND KONGO-CLASS HIT WITH ROCKETS AND HALF- AND QUARTER-TON BOMBS X ALSO AT THIS

225

POSITION 1 DD WITH BOW BLOWN OFF BUT STILL UNDERWEIGH AND 1 CA [heavy cruiser] DEAD IN WATER AFTER HITS WITH BOMBS AND 2 TORPEDOES X 1 CL DAMAGED IN TABLAS STRAIT X 1 SEAPLANE TENDER HIT IN GUIMARAS STRAIT BLEW UP AND SANK X WE SHOT DOWN 40 PLANES AND LOST 11, MOSTLY TO INTENSE JAP WARSHIP AA.

Thus ended the three-day, threefold Battle for Leyte Gulf. Six of our ships had been sunk and eleven damaged. Twenty-six enemy ships had been sunk, and twenty-five damaged. In my official report, I was able to write with conviction that the results of the battle were "(1) the utter failure of the Japanese plan to prevent the reoccupation of the Philippines; (2) the crushing defeat of the Japanese fleet; and (3) the elimination of serious naval threat to our operations for many months, if not forever."

COMINCH's endorsement of my second and third claim was reluctant at first. On the night of October 25, I had radioed CINCPAC, THE JAPANESE NAVY HAS BEEN BEATEN AND ROUTED AND BROKEN BY THE THIRD AND SEVENTH FLEETS. I heard later that COMINCH had told CINCPAC that nothing in the reports he had received could justify my optimism. On the twenty-ninth, however, COMINCH was telling Kinkaid and myself, A LARGE PART OF THE ENEMY NAVY HAS BEEN EFFECTUALLY DISPOSED OF FOREVER AND THE REMAINDER FOR SOME TIME TO COME X ALL OFFICERS AND MEN OF YOUR FLEETS HAVE THE HEARTIEST ADMIRATION OF ALL HANDS X WELL DONE.

That's something, coming from Ernie!

When I reported to him in Washington the following January, my very first words were, "I made a mistake in that battle."

He held up his hand. "You don't have to tell me any more. You've got a green light on everything you did."

But I wanted to get it off my chest. I said, "I still think it was a mistake to turn south when the Japs were right under my guns."

Ernie said, "No. It wasn't a mistake. You couldn't have done otherwise."

All the bigwigs sent us congratulations. General MacArthur's message was particularly warming: WE HAVE COOPERATED WITH YOU SO LONG THAT WE EXPECT YOUR BRILLIANT SUCCESSES X EVERYONE HERE HAS A FEELING OF COMPLETE CONFIDENCE AND INSPIRATION WHEN YOU GO INTO ACTION IN OUR SUPPORT. General Marshall told us, a splendid and historic victory x the army owes you a debt of thanks. From Secretary Forrestal, the third fleet has done it again.

Such praise from such men is agreeable to read, but I would gladly forgo every word of it if I could also forgo a few words of my own. These are the ones: "At 1115 c/c to 180."

I have attempted to describe the Battle for Leyte Gulf in terms of my thoughts and feelings at the time, but on rereading my account, I find that this results in an implication grossly unfair to Tom Kinkaid. True, during the action, his dispatches puzzled me. Later, with the gaps in my information filled, I not only appreciate his problems, but frankly admit that had I been in his shoes, I might have acted precisely as did he.

—Which urges me to reemphasize a point I made earlier: although our naval power in the western Pacific was such that we could have challenged the combined fleets of the world, the fact that it was not coordinated under any single authority was an invitation which disaster nearly accepted. What brought us victory instead was simply this: all hands thought alike. And that we did so is a tribute to our indoctrination in the United States Navy.

☆
☆ 14 ☆
☆ ☆

THE BATTLE for Leyte Gulf ended on October 26, 1944. On January 26, 1945, I was relieved in command of the Third Fleet. The intervening three months were a repetition of the months before—strike and strike again, in support of MacArthur's advance—but with this difference: each of the three months brought us a new and unforgettable experience. In November, it was *kamikazes;* in December, a typhoon; in January, our foray into the China Sea.

The *kamikazes* picked the date of their debut shrewdly. Our long weeks at sea, culminating in a three-day battle, had depleted our planes and exhausted our men. Since the end of August, TF 38 had lost 220 of its planes in combat and roughly fifty more in operational accidents. Now the normal level of these accidents was tilting upward, because of fatigue. For instance, a flight surgeon on the *Wasp* reported that only thirty of his 131 pilots were fit for further fighting. The whole task force was overdue for retirement to Ulithi for rest and replenishment, particularly because our next operation would be the most rugged of all—a smash into the heart of the Japanese Empire, Tokyo itself.

But we couldn't retire yet. They still needed us in the Philippines. Although General Kenney had assumed responsibility for direct air support of the Leyte area, Kinkaid asked us to stand by. He wasn't satisfied with the cover that Kenney was providing his Seventh Fleet, and so many of his CVE's had been sunk or crippled in the action off Samar that he couldn't provide his own. Accordingly, I postponed the strike against the Empire, sent two of our

228

task groups—McCain's and Ted Sherman's—back to Ulithi, and kept the other two at the front, as tired as they were. Davison's group cruised off Samar; Bogan's, which included my flagship, was northward, off Luzon.

It happened at 1214 on October 29. A flight of Japs bored in on our group. Our vigilant CAP managed to shoot down twenty-one of·them, and the ships' AA shot down another, but one plane broke through and dived into a carrier. Of course, it was Bogan's flagship, the *Intrepid*. I say "of course" because the *Intrepid* was the unluckiest ship in the Navy. Like the *Saratoga*, she could hardly poke her nose out of port without getting it rapped. She has the grim distinction of having taken a total of five *kamikazes*, and she has spent so much time in dry dock that the fleet calls her "the Decrepit" and "the Dry I." This *kamikaze*, her first, struck her a glancing blow in a gun gallery. Only six men were killed, and her slight damage did not impair her operating efficiency, so we were more concerned about the weapon than about its target.

I didn't know the term at the time, but I had seen a *kamikaze* before—the plane that had tried to crash the *Enterprise* during the Marshalls raid in February, 1942. That plane was already doomed; its pilot would have been killed anyhow. But the plane that struck the *Intrepid* had not been damaged; the dive was obviously a deliberate sacrifice. Intelligence had warned us that "the Divine Wind Special Attack Corps" had been organized, but even after we had seen this sample performance, I think that most of us took it as a sort of token terror, a tissue-paper dragon. The psychology behind it was too alien to ours; Americans, who fight to live, find it hard to realize that another people will fight to die. We could not believe that even the Japanese, for all their hara-kiri traditions, could muster enough recruits to make such a corps really effective.

We were violently disillusioned the very next day. They missed the *Enterprise*, in Davison's group, but they hit two of his other carriers, the *Franklin* and *Belleau Wood*, killing a total of 158 men, destroying forty-five planes, and requiring the withdrawal of both ships for repairs. Our CV's were obvious targets: their huge tanks of aviation gasoline were as vulnerable as they were inflammable, their fire power was light, their armor was thin, and damage to their flight decks meant the neutralization of around 100 planes.

229

On November 1, however, the *kamikazes* switched to Kinkaid's destroyers in Leyte Gulf; they sank one and damaged five. On the fifth, they struck at Sherman, whose group was fresh from Ulithi; one of them missed the *Ticonderoga*, and another missed the *Lexington*, but the third hit the *Lexington's* signal bridge, killing forty-seven men. We had dismissed the Special Attack Corps as a flash in the pan. Now it seemed less a flash than a blast.

CAPTAIN DOW:

For some mysterious Jap reason, their radio at Manila chose the day of the attack on Admiral Davison's group to scream, "We dare the American public to ask where Halsey is!"

When I reported this to the Admiral, he said, "If CINCPAC would let me, I'd send 'em my latitude and longitude!"

Incidentally, that day was his sixty-second birthday.

Our adjustment to the *kamikazes* was complicated by the enemy's stubborn refusal, despite his staggering naval defeat, to consider Leyte lost. He began to pour planes into his fields on Luzon, Mindanao, and the Visayan Islands, and to rush troops through his inland waterway, across the Sibuyan Sea. Kenney could neither stop them nor protect our own troops and shipping. His fighters were useless against convoys, and he had few bombers. Moreover, the rains had begun; construction of his new airfields was delayed; and his only serviceable field, Tacloban, was not adequate to handle enough planes for steady offense and defense. On one overcrowded night, a scattering of Jap bombs wiped out twenty-seven of his parked P-38's. The enemy became bolder; our Leyte advance slowed down; so MacArthur requested the fast carriers to lend him a hand again.

This meant a further postponement of the rest we urgently needed, and the abandonment of my cherished hope of making the first carrier raid on Tokyo since Jimmy Doolittle's (the honor fell to the Fifth Fleet, in February), but the critical situation at Leyte took precedence over everything else. There are two theories of how best to use carriers in support of shore operations: one is passive—keep them close by in a small area, as bases for CAP's; the other is active—crush enemy air power at its source. I have always held the second theory. I told MacArthur that we could

230

accomplish more if he would let us strike the feeder fields on Luzon, and as soon as he gave his permission, we struck. In fact, between November 5 and 25, we struck six times. We destroyed 756 planes; we wiped out a ten-ship convoy headed toward Leyte; and we sent a surface force to bombard the air installations at Iwo Jima, which was being used as a search-plane base and a staging point for aircraft en route from the Empire to the Philippines.

Meanwhile, we had also taken a vicarious hand in furnishing close air defense for Leyte. I had had under my command in the South Pacific a Marine air group which had proved its versatility in everything from fighting to blasting enemy vessels. I knew that this group was now under MacArthur's command, and I knew, too, without understanding why, that when Kenney was not keeping it idle, he was assigning it to missions far below its capacity. Kinkaid's complaint of insufficient air cover prompted me to take a step which was more than a liberty; to a man of meaner spirit than MacArthur's, it would have seemed an impertinence. I called these Marines to his attention. He ordered them forward, and within twenty-four hours of their arrival, they had justified my recommendation. Thanks to them and to our strikes on Luzon, Kinkaid's daily report began to read, "No bogeys."

The November 25 strike was our last in support of Leyte. There were moments when I was afraid it would be our last anywhere. Until then our new tactics had smothered the *kamikazes;* this time they were ready for us and staged a counterattack. One plunged into the carrier *Essex*, in Sherman's task group, but the rest concentrated on our group, so I saw them clearly. The first dived at the carrier *Hancock*, which shot him down directly overhead; a fragment of his wing fell on her flight deck and started a fire. The second and third, both loaded with bombs, crashed into the luckless *Intrepid*. The fourth dived through the light carrier *Cabot's* forward ramp; two minutes later, the fifth hit close aboard her port side.

The *Essex's* fire was soon extinguished; fourteen of her men were killed and damage was heavy, but she was able to stay at sea. The *Hancock* had no deaths and negligible damage. Although the *Cabot* lost thirty-four men and was badly damaged forward, she too could stay at sea. But the *Intrepid* went through hell. An instant after she was hit, she was wrapped in flames; blazing gasoline

231

cascaded down her sides; explosions rocked her; then oily black smoke, rising thousands of feet, hid everything but her bow. Despite this inferno, she kept her bearing, speed, and distance in the formation; and Jerry Bogan surrendered control of the task group for only half an hour, and only because his communications had been burnt away. It was as fine a display of guts as I've ever seen.

The *Intrepid* had sixty-nine men killed or missing, seventeen planes destroyed, and damage severe enough to send her back to Pearl. Thus, in less than a month, *kamikazes* cost the Third Fleet 328 men, around ninety planes, and the use of three carriers. Apparently they had proved their effectiveness, for when a carrier can be temporarily disabled, or a destroyer sunk, at the price—as the public believed—of one pilot and one ramshackle plane, it seems to be a bargain. So it might be, if that were the true price. But our statistics show that of all the *kamikazes* attempting to dive on use, about 1 per cent succeeded; the rest either crashed harmlessly or were shot down. The true price therefore becomes 100 pilots and 100 planes.

More important, while planes are expendable, pilots are not. Long before these attacks, it was clear that the quality of Jap pilots was degenerating. We suspected that we had killed off their good ones, deep into the reserves, and the *kamikazes* confirmed our suspicion. They were bungling amateurs who, having demonstrated their unfitness for combat flying, had been dosed with fanaticism and press-ganged into the Special Attack Corps. To me, the *kamikaze* was a weapon not of inspiration, but of desperation —an unmistakable sign that the Japanese war machine was close to collapse.

I would be a damn fool to pretend that individual *kamikazes* did not scare me; they scared me thoroughly and repeatedly. But the *kamikaze* conception did not scare me for a moment. I was confident that we could devise tactics to counter it, *if* our men were rested, our complement of planes was full, and our fleet was on the offensive. The early attacks, I reemphasize, caught us with tired men and few planes. Besides, the *Intrepid* was first hit while we were confined to a narrow area, searching for pilots downed by a storm the evening before; and the *Franklin* and *Belleau Wood* were hit just after part

232

of the CAP over their task group had been sent to cover our near-by tankers, which had been discovered by a snooper. (We would have been crippled by the loss of our indispensable tanker force, but the Japs were too stupid to strike it.)

Slew McCain had relieved Pete Mitscher as CTF 38 on October 30. With the help of Slew and his staff, we set to work on our defense against the *kamikazes*. It fell into three parts: short, medium, and long range.

Short-range defense was our AA. There was nothing we could do to improve it except devote more time to practice.

Medium-range defense took study. When we examined the attacks, we found that they followed three patterns. The *kamikaze* pilots were trailing our own planes home and thereby foiling our IFF (a radar device for the automatic Identification of Friend or Foe); or they were making a long, fast glide from high altitudes, tunneling through the nulls on our radars; or they were skimming the water so that our radars could not detect them until they were too close for interception by our CAP. We countered the first type by stationing picket destroyers well out from the force, and ordering our homing planes to approach them on specified bearings and circle them in a specified manner. We countered the second by sending our CAP higher and farther. And we countered the third by establishing "Jack" patrols to orbit at low altitudes.

Our long-range defense was the "constant CAP," which entailed keeping a blanket of fighters over all enemy airfields on a twenty-four hour, heel-and-toe schedule. Our day fighters shot down the Japs when they tried to take off, and our night fighters discouraged them from even trying it.

Of course, a constant CAP requires a great many fighter planes. We obtained them by changing the complements of our large carriers from thirty-seven fighters, thirty-six bombers, and eighteen torpedo planes to seventy-three fighters, fifteen bombers, and fifteen torpedo planes. (Our powerful new F6F's and F4U's had proved that they could double as bombers on demand, and we were finding only limited use for our torpedo planes.) We also asked for, and eventually were given, two large carriers with air groups trained in night flying to supplement the one group we already had.

None of these improvements was developed by merely rubbing

233

a lamp. Each had to be discussed, tested, and modified. Nor did their adoption put an abrupt end to the *kamikazes*. A few of them, though fewer than before, occasionally broke through our defenses and scored damaging hits. But what had once loomed as a monstrous, bone-crunching jinni was soon brought into perspective and reduced to the size of a normal occupational hazard.

Strategic as well as tactical adjustments were required. The withdrawal of the crippled *Franklin*, *Belleau Wood*, and *Intrepid*, with destroyers to escort them, forced the consolidation of TF 38 from four task groups into three; and the strain of the *kamikaze* attacks, on top of our long stretch of combat, made an adequate rest period obligatory at once. MacArthur's next move, the invasion of Mindoro, was scheduled for December 5. We hated to request a postponement, but there was no help for it. Almost as soon as his obliging reply was decoded, we turned our prows toward Ulithi.

When we entered the atoll on November 27, the *New Jersey* had steamed 36,185 miles since leaving Pearl Harbor in August; and of those ninety-five days, she had spent only ten in port. I was tired, in mind, body, and nerves. So were we all. I did not carry a physical burden, as did the crews of our ships and planes, but the burden of responsibility seemed quite as heavy. Heaviest was the tension that built up under the constant threat of air attack; the attack itself was almost a relief, because you knew that things couldn't get any worse. This tension did not begin to slack off until late on the final day of a strike series, when the force had come to its retirement course. Even then it took me a long time to unwind. Other men may have done it with the help of noble literature; I used to read *The Police Gazette*.

My day at sea began around 0500, when I turned out to watch the first strikes take off, and it ended around 2400. Our only recreations were the movies and, when we were clear of the combat area, a game of deck tennis.

CAPT. CARNES WEEKS, ADMIRAL HALSEY'S STAFF MEDICAL OFFICER:
The Admiral hated anything to interrupt his game. One afternoon he had to quit for a rain squall. As soon as it stopped, word was passed over the bull-horn, "Dry down all weather decks!" He didn't wait for a working party; he grabbed a swab and turned to.

I guess it's just as well that Farragut and Dewey were dead already.

234

After the movie, I sat in on the nightly meeting of my Dirty Trick Department—Mick Carney, Ham Dow, Doug Moulton, Harold Stassen, and Johnny Lawrence—and listened to them concoct new methods of bedeviling our gullible enemy. (The Navy prefers me to drop this topic right here.) They were still at it when I left, just before midnight. I went out on flag bridge for a last look around the formation, and into flag plot for a last look at the charts and dispatches. In my sea cabin, I had one more cup of coffee (my tenth) before turning in, and one more cigarette (my fortieth). I always hoped for five hours' sleep, but I seldom got it. This cruise was a poor sedative for a natural worrier. Besides, it's hard to sleep soundly when you know that the next second may bring the clangor of the gong calling you to general quarters.

Our two weeks at Ulithi were like two weeks in the country, God-forsaken though the country was. Most of the time we rested and tried to relax. We couldn't relax completely, because something still goaded our minds: the *kamikaze* attack on November 25. With the understandable exception of Formosa, which had been alerted for us on October 12 by our strike against the Nansei Shotos on the tenth, this was the very first time that we had failed to achieve complete tactical and strategic surprise. Why? What had tipped off the Japs? After days of discussion, we narrowed the possibilities to these three:

1. A leak in SOWESPAC.
2. The sudden inactivity of Kenney's planes.
3. The pattern of our radio traffic.

The last, we agreed, was the most likely, so we tested it by setting up "the Picnic Strike," so called because the day it was "launched," my staff and I had a picnic ashore at "Kessing's Last Resort," a beach named in honor of Scrappy Kessing, the atoll commander.

The "strike" consisted of no more than dummy radio traffic in a pattern exactly duplicating the pattern normally preceding a strike. At once all Jap merchant shipping around Luzon fled to safety across the China Sea. We had our answer. From then on, we varied our radio patterns broadly and resumed our pleasant practice of catching the Japs asleep.

The fleet sortied from Ulithi on December 11, primed to

235

support the invasion of Mindoro, on the fifteenth. Mindoro lies about 250 miles northwest of Leyte, under the shadow of Luzon, so our job was to hold down the enemy's fields there and keep him from intercepting our transports. We indexed every known or suspected field in the entire area and assigned each one to a specific carrier for neutralization. Then we struck with all our strength, for three days running. When we retired on the evening of the sixteenth, we had destroyed 270 planes at a cost of twenty-seven; we had sunk thirty-three ships; and not a single bogey had been able to penetrate closer to our formation than 20 miles.

COMMANDER KITCHELL:

There was no possible way for our pilots to know it at the time, but one of these ships was carrying American prisoners of war. We learned of the tragedy only because two of them managed to swim ashore and were subsequently rescued. Months later, the mother of a prisoner who had been lost on the ship wrote the Admiral a letter in which she said, "Even the detestable Germans occasionally stop and pick up people, whereas you run off and leave them. You ought to be hung as a war criminal!"

It made him miserable. He kept referring to it for days: "Doesn't she realize that these things are bound to happen in a war?" And he asked us over and over, "How could our pilots have known?"

We planned to fuel on the seventeenth and begin another three-day series of strikes on the nineteenth, when the congestion of supplies on the Mindoro beachhead and of ships offshore would demand all available air cover. But by the time we were able to strike Luzon again, MacArthur was striking it himself, and a disaster had struck us—a typhoon that rolled the fleet on its beam ends, swamped three destroyers, cost the lives of 790 men, wrecked some 200 planes, and damaged twenty-eight ships, nine so severely that they had to be detached for repairs. It was the Navy's greatest uncompensated loss since the Battle of Savo Island.

Our earliest hint of foul weather ahead appears in my war diary for the forenoon of the seventeenth: "A moderate cross swell and a wind varying from 20 to 30 knots made fueling difficult." We were then about 500 miles east of Luzon, with the destroyers trying to "drink" from the heavy ships, which would later fill their own bunkers from the fleet oilers. The *New Jersey's* first customer was

236

the *Spence*. My war diary shows the trouble that soon beset her and the other destroyers:

1128. Both forward and after hoses to the *Spence* parted.

1208. The *Collett* reported conditions very bad alongside the *Wisconsin*, and that both hoses had carried away.

1220. The *Stephen Potter* reported that she had just parted forward fueling hose.

1227. The *Mansfield* reported that she had broken loose from her station.

1229. The *Lyman K. Swenson* reported both hoses parted.

1238. The *Preston* reported casualties to both hoses and lines.

1240. The *Thatcher* reported parting one hose and being forced to cut loose.

With the wind and sea increasing, I ordered fueling suspended at 1310 and appointed a new rendezvous with the tanker force for 0600 next morning, 200 miles northwestward. We chose this position because my staff aerologist now estimated that a "tropical disturbance"—not necessarily a typhoon—was located about 500 miles east of us; he estimated further that it was moving north-northwest at 12 to 15 knots, and would presently collide with a cold front and recurve to the northeast.

An hour later, however, I received an unaccountably delayed dispatch from the aircraft tender *Chandeleur*, reporting that at 1000 she had observed a definite storm center less than 200 miles southeast of our present position. This was our first positive information. I immediately canceled the rendezvous I had just set, since it would be dead in the storm's probable path, and set another, southwest of us. Still later, I had to change it for one closer; the weather would not permit the tanker force to cover the original distance. My choice was restricted, of course, by the necessity of staying close enough to strike Luzon as we had promised.

We ran southwest all that night. At 0508 on the eighteenth, our aerologists placed the storm center northeast of us, about 250 miles, and still moving north-northwest at 12 knots. At our position, the wind was blowing 38 knots from almost due north, and the barometer stood at 29.67, which was .09 off from seven hours before. (Fair weather at sea level is 29.92.) Fueling would be even harder than on the day before, but we had to try it, not only for MacArthur's sake

237

but for ours. Our destroyers had operated at high speeds for three days and had fought the weather on the fourth; by now their fuel was so near exhaustion that their speed and range were severely restricted; worse, the less their fuel, the higher they rode and the less seaworthy they became. The *Colahan, Brush, Franks,* and *Cushing* were down to 15 per cent of capacity; the *Maddox, Hickox,* and *Spence* had somewhere between 10 and 14 per cent.

We began our attempt to fuel at 0700, but I soon had to face the fact that it was impossible, and I regretfully notified MacArthur that we could not meet our commitment. The weather continued to deteriorate. The escort carriers with the tanker force were pounding heavily in the mounting seas. The wind increased to 43 knots, and the barometer fell another six points. Typhoons are notoriously capricious; by 0830 it was plain that this one was no exception; instead of recurving to the northeast, as our aerologists expected, it had turned westward. Its center was now only 150 miles away, and from all indications, it would pass us close aboard.

My war diary gives an outline of the next few hours:

0841. The *Wasp* reported a life raft to her port, which appeared to have three persons on it.

0907. The *Independence* reported man overboard.

0911. The [light carrier] *Monterey* reported that, due to excessive roll, planes on her hangar deck had broken loose and caught fire.

0925. The *Monterey* reported she had lost steerageway.

0931. The *Independence* reported two men overboard.

0942. The [escort carrier] *Kwajalein* reported she had lost steering control.

1007. Wind 62 knots from 356. Barometer 29.52.

1012. The *Wisconsin* reported 1 Kingfisher [an observation-scout plane] overboard.

1016. The [heavy cruiser] *Boston* reported 1 Kingfisher overboard.

1017. The [escort carrier] *Rudyerd Bay* reported she was dead in the water.

1051. The [light carrier] *Cowpens* reported fire on her hangar deck.

1100. Wind 55 knots from 350. Barometer 29.47.

1128. The [escort carrier] *Cape Esperance* reported fire on her flight deck.

1300. Wind 66 knots from 358. Barometer 29.30.

1310. Wind velocity increased sharply from 75 to 83 knots, with gusts reaching 93 knots between 1330 and 1400. Barometer 29.23.

1358. Commander Task Force 38 reported the center of the typhoon showed on his radar at 000 [due north], distance 35 miles.

This was the peak of the storm. No one who has not been through a typhoon can conceive its fury. The 70-foot seas smash you from all sides. The rain and the scud are blinding; they drive at you flat-out, until you can't tell the ocean from the air. At broad noon I couldn't see the bow of my ship, 350 feet from the bridge. The *New Jersey* once was hit by a 5-inch shell without my feeling the impact; the *Missouri*, her sister, had a *kamikaze* crash on her main deck and repaired the only damage with a paintbrush; yet this typhoon tossed our enormous ship as if she were a canoe. Our chairs, tables, and all loose gear had to be double-lashed; we ourselves were buffeted from one bulkhead to another; we could not hear our own voices above the uproar.

What it was like on a destroyer one-twentieth the *New Jersey's* size, I can only imagine. I was told that some of them were knocked down until their stacks were almost horizontal and were pinned there by the gale, while water rushed into their ventilators and intakes, shorting the circuits, killing their power, steering, lights, and communications, and leaving them to drift helplessly. For instance, here is a report on the damage suffered by the *Hickox:*

Both steering motors out of commission. Main switchboard and emergency Diesel boards out. Numerous power panels and electrical wiring damaged. One boiler salted. All radar antenna down or carried away. Twenty-six-inch searchlight stripped. Longitudinal frame 14, starboard side, deflected inward. After deckhouse overhead buckled upward. Depth charge rack extension smashed with 6 holes in main deck where extension pulled out. Carpenter shop and clipping room aft flooded. Motor whaleboat and forward starboard davit carried away.

The *Hickox* was on our northern perimeter, the sector that caught the worst of it. As soon as the course of the typhoon was established, I had turned south to leave the storm center astern and bring the fleet within the left, or navigable, semicircle. Most of our ships cleared the center, but a few stragglers didn't. Some of them managed to ride it out. The rest we never saw again.

Soon after 1400, the weather mended. By 1500, the wind had dropped to 56 knots and the barometer had risen to 29.40; an hour

239

later, the wind was 35 knots and the barometer 29.46. By dusk we were able to start searching the area for survivors.

2002. The [light cruiser] *San Juan* reported hearing a whistle.
2006. The *Cabot* reported a whistle.
2016. The *Hancock* reported a light in the water astern.

There were many such reports, but a man in a life jacket is almost impossible to spot in a rough sea on a black night. The destroyers found nothing.

We continued the search while we fueled next day, the nineteenth, and for the two days following. It was the most exhaustive search in Navy history. Every ship and plane in two task groups took part. We had marked off an area large enough to include the extreme limits of drift, and destroyer divisions crisscrossed it abreast, with lookouts doubled. An occasional swimmer was picked up, and sometimes a raft-load. With their help, we compiled our casualty list. Three ships had been lost, the destroyers *Spence*, *Hull*, and *Monaghan*, with almost all hands. The survivors of the *Spence*—there were twenty-four of them—told us that her rudder had jammed full right in the wildest hour of the storm, capsizing her instantly. Forty-four men were recovered from the *Hull*, and six from the *Monaghan;* both these ships had also capsized and foundered.

For awhile we feared that a fourth ship, the destroyer escort *Tabberer*, would be added to the list. No one sighted her, and nothing was heard from her. Finally a message was relayed to us: her foremast had carried away, and all her radios and radars had been wrecked, but she was otherwise sound and was bringing in ten more survivors of the *Hull*. These men reported that they owed their lives wholly to the *Tabberer's* captain. While ships around them were barely keeping afloat, he maneuvered alongside and hauled the men aboard; even the shellbacks among them had never seen such seamanship.

His name, I found out, was Lt. Comdr. Henry L. Plage, of Atlanta. I sent him a "Well done for a sturdy performance!" and later I had the pleasure of awarding him a Legion of Merit. His shiphandling had been so brilliant that I inquired about his experience. I expected to learn that he had cut his teeth on a marlinespike, but he proved to be a Reserve who had been to sea exactly once before, for a short cruise during his ROTC course at Georgia Tech! How could any enemy ever defeat a country that can pull boys like that out of its hat?

Our postponed strike was finally set for December 21, but during our run-in the weather again became so foul that flight operations would have been impossible, and again I had to give MacArthur an excuse instead of an attack. By now we could stay at sea no longer; we had to retire to Ulithi and repair our storm damage. We stood in on the morning of the twenty-fourth. That afternoon Chester Nimitz arrived from Pearl by plane. He was not quite a week old in his rank as fleet admiral, and when he was piped aboard the *New Jersey*, a five-star flag was broken for the first time in the Pacific Fleet.

With characteristic thoughtfulness, Chester had brought us a Christmas tree decked with ornaments. Everybody enjoyed it, but even if Santa Claus had come down one of the *New Jersey's* stacks that night, I doubt if we could have summoned the proper holiday spirit. As for myself, four consecutive Christmases away from home, four Christmases of sea and sand instead of snow and holly, had so saturated me with war on the ocean that I couldn't get into the mood of peace on earth.

The ten days preceding our return to Ulithi had brought us several reports of Jap warships in the China Sea; two fat plums, the battleships *Ise* and *Hyuga*, were specifically located in Camranh Bay, on the Indo-China coast. I had wanted to raid the China Sea area ever since I took command of the fleet. This stolen empire supplied oil, rubber, rice, and other materials essential to Japan's survival, and I was certain that a slash at her shore facilities and shipping would stagger her severely. Three months before, in conversations with MacArthur's staff at Hollandia, we had stressed the necessity of his opening Surigao Strait at the earliest possible moment, to give us access to the South China Sea through the central Philippines; and on October 21, I had reminded him again by dispatch.

Ernie King read a copy of it and at once asked Nimitz, "What has Halsey in mind?"

Chester passed the question to me. My answer brought a firm order to stay out until I received CINCPAC's authority. (I am afraid that my superiors worried about my judgment in the presence

241

of a juicy target.) I was disappointed, but not yet frustrated. There was one target in the area which I could hit without violating Ernie's injunction—a concentration of Jap warships in Brunei Bay, on the northwest coast of Borneo. My plan was to slip in close to the east coast and throw a strike across the island. If it worked—and we were quite confident that it would—we might revenge Pearl Harbor then and there. What balked us was neither COMINCH nor CINCPAC, but Kenney's inability to give Leyte effective air support. I had to stand by and attend to his knitting for him. We found some compensation in sinking the convoys attempting to reinforce General Yamashita, commanding the Japanese forces on Leyte, but that too should have been Kenney's business.

We were free again at the end of December, however, so I asked Chester's permission to enter the China Sea on completion of our next assignment—covering MacArthur's landing at Lingayen Gulf on January 9. Chester approved. The day after we sortied was New Year's Eve. That night I picked up the TBS and broadcast a message to all hands, under my code name.

"This is Blackjack himself," I said. "Your work so far has been superb. I expect even more. Keep the bastards dying!"

Incidentally, the last entry in my war diary for 1944 gave us particular satisfaction:

Prisoner of war interrogation in the Southwest Pacific confirmed previous sinkings claimed by the Commander Third Fleet, and also confirmed extensive damage to the remaining Japanese battleships. It is now definite that the Japanese suffered a greater loss in the Second Battle of the Philippine Sea [as the Battle for Leyte Gulf was originally known] than in any other naval engagement.

The last entry in my flag log for 1944 also gave us satisfaction. It says simply, "Steaming as before."

We had hoped that the price we paid for the typhoon would buy us clear skies for awhile, but more foul weather dogged us off and on for the next three weeks. It aborted half our strikes against Formosa on January 3 and 4, and kept our score down to 111 planes destroyed and sixteen ships sunk; it also helped send our own losses up to seventeen planes. The only bright spot was a childish attempt at deception on the part of some Jap pilots; pretending to

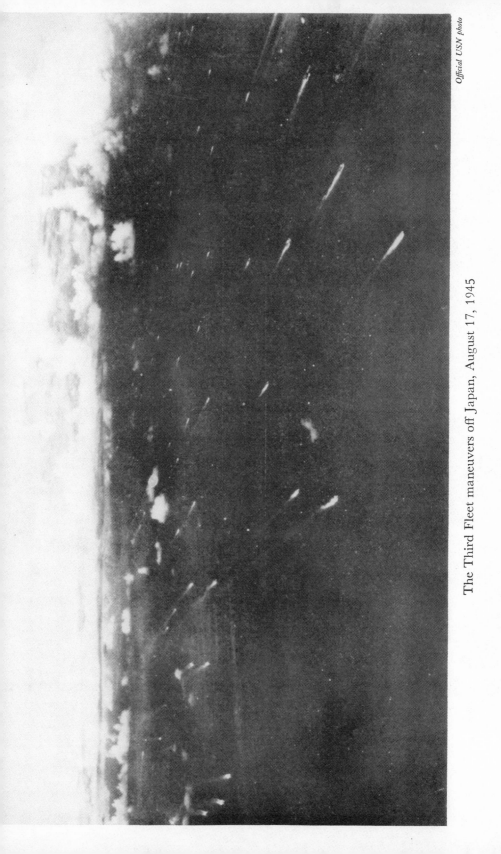

The Third Fleet maneuvers off Japan, August 17, 1945

Official USN photo

The heavy cruiser *Tone*, after the attack of July 28

The Third Fleet's first night in Sagami Bay, August 27, 1945,
when the sun seemed to sink directly into Fujiyama's crater

The surrender ceremony, aboard my
1, General MacArthur; 2, Chester Nimitz; 3, myself; 4, Forrest Sherman; 5,
Howard Fellows; 11, Dick B

U.S.S. Missouri, September 2, 1945

Cain; 6, Jack Towers; 7, Kelly Turner; 8, Lloyd Wiltse; 9, Mick Carney; 10,

ary Jones; 13, Jimmy Thach

Press Association

The White Horse, with me aboard, and Bill Chase, commanding the first Cavalry Divisi
Tokyo, September, 1945

Official USN

My flagship, the *U.S.S. South Dakota*, leads TG 30.2 under Golden Gate Bridge, October 1

The end of my sea duty. I am piped over the side for the last time, by Mick Carney, at Long Beach, California, November 20, 1945

ome again, to a welcome from two of my grand-children, Margaret and Halsey Spruance.

be lost American pilots, they begged over the radio for vectors to our force, but their English was so crude that we laughed at them.

MacArthur had previously forbidden TF 38 to strike below the top half of the dome of Luzon except in self-defense, the rest of the Philippines being reserved for the Army and the CVE's of the Seventh Fleet. Now he requested us to cross the line, since his planes were not neutralizing the enemy's Luzon fields as thoroughly as he had expected. We fueled on the fifth and struck on the sixth, through weather that made it impossible to maintain a holeproof blanket, and enough *kamikazes* broke out to plunge on sixteen Seventh Fleet bombardment and mine-sweeping units which were preparing Lingayen Gulf for the landing.

We had intended returning to Formosa on the seventh, but MacArthur asked us to stand by one day more. I consented reluctantly; I have already said that my conception of carrier warfare rejects passive defense of an area in favor of stifling the opposition at its source—in this case, Formosa. Our photo interpreters pored over their pictures of Luzon, searching for planes which the enemy had dispersed and concealed; and thanks to their diligence, we located and destroyed seventy-five on the ground. Only four others managed to take off—briefly.

This was our last strike in the Philippines. We fueled on the eighth and hit Formosa next day with everything we had, to cover the landing. That night, when all our planes were back aboard, we headed into the China Sea. Even now it is hard for me to realize that we slipped past the Japs; at one point in our passage through Bashi Channel, just south of Formosa, we were only 80 miles from their air base at Koshun. I imagine that either MacArthur's appearance at Lingayen panicked them into forgetting to send out patrols, or all their planes were being diverted to evacuating their key men from Manila. Three large transport planes, on a course from Manila to Formosa, closed us before daylight next morning, and all three were splashed by our night fighters; the second one went down only a few miles from my flagship and burned brilliantly until it sank. The Jap radios immediately became so hysterical that we guessed our bag was fairly heavy. Our code experts confirmed it: the transports were evacuating the entire operations section of the Philippine Air Command.

243

The China Sea venture—PLAN GRATITUDE—was extremely ticklish. Jap airfields encircled the area almost completely, and no part of it was beyond easy range of their fighter planes, yet our huge fleet was trying to cross it undetected. If the enemy spotted us, his ships would run for Singapore, where we did not dare follow. On the other hand, if we could creep up and pounce, not only might we disrupt his supply lines from southeast Asia, but we might even sink enough shipping, both merchant and combat, to affect the course of the war drastically. Everything depended on surprise.

Mick Carney usually wrote his night orders in black ink. On the night of the tenth, he made this entry in heavy red crayon: "Skunks to be sunk!" (A "skunk" was our code term for a surface contact, a companion term to a "bogey" in the air.) And on the following night he wrote, "Concealment is paramount!"

Several pages back, I listed certain *kamikazi*-inspired modifications in our air arm. These had already been put into effect: additional fighter planes had been assigned to the *Essex* and *Wasp*, replacing their dive bombers (the new fighter pilots on the *Essex* were Marines, making their debut in TF 38); and the *Independence*, our only carrier with an air group specially trained in night work, had been supplemented by another, the *Enterprise*.

As soon as we were through the gate to the China Sea, we organized the two night carriers and their screens into a separate task group, commanded by Rear Adm. Matthias B. Gardner, and put it in the van of the force, along with Bogan's group, which we had beefed up with two more heavy cruisers and a division of destroyers. Our battle plan was this: Bogan and Gardner would lead our run-in toward Camranh Bay, where we expected to make our richest haul; Gardner's planes would make a predawn search for enemy shipping, and when they had marked it down, Bogan's would cripple it for eventual destruction by the planes and guns of the other two groups, Ted Sherman's and Rear Adm. Arthur W. Radford's.

We fueled on the eleventh from Capt. Jasper T. Acuff's courageous tanker force, which, though virtually defenseless, was following us into these dangerous waters, and at 1400 the run-in began. Almost at once we had a close call—three bogies loomed on our radar screen. They were Jap fighters, "Jakes," pursuing a

SOWESPAC patrol plane, but our CAP overhauled them and shot them down before they could cry the alarm. That night I sent a message to the force: GIVE THEM HELL X YOU KNOW HOW TO DO IT X GOD BLESS YOU ALL. Next morning would tell the story.

Gardner's planes flew off at 0300 and fanned out to search the Indo-China coast from Saigon north to Tourane, a distance of 500 miles. At dawn we launched our strike, and at 0707 we formed TG 34.5—two fast battleships, two heavy cruisers, three light cruisers, and twelve destroyers—and sent it forward to intercept any warships that might try to break out of Camranh Bay. None were there, unfortunately, but our planes caught a convoy of eleven ships near Cap St. Jacques and sank them all; two other convoys were severely battered; and still other ships were sunk or damaged in various ports. We also tore up docks, air installations, and fuel dumps until the whole coast was a shambles.

As later verified by French Intelligence, we sank forty-one ships that day, totaling 127,000 tons, and damaged twenty-eight, totaling 70,000 tons. Moreover, many of the damaged ships were driven ashore and wrecked by an obliging monsoon which swept in as we stood out. We missed the *Ise* and *Hyuga*, which had gone to Singapore, but we sank the captured French cruiser *Lamotte-Picquet* at Saigon and the Jap light cruiser *Kashii* at sea. It was one of the heaviest blows that Jap shipping ever sustained. It was also a strongly worded notice that control of the South China Sea had changed hands. The Jap supply route from Singapore, Burma, Borneo, and the Dutch East Indies was shattered. We left the pieces to be picked up by our submarines and land-based planes.

AA was intense and effective, costing us sixteen planes, but air opposition was light; we found only fifteen planes to shoot down and only forty-seven to burn on the ground. That evening the Japs showed that experience had taught them a lesson. Their air commander at Singapore sent fifty Bettys up to Saigon to arm and refuel before attacking our force. He timed their arrival with the departure of our last strike, which was smart, but he wasn't quite smart enough; he didn't allow for our night fighters. They caught the Bettys in a neat line on the Saigon field and burnt up every one of them.

The monsoon that backed our attack brushed us harmlessly

245

with its northern edge, but it was the forerunner of a week of weather that dislocated our entire schedule. It delayed our first fueling a full day; it hindered our next series of strikes by ceilings that hid the targets—Formosa, Hong Kong, Canton, and Amoy; and it not only postponed our second fueling for two days, until the nineteenth, but forced us to set the rendezvous inconveniently far south, under the lee of Luzon.

By now, however, we had wrung the China Coast dry of profits and had proved that its defenses were flimsy. Only one mission was left on our agenda—photographic coverage of Okinawa, in preparation for the spring invasion. The shortest course was through Balintang Channel, north of Luzon, but the seas were still so heavy that our passage would be dangerously slow—an invitation to air attack. The other course, through Surigao, was sheltered, but it was far longer and would concentrate the force in narrow waters. CINCPAC directed us to use Balintang. We approached it uneasily on the afternoon of January 20. As we reached a point on the flight line between Luzon and Formosa, bogeys began to clutter our screen. In the next two hours, our CAP shot down fifteen. The night promised to be rugged. But just as we entered the channel, the wind and sea abated, and we sprinted through safely.

During the eleven days and 3,800 miles in the South China Sea, not one of our ships had suffered battle damage, and as at Mindoro, no enemy combat plane had been allowed within 20 miles of our force. We were congratulating ourselves on our luck when it washed out abruptly. On the twenty-first, heading northeast toward Okinawa, we sent a final strike against Formosa as we ran past. It was extremely successful; we sank twelve ships and destroyed 149 planes, but the Japs came boiling out, and four of them broke through our CAP and AA. One dropped a small bomb on the carrier *Langley*, killing one man and inflicting negligible damage. (Worse, one of the *Hancock's* own bombs accidentally detonated on her flight deck that same day, killing forty-eight men.) The other three were *kamikazes*. The first and second plunged headlong into the *Ticonderoga*, killing 140 men and severely damaging the island structure, the flight deck, and the hangar deck. The third hit the destroyer *Maddox*, killing four men. This attack was the last, with one exception, that succeeded in damaging a ship of TF 38 while I

246

commanded the Third Fleet; the exception was when a *kamikaze* hit the destroyer *Borie* only a week before the surrender.

For awhile, next day, I thought that our curse was still riding us. Of the three photo planes assigned to map the most important section of the Okinawa coast, two turned back with engine trouble, and the third's camera failed, which meant that we would have to cancel our retirement and stand by for another run. Just as I was working myself into a rage, word came that a photo pilot assigned to a low-priority area had been weathered out of it, and on his own initiative had covered the important one. I immediately asked his carrier, the *Lexington*, whether he preferred Scotch, rye, or bourbon, and when we returned to Ulithi on the twenty-fifth, I obtained six bottles of his choice and had them delivered to him.

At 2400 on January 26, Ray Spruance relieved me, and Pete Mitscher relieved Slew McCain in command of TF 38. So ended my first cruise with the Third Fleet. In our five months at sea, we had destroyed 7,315 enemy planes, and had sunk 90 warships and 573 merchant vessels totaling more than 1,000,000 tons. I sent a dispatch to all hands, NO WORDS CAN EXPRESS MY PRIDE. . . . SUPERLATIVELY WELL DONE. The possibility that I was telling these splendid men good-by forever clouded my pleasure at the prospect of going home and seeing my family again. I was moping around, waiting to shove off for Pearl, when something happened that blew away my depression and made me break out laughing. A communications officer brought me a dispatch from General MacArthur. I assume it was meant to read, YOUR DEPARTURE FROM THIS THEATER LEAVES A GAP THAT CAN BE FILLED ONLY BY YOUR RETURN. But the word FILLED had been garbled. It came out FOULED.

☆
☆ 15 ☆
☆ ☆

Less than two weeks after Ray Spruance took over the Third Fleet—which thereupon became the Fifth Fleet again—Mick Carney and I were spending a lazy afternoon at the flag officers' rest home on Oahu. Suddenly the radio announced that Army troops had entered Manila. I called Tulao, my Filipino chief steward, and hugged him and gave him the great news. He was on the verge of tears when Mick told him firmly, "Tulao, bring me an old fashioned, please."

Tulao brought it. "Now," Mick said, "I want you to join us in a toast to your wonderful people."

Tulao appealed to me. "The Admiral knows I don't drink, sir."

"This is one time you do," Mick said. "It's an order." And the three of us drank the health of the Philippine nation.

Most of my staff had some leave coming, and most of us spent it on the mainland. My medical officer, "Piggy" Weeks, arranged for Mick and me to be invited to a Georgia plantation, where—as Harold Stassen wrote in my war diary—"AA proficiency was maintained with quail and wild turkey as targets." Mick proved to be an excellent wing shot, among his other accomplishments, and on the rare occasions when he missed, he always had an unimpeachable ballistic explanation of why the shot had been impossible in the first place.

I spent March in Washington on temporary duty. On the seventh, President Roosevelt summoned me to the White House and awarded me a Gold Star in lieu of a third Distinguished Service Medal.

248

EDITOR'S NOTE:
The citation follows:

"For exceptionally meritorious service to the government of the United States in a duty of great responsibility as Commander, Third Fleet, operating against enemy Japanese forces from June 15, 1944, to January 25, 1945. Carrying out a sustained and relentless drive against the enemy, Admiral Halsey skillfully directed the operations which resulted in the capture of the Western Carolines and a crushing defeat on the Japanese carrier force in the battle off Cape Engaño on October 25, and associated attacks on the Japanese fleet in waters of the Philippines. Conducting a series of brilliant and boldly executed attacks on hostile air forces, shipping and installations in the Ryukyus, Formosa, the Philippines, South China, and Indo-China, Admiral Halsey was directly responsible for the great damage inflicted on enemy aerial forces and the destruction of shipping vital to the Japanese in fighting an increasingly defensive war. Under his forceful and inspiring leadership, the recovery of the Philippines was painstakingly prepared for, covered and effectively supported during operations which evidenced his daring tactics and the devotion to duty of his gallant command."

My wife came to the ceremony. Gold Stars, combat stars, and such have to be stuck through the front of the ribbon and clipped from behind. My D.S.M. ribbon was sewn to my blouse, but somehow Fan managed to pin the star onto it—I have never figured how. I wasn't watching her, because just then the President remarked that he had given me a Gold Star before, "for being a very good destroyer skipper," when he was Assistant Secretary of the Navy. He hadn't, but I didn't correct him.

After lunch, he took me to his upstairs office and told me a number of things so secret that I would have preferred not to know them. One was Russia's pledge to declare war on Japan; the others are still secret. Our conversation lasted about an hour. I never saw Mr. Roosevelt again.

My temporary duty was almost finished when COMINCH informed me that certain high officials were apprehensive about the possibility of a Jap carrier raid against San Francisco, where the United Nations conference was in session.

I began to laugh. "Good Lord, Ernie, that's ridiculous! You know as well as I do that the Japs have almost no carrier air groups left and no carriers to put them on!"

Ernie said, "I agree with you. It's highly improbable, but it will be an excellent drill for us."

He appointed me Commander of the Mid-Pacific Striking Force, composed of all surface units available in the Hawaiian area and in our West Coast ports, and we drew plans to meet the attack. The Army concentrated some AA around San Francisco, but otherwise our defenses went no further than paper.

I met my staff in Pearl on April 7. Our first assignment was to prepare four possible operations:

1. Employment of the fast carriers as strategic cover for the seizure of an area on the China Coast in the vicinity of Nimrod Sound [about 100 miles south of Shanghai].

2. Seizure of an area on the Shantung Peninsula [about 350 miles north of Shanghai].

3. Establishment of a line of communications with Russia across the North Pacific, including an entry into the Sea of Japan through La Pérouse Strait [north of Hokkaido, the northernmost home island].

4. Entry into the Sea of Japan through Korea Strait [between Korea and Kyushu, the southernmost home island].

We submitted plans for all four operations. The first was already tentatively scheduled, so it was too late for us to raise objections, but we recommended that the other three be combined into a direct assault on Kyushu itself, between Kagoshima Bay and Ariake Bay. The strategy of gradual encirclement and strangulation, as represented by landings at Nimrod Sound and Shantung, and as endorsed by Ray Spruance, I considered a waste of time—two bites at a cherry. None of these operations was ever mounted, of course; Japan collapsed too soon for either school of strategy to be given a test; but although it is futile to debate the empty questions at this late date, I still maintain that an assault on Kyushu in sufficient force would have been an economical short cut.

Toward the end of April, I made a brief trip to CINCPAC's advanced headquarters at Guam, where Chester Nimitz told me that I would relieve Ray Spruance in about a month and that my new flagship would be the *Missouri*. I was sorry not to have the *New Jersey* again, but she was being overhauled. From Guam I went to Okinawa to confer with Ray, then returned to Pearl. We were there when Germany surrendered. Perhaps I should have been tremendously jubilant, but my principal feeling was eagerness—to get the men and gear that were now released from Europe. Eisenhower's job was finished; ours was not.

I hoisted my flag in the *Missouri* on May 18. Capt. Stuart S. Murray, her captain, met me on the quarterdeck as I came aboard, and I told him, "This is a significant day. I served in the *Missouri* forty years ago, and here I am back again!"

We sailed for Okinawa and anchored off Hagushi, on its west coast, on the twenty-sixth. The day passed in further conferences —aboard ship in the morning with Ray and his staff, and ashore in the afternoon with Lt. Gen. Simon Bolivar Buckner, commanding the Tenth Army. Many of our old SOPAC friends stopped by his tent: Lt. Gen. John R. Hodge, commanding the XXIV Corps; Roy Geiger, commanding the III Marine Amphibious Corps; and Maj. Gen. Francis Patrick Mulcahy, commanding the Tactical Air Force. Ray had told me that several features of the shore establishment were unsatisfactory, especially its radars, so I mentioned them to General Buckner. This was the first he had heard of them, and he set about correcting them at once. I will always maintain that if you want something done quickly, a five-minute conversation is infinitely better than a 5,000-word report in triplicate.

It had been agreed that the change of command would become official at midnight on the twenty-seventh. As the *Missouri* stood out, a few hours before then, I gave orders for her to drop some 16-inch calling cards on the enemy's doorstep; I wanted him to know I was back. Next morning we rendezvoused with the fast carrier forces, and a second change of command was arranged: Slew McCain relieved Pete Mitscher as CTF 38.

This was the last time that Pete served under my command. I hated to see him go. The farewell dispatch that I sent him represented the opinion of the whole Third Fleet: IT IS WITH THE VERY DEEPEST REGRET THAT WE WATCH A GREAT FIGHTING MAN SHOVE OFF X I AND MY STAFF AND THE FLEET SEND ALL LUCK TO YOU AND YOUR MAGNIFICENT STAFF.

My talks with the Navy and Army at Okinawa had shown me that once again the fleet was being held in static defense instead of being sent to hit the enemy where it would hurt. This strategy was

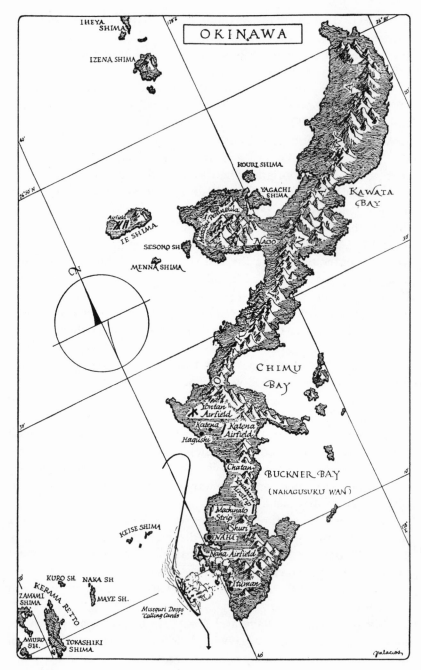

OKINAWA

IHEYA SHIMA

IZENA SHIMA

KOURI SHIMA

YAGACHI SHIMA

KAWATA BAY

Airfield
IE SHIMA

SESOKO SH

MENNA SHIMA

Motobu Peninsula

NAGO

CHIMU BAY

Yontan Airfield

Katena   Katena Airfield

Hagushi

Chatan

BUCKNER BAY
(NAKAGUSUKU WAN)

Yonabaru Airfield

Machinato Strip

Shuri

NAHA

Naha Airfield

KEISE SHIMA

Itoman

KURO SH.   NAKA SH

KERAMA RETTO

ZAMAMI SHIMA

MAYE SH.

AMURO SH.

TOKASHIKI SHIMA

Missouri Drops
"Calling Cards"

palacios

252

worse than unprofitable; it was expensive. The popular conception of an amphibious operation assigns heavy casualties to the foot soldiers and few to the sailors, yet my war diary for May 29 has this entry: "Ground forces KIA & MIA [killed and missing in action] to date, 5,492. KIA & MIA from 218 ships, 2,475."

Kamikazes had been attacking the Fleet ferociously. Our picket ships—destroyers and destroyer escorts—were being smashed almost daily. We had given the enemy the initiative, instead of blanketing his home fields and burning every plane we could find. A few days before, I had asked Ray Spruance how well the SOWESPAC air force, based in the Philippines, was neutralizing Formosa.

He said bitterly, "They've destroyed a great many sugar mills, railroad trains, and other equipment."

I blew up. "Sugar mills can't damage our fleet! Why the hell don't they destroy their *planes?*"

The immobilization of the fleet could be blamed on two facts: first, the Japs' stubborn defense, which had prevented our ground forces from obtaining airfields where they could base enough planes for their own protection; second, the ground forces' failure to install enough radars to permit the withdrawal of our patrols and pickets. As a result, Ray had had to continue his support, despite the dangerous exposure of the fleet and the fact that his ships were long overdue for repair and his men for rest.

I would have liked to haul out at once, but the ground forces still were far from self-sufficient, particularly as the British Pacific Fleet's fast carrier task force, which had been striking the Sakashima Gunto, south of Okinawa, had just retired to Sydney for a month. However, there was a Marine air group based in the Philippines, MAG 14, which I knew was quite capable of taking over our job. I recommended that it be brought forward, and CINCPAC approved. Pending its arrival, I sent Ted Sherman's task group ahead to Leyte, to begin its rest period, and turned over all the support missions to the remaining two groups, Radford's and Rear Adm. Joseph J. Clark's. ("Jocko" Clark had relieved Dave Davison in command of TG 38.1.)

Our fighters struck southern Kyushu on June 2 and 3, but all air operations on the fourth were canceled by the sudden approach of a typhoon. It soon became evident that our tragic experience in

December had taught us nothing. Again the early warnings were critically delayed; again the estimated positions of the storm center were at wide variance; again the predictions of its course were faulty; and again the fleet suffered heavy damage. The bow of the heavy cruiser *Pittsburgh* was wrenched off, thirty-two other ships were battered, and 142 planes were destroyed. Our only consolation in the whole affair was that no ships were sunk and only six men were lost.

As far back as January, I had vigorously urged the establishment of weather reconnaissance squadrons to track typhoons and report their movements. In May, I had made supplementary recommendations that these reports be transmitted with the highest priority. I now repeated my recommendations in the strongest terms at my command. This time they brought results. Typhoons continued to rage around our area—another threatened us on June 11, and still another on the nineteenth—but thanks to alert reconnaissance and ample warnings, we dodged them easily.

Meanwhile, Ted Sherman and his task group were safe, they thought, in Leyte Gulf, but on the seventh a disaster struck them, too. An Army P-38 began flat-hatting Ted's anchorage, making dives and dummy runs on his ships. One dive ended abruptly, when the pilot misjudged his altitude and crashed into the flight deck of the *Randolph*, killing eleven men and injuring fourteen, destroying a number of parked planes, and ripping up a length of the deck.

Ted had been in combat almost since the beginning of the war; the old *Lexington* had been sunk under him in the Battle of the Coral Sea. He is a real fighter and, like most such, he has small patience with show-offs. He notified CINCPAC and all authorities in the Philippines that he had given orders to open fire on the next plane that buzzed his ships. Quite rightly, CINCPAC cooled him down and canceled his orders, but I am in complete sympathy with the indignation that dictated them.

While MAG 14 was moving into Okinawa, we staged another strike on Kyushu and a surface bombardment of two Bonin islands. These were our last chores; we headed south and anchored at Leyte on June 14. Every man in the fleet was eager to get ashore, but the excitement among our Filipino bluejackets was intense; we were giving them leave, and they would be able to visit their homes

254

and families for the first time in several years. I myself visited Manila for the first time in many more years—since the Round-the-World Cruise in 1908. My pilot took me on an air tour of the harbor, which I was delighted to see littered with sunken enemy ships, and next morning I made a surface tour with Commo. William A. Sullivan, who was restoring the port facilities. We had reckoned that our many attacks between September and January had sunk about 120 craft of all sizes, but Sullivan told me that the correct figure was close to 600. The Third Fleet could not take credit for them all, of course, but enough were ours to make me as happy as a dog with two tails.

I lunched with General MacArthur (it was our first meeting since the June before) and found him in spirits as high as my own. Not only was his Philippines campaign—a model of generalship throughout—now nearly at its end, but he and Mrs. MacArthur had discovered that their house in Manila was only slightly harmed, instead of wrecked, as they had expected. I believe it owes its escape to the fact that the Japanese Ambassador to the Philippines lived in it during the occupation.

The Okinawa campaign was also winding up. The drama of its last few days is condensed in my war diary as follows:

17 JUNE. Adm. Minoru Ota, Commander Naval Base Force, was found with his throat cut, sitting in a ceremonial pose in a cave in the 4th Marines' zone on the Oroku Peninsula.

18 JUNE. Lt. Gen. S. B. Buckner was killed by enemy shellfire while observing an attack.

19 JUNE. The collapse of Japanese defenses was evident across the entire line. At 0440/I [Okinawa time] Maj. Gen. Roy S. Geiger, USMC, assumed command vice the late General Buckner.

20 JUNE. Civilians surrendered in masses.

21 JUNE. Major General Geiger announced that organized resistance had ceased.

27 JUNE. The bodies of Lieutenant General Ushimajima and Lieutenant General Cho, Commanding General and Chief of Staff of the Japanese forces on Okinawa, were found with indisputable evidence of hara-kiri.

A major naval and land phase of the Pacific War had been successfully concluded. The final phase opened at dawn on July 1, when the fleet sortied from Leyte. There had been two changes in

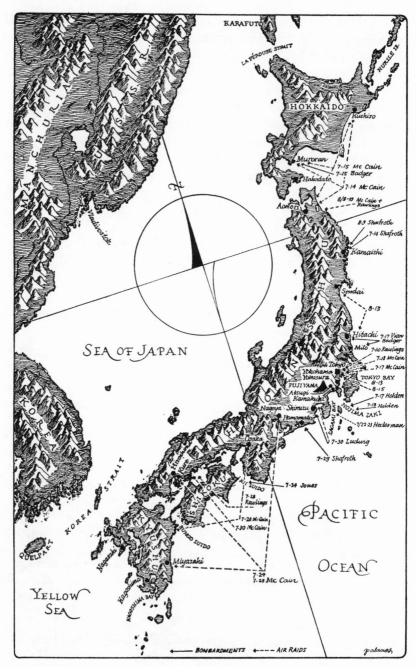

KARAFUTO

LA PÉROUSE STRAIT

KURILE IS.

HOKKAIDO

Kushiro

Muroran — 7-15 Mc Cain
7-15 Badger

Hakodate — 7-14 Mc Cain

Aomori — 8/9-10 Mc Cain +
Rawlings

8-9 Shafroth

7-14 Shafroth

Kamaishi

Sendai

8-13

Hitachi — 7-17 Vian
Badger

Mito — 7-30 Rawlings

Tokyo — 7-18 Mc Cain

7-17 Mc Cain

Yokohama
Yokosura — TOKYO BAY
8-13

FUJIYAMA — 8-15

Atsugi
Kamakuki — 7-17 Holden

Nagoya *Shimizu* — 7-18 Holden

Hamamatsu — NOJIMA ZAKI

7/22-23 Hederman

Osaka — 7-30 Luding

7-29 Shafroth

KII SUIDO — 7-24 Jones

7-28
Rawlings

7-28 Mc Cain

7-30 Mc Cain

BUNGO SUIDO

Miyazaki — 7-24
7-29 Mc Cain

QUELPART

Nagasaki

Kagoshima *Kagoshima Bay*

SEA OF JAPAN

Vladivostok

MANCHURIA

KOREA

KOREA STRAIT

N

PACIFIC

OCEAN

YELLOW
SEA

SHIKOKU

←— BOMBARDMENTS ←---- AIR RAIDS

palacios

256

task group command: Rear Adm. Thomas L. Sprague had relieved Jocko Clark as CTG 38.1, and Jerry Bogan had relieved Ted Sherman as CTG 38.3. A third change, in task force command, I will quote from my war diary:

Rear Admiral John F. Shafroth relieved Vice Admiral Willis A. Lee in command of Battleship Squadron 2 and of TF 34. Vice Admiral Lee's orders provide for resumption of command of BATRON 2 on completion of temporary duty.

Ching Lee was an expert on every form of gun from a .45 to a 16-inch. He was a champion pistol shot and had been a member of the American Rifle Team in the 1920 Olympics. The temporary duty that called him away was the organization of a force specially armed against *kamikazes*. He hated to leave the combat zone. I remember his telling Jack Shafroth as he shoved off, "Don't get yourself settled in that job, because I'm coming back!"

But he didn't come back. Two months later he was dead of heart failure—the first of four task force commanders that I have lost since the war. He was a sterling officer and a true friend, and I miss him.

We sortied from Leyte under a broad directive: we would attack the enemy's home islands, destroy the remnants of his navy, merchant marine, and air power, and cripple his factories and communications. Our planes would strike inland; our big guns would bombard coastal targets; together they would literally bring the war home to the average Japanese citizen.

With our campaign thus focused on Japan proper, we did not expect to see Leyte again, and we didn't—but for a reason far different from what we thought. For the sake of a shorter supply line, we were planning to base in the future at Eniwetok, which is about the same distance as Leyte from Tokyo, but some 2,200 miles nearer our main base at Pearl Harbor. We did not see Eniwetok either. Our next port of call was Tokyo itself.

On our way north, we received a dispatch from CINCPAC, warning us that a Jap hospital ship, the *Takasago Maru*, en route from Wake Island to the Empire, might pass through the waters where we were operating and therefore might have to be diverted for security. CINCPAC added that a boarding party from one of his destroyers had already inspected her and released her;

257

she was transporting only wounded troops and troops suffering from malnutrition.

That made me mad. Although Japan had never signed the Geneva Convention, she professed to observe it; yet I had suspected throughout the war that she was using her hospital ships for unauthorized purposes. This was an instance. Battle casualties are legitimate evacuees; malnutrition cases are not. For three years we had been blockading the by-passed Jap islands in an attempt to force their surrender. The starving men on the *Takasago Maru* had constituted a large part of the Wake garrison; their evacuation meant that Wake's scanty provisions would last that much longer. I sent a destroyer to intercept the ship and escort her to Saipan, and I intended recommending either that all but her battle casualties be returned to Wake, or that an equal number of Japs be sent there from our Saipan prison camps as replacements. However, CINCPAC directed me to let her proceed, and I had to comply. Ironically, she arrived at Yokosuka, near Tokyo, just as we struck it, and I am told that a stray bomb narrowly missed her.

Our preparations for the attack on the Empire were extremely careful. B-29's had made a thorough reconnaissance of Hokkaido and northern Honshu. Navy B-24's, covered by Army P-51's, had photographed Tokyo, our first objective. Submarines had probed for mine fields offshore from our bombardment areas. As we closed in, land-based planes flew barrier patrols ahead of us, to screen our approach from enemy scouts; and seven submarines advanced on a 100-mile front to destroy enemy pickets and to act as lifeguards for our pilots.

Strike day was July 10. The afternoon of the ninth, just before our run-in, we made a sound contact with an enemy submarine on the fringe of the force. While our destroyers attacked, I prayed that the sub had had no chance to cry the alarm. The report came presently. It was not a sub but a whale; one destroyer had cut its tail off. I have already told how we often mistook fish for torpedoes in World War I. Our confusion multiplied in this war. Porpoises and drifting logs are thick around Japan, and sometimes they will deceive even the sharpest eyes. Five-inch shell cases, floating end up, gave us many a periscope scare. Worst of all were the big glass balls that Jap fishermen use as net buoys; their resemblance to mines kept our nerves raw and jumping. (There was hardly a day on this cruise when we did not encounter at least five drifting mines and explode them with gunfire.)

Our luck held. It even improved. We picked up a weather front and rode it almost to our launching point, and when our strike arrived over Tokyo at daybreak, not a single interceptor was in the air, and only two snoopers came near the force. Both were shot down. Tokyo was a poor target. The few planes our pilots managed to find were degassed, revetted, and widely dispersed. The Japs had been slow to learn the obvious economy of degassing their planes, and we were sorry they ever learned it; a plane with empty tanks does not always burn under strafing, so damage appraisal becomes difficult. Still, we could count 109 definitely destroyed and 231 damaged. We also damaged hangars and other installations.

Previous attacks on Tokyo by B-29's and Army fighter planes had led us to believe that opposition would be light, but our pilots reported it almost nonexistent. Even the AA was meager—the AA protecting the heart of the Empire, the home of the Son of Heaven. We began to reestimate the probable duration. . . .

Every turn of our screws now took us further north than any ships of the fleet, except submarines, had ever ventured before. Our schedule called for strikes against Hokkaido and northern Honshu on the thirteenth, but the fog belt that hangs down from the Kuriles blanketed our targets, and we had to postpone for a day, much as I would have enjoyed staging the first surface bombardment of the Japanese homeland on a Friday the thirteenth.

The lack of mine sweepers hampered our bombardments by forcing us to stay outside the 100-fathom curve, but Jack Shafroth maneuvered his force—three battleships, two heavy cruisers, and nine destroyers—close enough in to permit a leisurely, broad-daylight, two-hour shelling of the large steel plant at Kamaishi. In this case, "close enough" meant that the force was clearly visible from the beach. However much propaganda a Japanese civilian will swallow, it must have been hard for him to digest the news that certain American warships had been sunk when he had just watched them blast his job from under him.

At midnight we sent out a destroyer-light cruiser sweep to ambush coastwise shipping, and next morning Rear Adm. Oscar C.

Badger took another heavy bombardment force, including the *Missouri*, right into the enemy's jaws. The chart justifies my metaphor; during the hour that we shelled our objective—the city of Muroran, a coal and steel center on southern Hokkaido—we were landlocked on three sides. We opened fire from 28,000 yards and poured in 1,000 tons of shells. It was a magnificent spectacle, but I kept one eye on the target and the other on the sky. Our three-hour approach had been in plain view, as would be our three-hour retirement, and I thought that every minute would bring an air attack. None came; the enemy's only resistance was desultory AA fire against our spotting planes; but those were the longest six hours in my life.

The fast carriers, meanwhile, had been working over Hokkaido's railways, shipping, and air facilities, also against light resistance. Here is their score for the two-day attack:

	DESTROYED	DAMAGED
Ships	44	61
Small craft	96	174
(Tonnage	71,000	88,000)
Planes	38	46
Locomotives	84	28

In addition, they burned out twenty city blocks at Kushiro. Our losses were sixteen men and twenty-three planes to AA, and nine men and eighteen planes operationally.

A large amount of Honshu's coal and iron came from Hokkaido via train ferries, and their destruction was Rollo Wilson's pet project. When the first action reports began to sift in, he snatched them up and pored over them; the ferries were not mentioned. Later reports also ignored them. Rollo was sulking and cursing when the final reports arrived. I heard him whistle and saw him beam. "Six ferries sunk!" he said, "Pretty soon we'll have 'em moving their stuff by oxcarts and skiffs!"

To a few members of my staff, the enemy's failure to hit us while we were in the cul-de-sac at Muroran implied that he was hoarding his air power against an expected invasion, but most of us believed that he had little air power left to hoard, that he was short of planes, spare parts, pilots, and fuel. In my own opinion, his shortages were even reaching the point of no-return, the point where collapse of his whole war machine would become inevitable. Since three years before, in our South Pacific days, I had argued that Japan's ultimate end would be collapse. The only member of my staff who agreed with me then was Brig. Gen. Dewitt Peck of the Marines, my War Plans officer before Bill Riley. The rest maintained that she would commit national suicide rather than surrender. Muroran fortified my conviction that Dewitt and I were right. However, lest I seem to be parading my prescience, I should add that I now picked October as the date of her surrender. Not for two weeks more did I realize that she would never last through August.

We fueled on July 16, and everyone was able to relax except me. The flag log for that morning tells why: "At 0645, CTF 37 reported for duty and took station astern of TG 38.4. At 0845, HMS *Quadrant* came alongside with CTF 37 and staff for conference. At 0907, HMS *Terpsichore* came alongside with CTG 37.1 and staff."

TF 37 was the fast carrier task force of the British Pacific Fleet—one battleship, four large carriers, six light cruisers, and eighteen destroyers, under Vice Adm. Sir Bernard Rawlings; CTG 37.1 was Vice Adm. Sir Philip Vian. I knew both these gentlemen by their splendid reputations, but we had never met, and I am afraid that my appearance did little to recommend me. They were wearing smart blues; I was wearing a Marine woolen jacket, a blue flannel shirt, green flying trousers, and a long-billed cap like a swordfisherman's. I explained that I found these motleys more comfortable for fighting, and reluctantly I opened the conference. I say "reluctantly" because I dreaded it. When I was informed at Pearl Harbor that the British Pacific Fleet would report to me, I naturally assumed that I would have full operational control, but when I reread the plan at Leyte, I discovered that tactical control had been reserved. This would force me to present Admiral Rawlings with three alternatives, and I did so now:

1. TF 37 would operate close aboard us, as another task group in TF 38; it would not receive direct orders from me, but it would be privy to the orders that I gave TF 38; these it would consider as

261

"suggestions" to be followed to our mutual advantage, thereby assuring us a concentrated force with concentrated weapons.

2. TF 37 would operate semi-independently, some 60 or 70 miles away, thereby preserving its technical identity at the cost of a divided force. (I stipulated that I would consent to this choice only if the request were put in writing.)

3. TF 37 would operate completely independently, against soft spots in Japan which we would recommend if so desired.

Bert Rawlings did not hesitate. He said, "Of course I'll accept Number 1." My admiration for him began at that moment. I saw him constantly thereafter, and a finer officer and firmer friend I have never known.

Whereas TF 38 could strike on three successive days, we were counting on the British to strike on only two, because of their ships' lower fuel capacity and slower rate of fueling; however, by fueling them from our own tankers when the need arose, they were able to match us strike for strike. One of my most vivid war recollections is of a day when Bert's flagship, the battleship *King George V*, fueled from the tanker *Sabine* at the same time as the *Missouri*. I went across to "the Cagey Five," as we called her, on an aerial trolley, just to drink a toast to this unique episode in the histories of the American and Royal Navies. (I would have invited Bert back for a return toast if it had not been for Secretary Daniels' Order 99.)

Our strike against Tokyo on the tenth had been chiefly exploratory; our photographers had obtained good coverage of the area, so we returned on the seventeenth to develop the targets they had pin-pointed. Top priority was assigned to the battleship *Nagato*, which photo intelligence had discovered badly damaged but still afloat at the Yokosuka Naval Base. Again foul weather required a day's postponement, but we improved our wait with a midnight bombardment of an engineering works and arms factory at Hitachi, about 50 miles north of Tokyo. The afternoon of the eighteenth was clear, and our fliers went in. The AA was the heaviest they had ever encountered; it cost us and the British together eighteen men and fourteen planes. We destroyed forty-three enemy planes and damaged seventy-seven, sank several ships, and wrecked a number of locomotives, dumps, and barracks, but although the *Nagato's* superstructure was battered further, she still floated.

VICE ADMIRAL CARNEY:

I had a good look at her on August 30, when I accepted the surrender of the Yokosuka Base. Her topsides were chewed up, but she was
floating at about normal draft, and her hull and turrets appeared intact.
It takes torpedoes to sink a heavily armored ship; bombs are not enough.
Of course, I am excluding atomic bombs. Almost exactly a year after this
strike, an atomic bomb sank the *Nagato* at Bikini.

Before our next strikes, we withdrew to a rendezvous with our
supply force, brilliantly organized and led by Rear Adm. Donald
B. Beary. This is what TF 38 took aboard: 6,369 tons of ammunition, 1,635 tons of stores and provisions, 379,157 barrels of fuel oil,
99 replacement planes, and 421 replacement personnel. I give the
figures because I believe that this was the largest replenishment
ever achieved by a fleet at sea.

On our way to the rendezvous, I sent a destroyer-light cruiser
force on a shipping sweep up to Nojima Zaki, which is one of
Tokyo's gateposts; and as we returned, on the twenty-second, I
sent two destroyer forces to the same waters. One bombarded a
town; the other found a convoy of four ships, sank two, and damaged the others. These sweeps and bombardments accomplished
more than destruction; they showed the enemy that we made no
bones about playing in his front yard. From now on, we patrolled
his channels and shelled his coast almost every night that the
weather permitted.

I notice that in the past few pages I have made several references
to the weather. It had been troublesome enough thus far, and from
here on it became worse. Summer is the season for typhoons around
Japan. We once had three of them on our chart in a single day,
moving trunk-to-tail like circus elephants. Between typhoons we
had long periods of rain and low overcasts. My operations report
reminds me that though we were trying to redouble the intensity
of our attacks, in an effort to precipitate Japan's now imminent
capitulation, the weather balked us time and again.

25 JULY. Bad weather reduced the effectiveness of the heavy strikes on
primary targets. Afternoon strikes were canceled.

30 JULY. Unfavorable weather conditions.

31 JULY. Threat of a typhoon caused radical departures from planned
operations.

263

2 AUGUST. Still waiting for the typhoon to clear.

8 AUGUST. Bad weather, consisting of fog and low visibility, prevented scheduled strikes.

9 AUGUST. Fog prevented getting into Hokkaido.

We might have been able to mount fifteen attacks in the short time left us, but the weather allowed only seven. The first three were concentrated on the Inland Sea area. The series began on July 24 with a fighter sweep against airfields between northern Kyushu and Nagoya, and a strike on the Kure Naval Base with bombs, rockets, and torpedoes. Kure is the port where Jap warships went to die. We hit them hard that day but did not finish them off; next day's strike was partly weather-bound, and we could not resume the action until the twenty-eighth. By sunset that evening, the Japanese Navy had ceased to exist. Photographs showed the battleship *Ise* down by the bow and resting on the bottom; her sister ship, the *Hyuga*, was awash amidships; the *Haruna* was beached and burning, with a large hole in her stern. The *Katsuragi's* flight deck was torn and buckled; the *Amagi's* could have been used as a ski slide. The heavy cruisers *Tone* and *Aoba* were beached. The Commander in Chief of the Combined Japanese Fleet could reach his cabin in his flagship, the light cruiser *Oyodo*, only in a diving suit.

Japan had twelve battleships in the war; only one was now afloat—the crippled *Nagato*, at Yokosuka. Of her twenty-five aircraft carriers, five were still afloat but damaged. Of eighteen heavy cruisers, the only two afloat were at Singapore, both damaged. Of twenty-two light cruisers, two were afloat. And of 177 destroyers, forty-two were afloat, but only five were fully operational.

I will not itemize the buildings, tanks, dumps, merchant vessels, small craft, and locomotives that also were destroyed during these three days, but our American and British pilots shot down or burned up 306 enemy planes and damaged 392. Together, our losses from all causes, operations as well as combat, were 102 men and 133 planes. This ratio may seem unfavorable in comparison with our usual 10 or 15 to 1, but three factors must be considered: the enemy's AA was extremely heavy, particularly over his warships; his air-borne opposition was more determined than any he had shown us in a long while; and he had dispersed his planes so widely—among crops, under trees, and even in graveyards, sometimes as much as 5 miles from their base—that our pilots had great trouble ferreting them out for destruction. A Jap air commander later complained to us that this new doctrine of dispersal meant not only that he was unable to scramble his pilots within reasonable time, but that he could not even communicate with them.

Slew McCain strongly opposed our strikes against Kure. He and his staff considered the Japanese Fleet only a minor threat; they wanted to use our air strength against other, more profitable targets. But there were three good reasons why this fleet had to be destroyed:

1. *For the sake of our national morale.* This was the only appropriate retaliation for Pearl Harbor.

2. *For the sake of the Russians.* Our high command knew of their impending declaration of war and knew that if we had to establish a supply line to them, it would run between Kamchatka and Hokkaido—a route so exposed that even a few enemy cruisers and destroyers could dominate it.

3. *For the sake of the peace terms.* We could not afford to have a surrendered Japan use the existence of part of her fleet as a bargaining point, as Germany had after World War I.

There was also a fourth reason: CINCPAC had ordered the Fleet destroyed. If the other reasons had been invalid, that one alone would have been enough for me.

A last bit of background needs to be filled in: the strikes against Kure were made only by American planes. At Mick Carney's insistence, I assigned the British an alternate target, Osaka, which also offered warships, but none of prime importance. Mick's argument was that although this division of forces violated the principle of concentration and superiority, it was imperative that we forestall a possible postwar claim by Britain that she had delivered even a part of the final blow that demolished the Japanese Fleet. I hated to admit a political factor into a military equation—my respect for Bert Rawlings and his fine men made me hate it doubly—but Mick forced me to recognize that statesmen's objectives sometimes differ widely from combat objectives, and that an exclusively American attack was therefore in American interests.

All through the war, senior admirals and generals in the combat zone were under steady pressure to broadcast in behalf of bond drives and such. My turn came during the Kure strikes. As well as I can recall, I said something to this effect: "What is left of the Japanese Navy is helpless, but just for luck we're going to hunt them out of their holes. The Third Fleet's job is to hit the Empire hard and often. We are doing just that, and my only regret is that our ships don't have wheels, so that when we drive the Japs from the coast, we can chase them inland."

Within a week I received a letter from a man who had heard my broadcast. He wrote that my worries were at an end. He had invented an apparatus enabling ships to travel overland.

After Kure, we worked our way east. On July 29, our heavy ships bombarded Hamamatsu; on the thirtieth, our planes struck Tokyo and Nagoya; and that night a destroyer squadron bombarded the railroad yards and an aluminum plant at Shimizu. We refueled on the thirty-first and first, in preparation for a swing back west and a three-day smash at Kyushu and Korea, beginning on the third. However, a typhoon held us up, and we had to reschedule for the fifth. We were making our run-in on the evening of the fourth when a dispatch from CINCPAC abruptly shifted our strikes to northern Honshu and Hokkaido. The Twentieth Air Force was ready to drop the atomic bomb on Hiroshima.

Around the middle of July, CINCPAC had forbidden us to attack certain cities, including Hiroshima and Nagasaki. No explanation was given, and I was puzzled until Rear Adm. William R. Purnell came aboard on the twenty-second, under CINCPAC's instructions, and gave me my first word of the bomb. He said that the drop was planned for August 2, on a Kyushu target, and that I was to keep all my planes at least 50 miles from the area. (This is why we set our own Kyushu strike for the third.) The typhoon that delayed us also delayed the drop—it was eventually made, of course, on the sixth, and although we could have struck on the fifth and hauled clear, we were needed elsewhere in a hurry.

Our shift to Honshu-Hokkaido was at the request of General MacArthur, who suspected that the Japs had massed several hundred planes at these northern fields for an attack on Okinawa, which had recently been placed under his command. We were weathered out on the eighth, and fog screened Hokkaido on the

266

ninth, but our heavy ships bombarded Kamaishi again for two hours that afternoon, while our pilots combed the Honshu fields, destroying or damaging 392 planes. By now our contempt for Japan's defenses was so thorough that our prime consideration in scheduling this bombardment, which was broadcast from the *Iowa*, was the convenience of the radio audience at home. My war diary remarks with satisfaction, "an excellent day."

It was also the day that Russia entered the Pacific War. Since the fields in the area which we were hitting were the only ones in the Japanese home islands from which Russian territory could be attacked, we hit them again on the tenth. We were hoping to fatten our score at the same time, but our pilots had slim pickings until late in the afternoon, when they discovered "lucrative concentrations"—as my war diary calls them—at Mamurogawa and Obanazawa, and happily chalked up another 175 destroyed and 153 damaged.

I was sitting in the flag wardroom that night when a communications watch officer brought Mick Carney a transcription of a radio intercept. Mick read it aloud: "Through the Swiss Government, Japan stated that she is willing to accept Allied surrender ultimatum issued at Potsdam, provided they can keep their Emperor. . . . "

None of us was wildly surprised. Ever since the first of the month, radio and press reports, decoded Jap dispatches, and the rapid decay of our opposition had been clear signposts to the event that now approached us. We were ready to meet it. Our long-range plans, drawn in the late spring, had called for a retirement early in August, but I had recently canceled them and had ordered the logistic pipe line kept full for just such an emergency as this, which would require the indefinite extension of our operations in Empire waters.

VICE' ADMIRAL CARNEY:

No single decision contributed more to the Third Fleet's prompt, smooth, and successful adjustment to the radical changes which the surrender imposed.

We were the only military unit at hand with sufficient power to take Japan in custody at short notice and enforce the Allies' will until occupation troops arrived. Accordingly, we had organized a landing force of a regiment of Marines, three naval battalions from TF 38, and a fourth from TF 37. These men, plus a reserve force of five battalions, were fully equipped and had been briefed on their jobs. We had assembled groups of specialists and artificers to operate captured Jap facilities and equipment, and to establish temporary shore facilities of our own. We were prepared even to occupy and develop the naval base and air station at Yokosuka, to man enemy vessels with nucleus crews, to demilitarize enemy installations, to drop supplies at POW camps, and to rescue and evacuate the prisoners.

Such tasks as these are not normally expected of a striking force at sea, but they represented—as we learned next morning—only a fraction of the extraneous duties that we would have to assume. Our dispatch boards had doubled in thickness overnight. The queries and instructions pouring in on us concerned subjects as diverse as these: military government units, whole blood, amphibious landing craft, postoffice ships, staff cars, interpreters, ammunition for small arms, national anthems, sanitation ashore, refrigerator ships, protocol of official visits, wire recorders, and so on. We still had the full-time job of operating the fleet, but my staff shouldered this new load as well.

Although the avalanche of dispatches indicated official confidence that surrender was probable, there was no suggestion that we belay or even slacken our attacks. We fueled on the eleventh as planned, intending to strike Tokyo early next morning. However, it takes time to set up a strike, and as the deadline approached, a typhoon to the southward was still heading toward us, so I notified Slew McCain to hold his planes until the thirteenth, in case we had to run for fair weather.

A few hours later, shortly after midnight, Mick Carney came to my room with an intercept from the Army News Service: "The American Secretary of State, speaking for the Allied Powers, has accepted the surrender of Japan, provided that the Supreme Allied Commander rule Japan through the authority of the Emperor."

I realized that this report was unofficial, but I was reluctant to attack an enemy whose surrender was actual though not yet ratified; and certainly I was more than reluctant to risk my airmen's lives under such circumstances. But *had* Japan surrendered? That "provided" puzzled me. I called a meeting of my staff to discuss it, and a majority of us finally agreed that the honorable course was to cease fire. My decision was hardly on its way to Slew when Mick, stubborn as always, came to my room with a fresh set of arguments. My armistice was not only premature, he said, but might easily prove to be one-sided; we had never trusted the Japanese before, and this was a hell of a critical time to start.

I was persuaded. I signaled Slew, ATTACK TOKYO AREA TO-MORROW UNLESS THE NIPS BEAT US TO THE PUNCH BY THROWING IN THE SPONGE.

Slew was worried that they would throw in something deadlier than a sponge. He warned his task force, KEEP ALERT FOR TRICKS AND BANZAI ATTACKS X THE WAR IS NOT OVER YET X THE NIPS MAY BE PLAYING THEIR NATIONAL GAME OF JUDO, WAITING UNTIL WE ARE CLOSE AND UNWARY.

The typhoon curved away harmlessly during the twelfth, and we started our run-in to the launching point. By now I was convinced that it would be folly to spare an enemy who considered himself in a position to quibble over terms while he maintained his belligerent status. (Somebody on my staff remarked that we were becoming eligible for a Japanese de-Liberation ribbon.) Moreover, the prolonged negotiations were raising another dilemma. We were now in our forty-third consecutive day at sea; our stores were running short; our galleys were reduced to serving dehydrated carrot salad. If the war was over, we could reprovision on the spot; if it was not, we would have to retire, reprovision, and return. Until the diplomats made up their minds, we were restricted to short-range plans. Even these took a manhandling. At 0100 on the thirteenth, I received a dispatch from CINCPAC ordering me to cancel the strike and proceed to the Tokyo area "with caution."

I passed the word to the task force at once, adding, SITUATION NOT CLEAR BUT MAY DEVELOP RAPIDLY X MEANWHILE MAINTAIN STRONG DEFENSIVE CAP; and later, I WILL ORDER IMMEDIATE ATTACK IF ENEMY SEARCHES OR SNOOPS.

Almost as this message went out, I received a second dispatch from CINCPAC, voiding the first. I signaled the task force, FOLLOW ORIGINAL SCHEDULE OF STRIKES. Within an hour, the strike was

269

taking off for Tokyo. Within a few hours more, TF 38 had weakened Japan's air power by 422 planes—254 destroyed on the ground, 149 damaged, and nineteen shot down near the force by our CAP. Ten of these nineteen were probably snoopers; the others were unquestionably *kamikazes*. Japan might have surrendered, but a good many Japanese had not been given the word.

(I have credited our magnificent score for the thirteenth to TF 38 alone, but this does not mean that the British had no part in it. They had a strong part, as usual. The explanation is that about half of TF 37 had withdrawn to Manus on the twelfth, for repair availability, and the rest had been incorporated into TF 38 as TG 38.5.)

The fourteenth was a fueling day. Our communicators' earphones stayed hot, but nothing more about the surrender came through. I told Slew, I INTEND STRIKING SAME GENERAL TARGET AREA ON FIFTEENTH, and Slew told his task force, OUR ORDERS TO STRIKE INDICATE THAT THE ENEMY MAY HAVE DROPPED AN UNACCEPTABLE JOKER INTO THE SURRENDER TERMS X THIS WAR COULD LAST MANY MONTHS LONGER X WE CANNOT AFFORD TO RELAX X NOW IS THE TIME TO POUR IT ON X SHOW THIS TO ALL PILOTS.

Mick was as exasperated as Slew. That night he wrote in his order book, "Peace be damned! Back to Tokyo tomorrow!"

Our first strike next morning, designated "Able 1" and consisting of 103 planes, was launched at 0415. Exactly at 0614—when Able 1 had struck and was returning, when Able 2 had been launched and was within five minutes of the target, and when our flight decks were being respotted for Able 3—I was handed a top-secret, highest priority dispatch from CINCPAC: AIR ATTACK WILL BE SUSPENDED X ACKNOWLEDGE.

I sent a message at once to hold Able 3 and recall Able 2. Some of Able 2's pilots suspected that the order was a Japanese trick. We had to authenticate it twice before they would obey.

A curious coincidence now happened. I have described how, on the morning of December 7, 1941, I was having breakfast on the *Enterprise* when my flag secretary, Doug Moulton, gave me the news that Japan had opened the war. On the morning of August 15, 1945, I was having breakfast on the *Missouri* when Doug, now my Air Operations officer, gave me the news that Japan had ended the war.

He burst in, waving a message blank, and shouted, "Admiral, here she is!"

It was a transcript of President Truman's official announcement.

Japan capitulated so soon after the atomic bomb and Russia's declaration of war that the public may overvalue these two factors. My own estimate of their importance—that they merely gave the Nips an excuse, and helped them save face—received authoritative support from Admiral Soemu Toyoda, Chief of the Japanese Naval General Staff, in a statement recently published by the Naval Analysis Division of the United States Strategic Bombing Survey.

"I do not think it would be accurate to look upon use of the atomic bomb and entry and participation of Soviet Russia into the war as direct cause of the termination of the war, but I think that [they] did enable us to bring the war to a termination without creating too great chaos in Japan."

I hope that history will remember this. I hope it will remember also that when hostilities ended, the capital of the Japanese Empire had just been bombed, strafed, and rocketed by planes of the Third Fleet, and was about to be bombed, strafed, and rocketed again. Last, I hope it will remember that seven of the men on strike Able 1 did not return.

My first thought at the great news was, "Victory!" My second was, "God be thanked, I'll never have to order another man out to die!" And my next was, "I am grateful for the honor of being in command of the Third Fleet on this day."

Then plain joy took over. I yelled, "Yippee!" and pounded the shoulders of everybody within reach. Suddenly Armistice Day, 1918, came back to me. When the news was announced, Admiral Beatty, the Commander in Chief of the British Grand Fleet, sent out this general signal: ALL HANDS SPLICE MAIN BRACE X NEGAT SQUADRON 5. To "splice the main brace" is to take a drink, and "negat"—short for "negative"—here means "except"; Squadron 5, being the American squadron, was dry. I now sent a signal to TF 38: ALL HANDS SPLICE THE MAIN BRACE X NEGAT TASK GROUPS 38.1, 38.3, 38.4—which left only 38.5, the British group.

I can best reconstruct the rest of this morning by quoting from my flag log, with notes:

1020. All strikes have returned.

I ordered the carriers to stow their bombers and torpedo planes on their hangar decks, to spot their flight decks only with fighters, and to maintain an augmented and extravigilant CAP. My trust in the Japs was still less than whole-hearted, and I was taking no chance that a *kamikaze* would seize a last-minute opportunity to win honor for his ancestors. In fact, I had our fighter directors call our CAP pilots by radio and instruct them, "Investigate and shoot down all snoopers—not vindictively, but in a friendly sort of way."

I was told later that one pilot had been overheard to ask, "What do you mean, 'not vindictively'?" And another answered, "I guess they mean for us to use only three guns instead of six."

1055. Received ALPOA 579 [a message to All Pacific Ocean Areas]: OFFENSIVE OPERATIONS AGAINST JAPANESE FORCES WILL CEASE AT ONCE [our first orders had been merely to suspend them] X CONTINUE SEARCHES AND PATROLS X MAINTAIN DEFENSIVE AND INTERNAL SECURITY MEASURES AT HIGHEST LEVEL AND BEWARE OF TREACHERY.

We were already doing so.

1110. Battle flags and Admiral's four-star flag broken on *Missouri*. Whistle and siren sounded for one minute. The fleet followed the motion.
1113. Admiral ordered the flag hoist "Well Done" run up.

I was putting on a little show. Mick and I watched it from the bridge.

1125. One Judy [a Jap dive-bomber]—

The high CAP called in, "Tallyho! One bandit diving!" But almost immediately afterwards, the same voice reported, "Splash one Judy!"

1300. Admiral made a broadcast to the Third Fleet.

In this broadcast, I said, among other things, "Now that the fighting has ended, there must be no letdown. There must be watchful waiting. Victory is not the end, but the beginning. We must establish peace—a firm, a just, and an enduring peace."

Thank God, the fleet took my warning to heart and did not let down! Even as I was speaking, a battle royal raged overhead—

272

1303. CAP splashed one Zeke and one Judy.

1316. CAP splashed one Judy.

1325. One Judy splashed by picket destroyer's gunfire.

Before the day was done, our CAP and AA had shot down eight planes trying to bomb us or dive into us. I was certain at the time that these Japs were irreconcilables, fighting a private war; but when I went ashore and saw the utter ruin of Japan's communications system, I became convinced that they simply had never received the word.

The last of these planes was splashed at 1445. After that minute, the Third Fleet never fired another shot in wrath. We added up its score for its two campaigns. Here it is:

Planes destroyed or damaged.................. 10,355
Warships sunk............................... 130
Warships probably sunk...................... 90
Warships damaged........................... 150
Merchant vessels sunk....................... 1,000

I hope that no nation ever dares challenge this record. But if it does, I hope that the Third Fleet is there to defend it.

EDITOR'S NOTE:

Captain Stassen had the forenoon watch that morning and kept the first part of the flag log which Admiral Halsey has quoted. Captain Stassen's last entry, before he was relieved at 1145, is as follows:

"So closes the watch we have been looking forward to. Unconditional surrender of Japan—with Admiral Halsey at sea in command of the greatest combined fighting fleet of all history. There is a gleam in his eye that is unmistakable!   —H. E. Stassen."

☆ 16 ☆

A N OLD NAVY precept runs, "Put down the sword and take up
the paintbrush." The Third Fleet's cheers at the news of
Japan's surrender had hardly died away when I ordered
all ships to turn to and spruce up. I was mindful of our morale as
much as of our appearance. The sudden change from war to peace
can be dangerous at sea; men accustomed to ceaseless vigilance and
strenuous duties can become flaccid instead of relaxed, if abruptly
left idle. General MacArthur, the newly appointed Supreme
Commander for the Allied Powers in the Pacific, desired all forces
and all services to make simultaneous landings on Japan, and since
the Army troops in the Philippines could not be transported in less
than ten days, we had that much free time ahead.

Aboard the *Missouri*, which had been designated as the scene
of the surrender ceremony—she was named for President Truman's
native state, of course, and had been christened by his daughter—
holystones began to scour through the gray battle paint to the white
teak decks beneath; brass also emerged from its dull coat; slip-
covers were broken out for our chairs and transoms; and when the
fleet entered Sagami Bay, at the mouth of Tokyo Bay, we were
smart and shining.

Meanwhile, my staff's preparations went forward. The landing
force was put aboard transports. We started a series of reconnaissance flights over Japan to locate the prisoner of war camps and to
drop food and medicine. Our task groups massed for an aerial
photograph—EXERCISE SNAPSHOT, then our planes had
their turn—EXERCISE TINTYPE. We organized a special task

force to furnish fire support during the occupation, if needed. Signatories came aboard for conferences: my old friend from the South Pacific, Air Vice Marshal Leonard Isitt, of the Royal New Zealand Air Force, who would sign for New Zealand; and Adm. Sir Bruce Fraser, Commander in Chief of the British Pacific Fleet, who would sign for the United Kingdom.

Every man jack among us was looking toward one moment, the moment we would anchor in Tokyo Bay. Our first anchoring in Japanese waters, at Sagami Bay, would be an appetizer. Mac-Arthur had set this for August 26, but two typhoons formed to the southward, and he postponed it for forty-eight hours on behalf of his air-borne troops. Many of my ships were small—patrol craft, subchasers, and the like; and even if they had not been crowded and short of stores, I would have been reluctant to keep them at sea in typhoon weather, so I requested and received his permission to put in on the twenty-seventh.

We raised the coast at dawn that morning. The Japanese Navy had been ordered to send us an escort through the mine fields, and to deliver officers empowered to arrange the surrender of the Yokosuka Base. When the escort came into view, we identified her as the destroyer *Hatsuzakura*. As stipulated, her guns were depressed, their breeches open, her torpedo tubes empty, and no crew was topside except enough men to handle a small boat. Mick Carney and I watched her from the *Missouri's* flag bridge. She was so frail, so woebegone, so dirty, that I felt ashamed of our having needed four years to win the war.

Mick pointed toward her. "You wanted the Jap Navy, Admiral. Well, there it is."

The fourteen emissaries were first put aboard the destroyer *Nicholas* for "processing." Not until their side arms had been confiscated and they had been made to bathe and undergo a medical examination, did we distribute them around the Fleet. Two captains and an ensign interpreter were then transferred to the *Missouri*. Here they were searched again, photographed, and marched under guard to Captain Murray's cabin, where the conference was to be held.

Our attitude may sound like a petty attempt to humiliate a beaten enemy, but it was not. It was part of a policy which grim

275

experience had taught us. We would not have omitted our precautions any more than we would have allowed the *Hatsuzakura* to approach us without our crews at quarters, our guns manned, and our planes overhead, ready to go into action at an inkling.

Mick presided over the conference, assisted by Oscar Badger, commanding our landing force. Also present were our Japanese language officer, Comdr. Gilven M. Slonim (known as "Tokyo Mose"), and several other officers of my staff. I did not attend, so I have asked Mick to describe what occurred.

VICE ADMIRAL CARNEY:

Captain Otani, representing Naval Headquarters, was a caricature of a treacherous Japanese brute. Captain Takasaki, representing the Yokosuka Command, was also a caricature, but of Bugs Bunny; I half expected him to greet me with, "Hiya, Doc!" The young ensign spoke cultured English with an American accent. Gil Slonim told me later that he may have belonged to the Imperial family, because his manner of address to the two captains was curt and condescending.

It took only a few minutes for us to obtain the information we needed and for Oscar Badger to issue his instructions, but during that time two incidents happened which may be worth mention. The first was when Otani lit a cigarette while my attention was elsewhere. As soon as I saw it, I took it away from him and told him firmly that he was not permitted to smoke in our presence. The second was when Otani requested the return of his side arms, as a requisite part of his uniform. I made it quite plain to him that we were prescribing his uniform from now on, and that side arms were not included in our prescription.

EDITOR'S NOTE:

Following are two paragraphs from orders which Admiral Carney issued to the staff at this time:

"8. With reference to the Japanese, an attitude of cold, impersonal formality will be maintained at all times; they are required to obey the orders of the forces of occupation, and such obedience will be demanded and enforced; but every effort shall be bent toward the avoidance of conduct not in keeping with the prestige of our traditions. . . .

"10. And finally, it must be remembered that these are the same Japanese whose treachery, cruelty, and subtlety brought about this war; we must be continually vigilant for overt treachery, and equally vigilant that we not become blinded by outward subservience and docility. They are always dangerous. . . . "

276

By late afternoon the whole fleet was at anchor in Sagami Bay, in full view of beautiful Kamakura, the Japanese Riviera, where the Summer Palace stands. We also had a view of Fujiyama. Its peak is usually cloud-capped, I am told, but that evening was clear, and the sun seemed to sink directly into the crater. Although the symbolism was strongly suggestive, we did not rely on it to the extent of not stationing picket boats and destroyers on the perimeter of our anchorage, nor did we light the ships. We were still being prudent. We had assigned targets to the heavy ships before we stood in, and our guns were not only loaded but trained. Moreover, we had left all but one of our carriers outside, in open water.

My apprehension lessened next day. We lighted ship at dusk and showed movies on the weather decks. (The staff officer who had the dogwatch wrote in the flag log, "At sunset, 1815/I [Tokyo time], all ships turned on anchor lights—'The lights came on again in Sagami Wan.'" [*Wan* is Japanese for *bay*.]) But we were at general quarters when we steamed into Tokyo Bay on the twenty-ninth—the supreme moment of my career—and it wasn't until September 3 that we began to stand at ease. Even then we still posted lookouts, our radars continued to search, and our ships maintained their high state of watertight integrity.

EDITOR'S NOTE:

Admiral Halsey's caution was justified, according to an Associated Press story in *The New York Times* for August 18, 1946, which says in part, "[An Army] report on the psychological warfare campaign against Japan . . . discloses that several hundred Kamikaze pilots plotted a mass suicide attack on the battleship *Missouri* in Tokyo Bay."

The story does not explain why the attack was canceled.

Meanwhile, on the twenty-eighth, elements of the Army's 11th Air-borne Division had started landing at Atsugi Airfield, near Tokyo. Navy ships had guarded their line of flight from Okinawa, and as they deplaned, I am told that the first sight to catch their eyes was a large sign, "Welcome to the U.S. Army from the Third Fleet." A brash young pilot from the *Yorktown* had dropped into Atsugi, wholly against orders, and had made the Japs paint it and post it.

MacArthur had directed us not to begin recovering POW's until the Army was ready to do so, but—as with the landings—circumstances forced us to jump the gun. Our first night at anchor in Sagami Wan, a picket boat patrolling close inshore heard a yell from the beach and picked up two British prisoners, whom it delivered to Commo. Rodger W. Simpson, commanding the rescue operation. The Britishers told Rodger a tale of such inhumanity as we found almost impossible to believe, until it was corroborated the following day by a Swiss doctor, representing the International Red Cross. Listening to these men convinced us that now was no time to defer to protocol. I ordered Rodger to take his task group, which included the hospital ship *Benevolence*, up to Tokyo and to stand by for a sudden signal. Chester Nimitz' plane arrived from Guam at 1420 on the twenty-ninth, and he had no sooner broken his flag on the *South Dakota* than I was explaining the urgency of the situation.

"Go ahead," Chester said. "General MacArthur will understand."

Rodger went ashore immediately with his rescue detail, which included Harold Stassen, whom I had lent him as his chief staff officer, and Commo. Joel T. Boone, who had relieved Piggy Weeks as my medical officer. Planes from the fleet guided their small boats up estuaries leading to the prison camps. One was the infamous Omori 8, whose commandant made a show of demanding credentials.

"I have no authority to release these men," he said.

Harold, unarmed as was the rest of the party, told him, "You have no authority, period!"

CAPTAIN STASSEN:

Our plan for OPERATION SWIFT MERCY was first presented to the Admiral before the capitulation was confirmed. He read it over, approved it, and returned it with this comment, "Those are our boys! Go get them!"

His directive echoed in my mind throughout the days of the actual operation. Whenever a camp commandant refused to admit us, as at Omori 8, we told him, "We are under Admiral Halsey's orders, and those are the only orders that count in Japan now!"

His name was an immediate open-sesame wherever we went. As soon as our interpreters spoke it, all resistance crumbled, and we walked straight in. I will never forget a certain bluejacket prisoner at the Kawasaki

Bunsha camp, when he learned who had sent us. His haggard face lit up. "I knew it!" he shouted. "I told these Jap bastards that Admiral Halsey would be here after us!"

There can be no question but that his decision to fetch out these men at once and give them medical treatment saved countless hundreds of lives.

At 1910 that evening, the first POW's, or RAMP's (Rescued Allied Military Prisoners) as they were now designated, were put aboard the *Benevolence;* by midnight, 794 had been brought out; and within fourteen days, every one of 19,000 Allied prisoners in our area, the eastern two-thirds of Honshu, had been liberated, docketed, bathed, examined, and either hospitalized or sent off for a quiet, comfortable convalescence.

The unspeakable brutality which they had endured at the hands of the Japanese Army—the Navy disclaims any connection with the camps—has been amply described by correspondents; besides, I still can not discuss the subject temperately. But before I leave it, I want to set down the only happy association that it has for me. Rodger Simpson's splendid record in the South Pacific included a daring destroyer raid on Simpson Harbor, at Rabaul; so, in answer to a query of his in Tokyo Bay, we replied, "Roger to Rodger Simpson of Simpson Harbor. If it had not been for that Rodger in Simpson Harbor, we might have been delayed in sending roger to Rodger Simpson in this harbor."

H Hour for our landing forces was 1000 on the thirtieth. Spearheaded by the 4th Marine Regimental Combat Team, British bluejackets occupied Azuma peninsula, U.S. Marines occupied Yokosuka Air Base, and U.S. bluejackets occupied Yokosuka Naval Base. The Japanese seemed anxious to avoid friction, and we met no opposition at any point. Mick Carney, as my representative, accepted custody of Yokosuka from Vice Adm. Michitare Totsuka at 1030; headquarters of the Third Fleet and of the landing force were established there at 1045, and my flag was raised over the station. (Chester Nimitz gave me hell for breaking my flag ashore in the presence of a senior officer and ordered me to haul it down; all the same, it is the first United States admiral's flag to fly over Imperial Japanese territory!)

Another flag incident had occurred earlier that morning, when

279

one of our nucleus crews boarded the battleship *Nagato*, and the American commanding officer directed her captain to haul down his colors. The captain tried to delegate the job to a bluejacket, but the American told him, "No. Haul them down yourself!"

This flag, along with the Japanese flag that had flown over Yokosuka, I presented to the Naval Academy Museum at Annapolis. A third Jap flag, from the old battleship *Mikasa*, I passed along to Ernie King, with a request that he present it to the Russians, since the *Mikasa* had been Togo's flagship at the Battle of Tsushima Straits.

I visited Yokosuka that afternoon. Despite the Japs' reputation for cleanliness and the fact that one of the surrender terms stipulated that "on delivery to the Allies, all facilities will be cleared of debris, scrupulously clean, and in full operating condition," the filth that I saw was appalling. The officers' club, which had been evacuated only a few hours before, was overrun with rats of an extraordinary size and character. They ignored our presence in some rooms but squeaked angrily when we entered others. They probably had a special membership which reserved certain parts of the club for themselves alone.

The civilians were also dirty. Worse, they were apathetic; I was told that their principal employment was walking up the streets on odd days and down on even. We found occasional evidence of malnutrition in urban areas, but the country folk looked well fed. I had heard from many sources that the average Jap considered me his personal archenemy, so I watched for signs of hatred. There were none. I was never accosted, and I doubt if I was ever recognized.

The only recalcitrance we met was on the part of the civil police. Possibly because we had allowed them to keep their side arms as a badge of authority, they gradually arrogated the additional privilege of not saluting Allied officers. This annoyed me. I directed Scrappy Kessing, whom I had appointed COMNAVBASE Yokosuka, to pass the word to the mayor that his police were to salute all Allied officers without exception, and that this order would be rigidly enforced.

The mayor protested, "How will they know who is an officer and who is not?"

Scrappy told him, "If they don't know, they'd better play safe by saluting every foreign uniform."

Now I come to our focal day, September 2, the day of the formal surrender. Supervised by Captain Murray, Bill Kitchell had worked like a Hong Kong coolie to organize the ceremony. He rehearsed every step of it, provided for every nuance of etiquette, and smoothed away even the possibility of a bobble. The result was the best job of its sort I have ever seen. No court chamberlain could have improved it.

The first guests, correspondents and photographers, arrived at 0710. Next came Navy representatives, then Army and foreign representatives, then Chester Nimitz and his staff, then General MacArthur and his party, and finally the Japanese envoys. Since Chester was SOPA (Senior Officer Present Afloat), I had shifted my personal flag to the *Iowa* near by; Chester's five stars were broken at the *Missouri's* aftermast, and as General MacArthur stepped aboard, his own flag was broken alongside.

The sight they made together was unique, but on the *Missouri* that morning was one flag that outshone them both. Washington had sent it by special messenger—the flag that Commodore Perry had flown in 1854 at almost our identical anchorage.

The destroyer bringing the Army men had not yet moored to us when old friends began calling back and forth. I shouted to Nate Twining, whom I was seeing for the first time since he had been my COMAIRSOLS, but when I spied Skinny Wainwright, whom I hadn't seen since War College in 1933, I could not trust my voice; I just leaned over the rail and grabbed his hand.

Chester and I were at the side to meet General MacArthur. As always, his manner to me and my staff was heart-warming. He greeted us by our nicknames and he remarked to Mick Carney, "It's grand having so many of my side-kicks from the shoestring SOPAC days meeting me here at the end of the road!"

Bill Kitchell escorted him to my cabin, with Chester following and me bringing up the rear. I imagine that history was fairly begging for something quotable from our conversation, or at least something dignified and sonorous, but what we actually said was this:

Halsey: "General, will you and Chester have a cup of coffee?"

MacArthur: "No, thanks, Bill. I'll wait till afterwards."

Nimitz: "So will I, Bill. Thanks all the same."

I had just added, "God, what a great day this is! We've fought a long, long time for it," when Bill Kitchell notified us that the Jap envoys were aboard. I had sent a signal to the destroyer fetching them that she was not to offer coffee, cigarettes, or any other courtesies, but I had been directed to revoke it.

A table with the two sets of surrender documents stood on the starboard veranda deck, almost in the shadow of No. 2 turret. MacArthur and Nimitz took their places behind it, and I joined the line of Navy officers. The ceremony opened with a short address by MacArthur, beautifully phrased and forcefully read. His voice was clear and firm, but his hands shook with emotion. When he had finished, he pointed to a chair at the opposite side of the table and almost spat out, "The representatives of the Imperial Japanese Government and of the Imperial Japanese Staff will now come forward and sign!"

(My flag log records it thus: "0903. Jap envoys were asked to sign. They did.")

The Foreign Minister, Mamoru Shigemitsu, who was to sign for the Emperor, limped toward the table, leaning on a cane. He had lost his left leg to a grenade thrown by a Korean in Shanghai; Nomura, later Ambassador to Washington, lost an eye at the same time. (I have been told that Hirohito presented Shigemitsu with an artificial leg which he has therefore had to wear ever since, although it doesn't fit.) He took off his gloves and silk hat, sat down, dropped his cane, picked it up, fiddled with his hat and gloves, and shuffled the papers. He pretended to be looking for a pen—an underling finally brought him one—but I felt certain that he was stalling for time, though God knows what he hoped to accomplish. His performance made me so mad that when we returned to my cabin after the ceremony, I told MacArthur, "General, you nearly had a contretemps this morning."

"How's that?" he asked.

"When Shigemitsu was stalling out there, I wanted to slap him and tell him, 'Sign, damn you! Sign!'"

MacArthur said, "Why didn't you?"

The second Jap, Gen. Yoshijiro Umezu, who was to sign for the

Imperial General Staff, did his job briskly; he didn't even sit down for it.

MacArthur was next, as Supreme Commander for the Allied Powers, then came their various representatives, led by Chester. His war plans officer, Rear Adm. Forrest P. Sherman, and I were invited to stand behind his chair while he signed. Newsreels show MacArthur putting his arm around my shoulders at this moment and whispering to me, and many of my friends have asked what he was saying. Again we fell short of the solemn occasion. MacArthur said, "Start 'em now!"

I said, "Aye, aye, sir!"

He was referring to a mass flight of 450 planes from TF 38, which we had ordered to orbit at a distance until we gave the word. We passed it to them now, and they roared over the *Missouri* mast-high.

Col. L. V. Moore Cosgrave, representing Canada, signed one line too low, so Len Isitt's signature was pushed down to the bottom of the page. He told me afterwards that he was "an humble footnote to the document."

The ceremony was finished by 0925, and all the Allied representatives came to my cabin. If ever a day demanded champagne, this was it, but I could serve them only coffee and doughnuts. I had a long talk with Skinny Wainwright and chatted, through interpreters, with Gen. Hsu Yung-Chang of China and Lt. Gen. Kuzma Derevyanko of Russia. General Hsu remarked that he was glad to see me alive, because the Japs had often reported me killed. General Derevyanko was more interested in the mass flight.

I was surprised to notice an aviation rating in the assembly until someone reminded me that a number of RAMP's had been asked to come. This one was an exceptionally husky lad, so Mick Carney remarked, "You look as if you could step into the ring and win the welterweight championship of the fleet. How did you manage to keep in such good shape in a prison camp?"

The lad grinned. "Sir, they had me working in the railroad yards that all their food passes through. Those bastards were lucky to get anything to eat at all!"

When the party broke up, Slew McCain lingered a few minutes. Since early August, he had been under orders to be relieved as

CTF 38 by Vice Adm. John H. Towers, the relief to take place when we put into Eniwetok. These orders made Slew thoroughly sore; he considered it an insult to be removed from his command in the middle of a campaign, and as soon as we received official news of Japan's capitulation, he requested immediate detachment. "I don't give a damn about seeing the surrender," he said angrily, "I want to get the hell out of here!"

I told him, "Maybe you do, but you're not going. You were commanding this task force when the war ended, and I'm making sure that history gets it straight!"

He returned to his flagship cursing and sputtering, but now he told me, "Thank God you made me stay, Bill! You had better sense than I did."

He left for home that night. Four days later he was dead of a heart attack. I want to quote my last dispatch to him as a memorial tribute: I HAVE GIVEN YOU WELL DONE SO MANY TIMES FOR INDIVIDUAL ACHIEVEMENTS THAT THIS FINE TRADITIONAL NAVY EXPRESSION OF APPROVAL IS INADEQUATE TO EXPRESS MY FEELING FOR THE SUM TOTAL OF YOUR CONTRIBUTION TO VICTORY X YOUR RESOURCEFULNESS, INGENUITY, STAMINA, AND FIGHTING SPIRIT HAVE BEEN SUPERB X INADEQUATE THOUGH IT MAY BE, I GIVE YOU ONE MORE ROUSING FAREWELL, WELL DONE X HALSEY.

Slew's own last dispatch to his command is characteristic of his regard for his men: I AM GLAD AND PROUD TO HAVE FOUGHT THROUGH MY LAST YEAR OF ACTIVE SERVICE WITH THE RENOWNED FAST CARRIERS X WAR AND VICTORY HAVE FORGED A LASTING BOND AMONG US X IF YOU ARE AS FORTUNATE IN PEACE AS YOU HAVE BEEN VICTORIOUS IN WAR, I AM NOW TALKING TO 110,000 PROSPECTIVE MILLIONAIRES X GOODBYE, GOOD LUCK, AND MAY GOD BE WITH YOU X MCCAIN.

It grieves me bitterly to realize that this great friend and fighting man is gone. I will never forget anything about him—his curses, his jumping-jack behavior, the leaky cigarettes he rolled, scattering tobacco all over the deck. Once I arranged for a steward's mate to follow him around with a brush and dustpan.

"What the hell's *this* for?" Slew demanded.

I told him, "So you won't dirty up my clean ship, that's what!"

Most vividly of all will I remember his cap, which not only was an affront to Navy regulations, but was the most disreputable one I ever saw on an officer. It was a green drab fatigue cap to which he had had his wife sew a "scrambled eggs" visor. Each part was bad enough by itself—the crown was threadbare, and the visor was crusted with verdigris—but together they were revolting. Yet Slew was as proud as if it were a royal diadem. Like most sailormen, he was extremely superstitious, and this was his "combat hat." He never wore it outside the combat zone; in the zone he was never without it.

When I visited Amon Carter at Fort Worth, he asked me to give him a cap of mine for his collection. There is nothing notable about my caps except their size, which is monstrous, but any collector who obtains that cap of Slew's will have something unique in naval costume.

Mention of Slew reminds me of another friend and fighting man whom I was soon to lose: Ping Wilkinson. I had seen him last at Peleliu almost exactly a year before. Now his famous Third Amphibious Force was bringing the 1st Cavalry Division to Yokohama. In fact, even as Shigemitsu was signing, Ping's flagship steamed past at the head of his transports. I had sentimentally given him his old SOPAC designation, CTF 32, and had urged him to attend the surrender; his fine face belonged at the ceremony to which he had contributed so much. But duty came first with him as always, and he refused to take time out until he had disembarked the troops. The following February, at Norfolk, Virginia, Ping's automobile plunged overboard from a ferry. He succeeded in freeing his wife, but he himself was drowned. His death was a blow to me and a loss to the whole Navy.

Even as I write this farewell to Slew and Ping, word comes that the fourth of my great task force commanders is dead: Pete Mitscher. All four were supreme in their lines, and I say it in full awareness that Pete's line and Slew's were the same: commanding the fast carriers. Not only was there nothing to choose between them as strategists and leaders, but their resemblance went far beyond their equal abilities. Both were small, brown, and wizened. Both had tremendous fighting hearts. Both were beloved by the men who served under them. Both were high-strung to tension hardly endurable. Almost their only difference was that where Slew blew off his pressure in curses and fidgets, Pete kept it bottled up inside. He never lost his temper and never raised his voice, but when he spoke, everybody listened. I would give much if I could hear him speak again.

Chester returned to Guam on September 3. Before he shoved off, he told me that a big celebration was being planned for Navy Day, October 27, in the principal ports of both coasts of the United States and that ships were to be detached and sent back as quickly as possible. I was to stay at Tokyo until September 20, when Ray Spruance would relieve me in command of the remaining forces; these would then become the Fifth Fleet, and the designation Third Fleet would be transferred to the ships proceeding to the West Coast ports in my charge. The *Missouri* would not be among them, Chester said; she was destined for New York, so that President Truman could broadcast his Navy Day speech from her bridge. I was disappointed not to be going home on my flagship, but I had no choice. I shifted my flag to the *South Dakota* and sat down to wait for my relief.

We continued to demilitarize enemy installations, to rescue and evacuate prisoners, and to arrange the quick return and discharge of men with sufficient points, but all this my staff handled. I had nothing to do, no decisions to make, and time would have dragged if I hadn't been able to get ashore for sight-seeing trips and reunions with my Army friends.

General MacArthur courteously invited me to accompany him to the formal occupation of Tokyo on September 8. We drove in together from his temporary headquarters at Yokohama, so I had a good view of the two cities. What impressed me most about the devastated areas, besides their vast extent, was the presence of iron and steel safes among the ruins; dozens and dozens of them stuck up from the ashes in every block. MacArthur told me that an edict had been issued, months before, requiring all safes to be turned in for conversion to war purposes, and when the B-29's' incendiary raids laid them bare, Tojo had felt so humiliated by the people's noncompliance that he apologized to the Emperor.

The American Embassy was intact, but the Chancellery had

taken three bombs and had suffered slightly. MacArthur pointed to it and nudged me. "Your fliers did that, didn't they, Bill?"

The Third Fleet didn't want credit for this trivial damage. "No, sir," I said. "Not my boys. Barney Giles is responsible." The B-29's based at Guam had been part of Lieutenant General Giles' command.

Later we drove past the Imperial General Headquarters, which had been bombed almost flat. "But my boys did *that*," I said.

The next time I saw General MacArthur, I called on him to protest against his order forbidding confiscation of Jap officers' swords. I considered this order unwise for two reasons. The first was that the sword was a universal symbol of militarism and tended to keep its spirit alive. When I was in Germany shortly after World War I, I visited a great many German homes; in almost every one I saw a bust of Napoleon on the mantel with a sword reverently hung above it. What Germany's militarism has cost us is sadly obvious.

"That's true," the General said, "but I was thinking of Appomattox, when Grant allowed Lee's troops to keep their side arms."

I said, "That brings me to my second point. Grant was dealing with an honorable foe. We are not."

MacArthur paced his office for a few moments, then said, "You're right! You're right! I'll revoke the order." And he did.

My most interesting day ashore I owe to Lt. Gen Robert L. Eichelberger, commanding the Eighth Army. Bob had invited me to make a tour of the Yokohama jail, where the war criminals were in custody, and had given me permission to bring along my Filipino steward, Tulao. One of the first cells we visited held the notorious Colonel Weissinger, the former "Butcher of Warsaw," who had later become chief of the German Gestapo in Japan. Everybody is familiar with the phrase "arrant coward"; Weissinger is the only one I ever saw. He had lost all control; his huge frame was shaking with fright, and we could hardly understand him for his blubbering.

Bob asked, "Well, Colonel, how are things going with you?"

Weissinger moaned, "Awful, General! Simply awful! I can't sleep or eat, I can't rest, I can't sit still, I'm so nervous!"

287

"Cheer up!" Bob said pleasantly. "Things will get much worse before they're better!"

Next we stopped to see Bob's fine collection of quislings—the former President of the Phillippines, Laurel, and his son; the former Philippine Ambassador to Japan, Vargas; two Burmese, a Dutchman, and others. Young Laurel, an officer on the staff of an American general when war broke out, had deserted to the enemy, taking along an assortment of secret orders and operation plans. He had been educated at a Japanese university, but his father did not have even this slight mitigation; he was a graduate of Yale. His classmates should have seen him—no shirt, no socks, and filthy shoes, trousers, and undershirt.

Vargas, on the contrary, was wearing a neat khaki suit and khaki tie. He talked volubly about his "many acquaintances" in the American Army. When he began to run down, I brought Tulao forward and told them, "I want you to see what a loyal fighting Filipino looks like. This man was on the destroyer *Porter* when she was torpedoed by your friends the Japanese, and many of his relatives have been tortured or killed by those same friends of yours. His name is Benedicto Tulao, and he's a damn fine man. Take a good look at him!"

They looked, but they said nothing. Tulao just glared. The prison captain remarked loudly, so that the quislings could hear, "If the regulations would let me, Tulao, I'd certainly love to give you three hours here by yourself!"

Incidentally, several of the American guards were of Polish descent, and I rather imagine that the Butcher of Warsaw dreaded the long, dark nights.

The most pathetic prisoner was an American sergeant. His story, which he told us in the voice of an educated man, was that he had been a novice in Buddhism before the war. After he was captured—I don't remember where—he declared his religion to the Japanese and eventually agreed to broadcast for them. At the time, he said, he sincerely believed that he was moved only by his Buddhistic desire for international peace, and it wasn't until after being taken into our custody that he realized what a crime he had committed against his native land. He assured us that he was not telling us this in any hope of clemency; he simply wanted to unburden himself, the poor devil!

Another renegade American was also there, a civilian captured at Wake Island. I have forgotten the details of his treachery, but I recall that he was said to be defiant and to have no sense of guilt. He looked at us curiously as we passed the exercise pen, then resumed his furious pacing.

As we left the prison, the captain of the guard showed Bob a Jap who had been freshly delivered—a small, fat, nasty little colonel. Bob talked with him through an interpreter and called me over. "The colonel here was with General Homma during the occupation of the Philippines."

I said, "So? Was he staff or with combat troops?"

When the interpreter asked him, the colonel hesitated to answer. Finally he admitted that he had been Homma's provost marshal general. He might as well have admitted that he had personally given Skinny Wainwright the "water cure," because a provost marshal general is charged with maintaining discipline, and all prisoners come under his direct command. What happened to Americans captured in the Philippines can be laid at the door of this same swine. If he hasn't been hung already, I would be glad to hold the other end of the rope.

My last tour of Tokyo was at the invitation of Maj. Gen. William C. Chase, commanding the 1st Cavalry Division. His message had merely mentioned lunch, so I was taken aback when he met me in a tin helmet and whisked me out to his camp in a car escorted by MP's and four tanks. In my innocence, I thought that all this martial display was for the benefit of the Japs, who can understand force if nothing else. My childlike trust took no alarm even when my host asked me to inspect his troops—as magnificent a body of men as ever I've seen. But presently the ugly trap was sprung: they led out the White Horse.

Someone has said, "Like poor relations, public relations is always with us." When I had been in Washington the preceding spring, the Public Relations section of the Navy Department dragooned me into giving an interview, and among the questions asked me was, "Is the Mikado's palace a military objective?"

I replied, "No. If by chance the B-29's or somebody came over there in an undercast, they might hit it by mistake, but it would have been a mistake." Instead of letting well enough alone, I added with thoughtless flippancy, "I'd hate to have them kill Hirohito's white horse, because I want to ride it."

The White Horse promptly jumped into the headlines, and soon I found myself connected with it as inseparably as if I were a centaur. The Chamber of Commerce of Reno sent me a beautiful saddle. The Lions Club of Montrose, Colorado, sent another, with a bridle, blanket, and lariat, and offered to ship me a mustang if the Imperial horse proved unavailable. The Military Order of the World Wars sent a toy horse. A Texas sheriff sent a pair of spurs. My cabin on the *Missouri* began to look like a tack room.

Now, seven months later, my sin was catching up with me. There was I, and there was a white horse—not *the* white horse, but a reasonable facsimile. I was relieved to see that, far from being a fiery stallion, he was old and sway-backed (a tiny spark of mercy burned in Bill Chase's black soul), so I managed to climb aboard. The horse had only two speeds, *very slow ahead* and *stop*, and he was as glad as I when our short cruise was over. However, it lasted long enough for me to conceive an ambition: I want to take Bill across the North Sea on a destroyer in midwinter.

My war diary for September 19 says, "At 1500/Z [Greenwich time, or Tokyo midnight] Com Fifth Fleet relieved Com Third Fleet of all tasks and responsibilities for naval operations in Empire waters," and next day, "At 0630/I [Tokyo time] Admiral Halsey departed by air for Pearl Harbor."

I had already paid my respects to General MacArthur, whose farewell words I shall always treasure: "When you leave the Pacific, Bill, it becomes just another damned ocean!" Now he sent me a dispatch that I treasure even more: PERSONAL FOR HALSEY X YOUR DEPARTURE LEAVES ALL YOUR OLD COMRADES OF THE PACIFIC WAR LONESOME INDEED X YOU CARRY WITH YOU THE ADMIRATION AND AFFECTION OF EVERY OFFICER AND MAN X MAY YOUR SHADOW NEVER DECREASE.

At Pearl, we formed TF 30 and sortied for the West Coast on the morning of October 9. After a parade past Diamond Head, the task groups separated and proceeded independently to their various

290

ports. TG 30.2, which included my flagship, the *South Dakota*, was assigned to San Francisco. I quote from my war diary for the fifteenth.

TG 30.2 in full parade dress entered San Francisco Bay. The *South Dakota* passed under the Golden Gate Bridge at 1300. Following in column were the [submarines] *Puffer, Baya, Kraken, Loggerhead, Pilotfish, Stickleback,* [the destroyers] *Dehaven, Samuel N. Moore, Blue,* [the light cruiser] *Vicksburg,* [and the battleships] *Alabama, Wisconsin, Colorado.* The *South Dakota,* with Governor Warren, Mayor Lapham, and Admiral [Royal E.] Ingersoll embarked, left formation to anchor in position to review the remainder of the column, then proceeded in to anchorage assigned.

I was home again.

Not for weeks did I learn that Chester Nimitz was only 50 miles away that afternoon. When friends asked him why he didn't come into town for the celebration, he told them, "Bill Halsey has done such wonderful work in the Pacific, the day ought to be his exclusively."

For generosity of spirit, I give you Fleet Admiral Nimitz!

Two days later the Department sent me out on a five weeks' speaking tour, but just as I was raising a bellow of complaint, I was gagged with a sugarplum—a Gold Star in lieu of a fourth Distinguished Service Medal.

EDITOR'S NOTE:

The citation follows in condensed form:

"For exceptionally meritorious service . . . in a duty of great responsibility as Commander Third Fleet, operating in waters off the Ryukyus and Japan from May 28 to September 2, 1945. Returning to the helm of the Third Fleet . . . Admiral Halsey placed in action the greatest mass of sea power ever assembled and initiated attacks on the enemy's naval and air forces, shipping, shipyards and coastal objectives. . . . In operations conducted with brilliant military precision and characteristic aggressiveness, [his] ships and planes . . . bombarded Okinawa, Okino Daito, and Minami Daito in the Ryukyus; they blasted every industry and resource which enabled Japan to make war; gallantly riding out the perilous typhoon of June 5, they effected repairs and went in to knock out remnants of the once mighty Japanese Fleet hiding in camouflage nets. . . . His professional skill and inspiring devotion to the fulfillment of a mission vital to lasting peace reflect the highest credit upon Admiral Halsey and the United States Naval Service."

I returned to my flagship at Long Beach on November 20. The last entry in the last war diary I will ever keep appears under the twenty-second: "Admiral W. F. Halsey, USN, relieved this date by Rear Adm. H. F. Kingman, USN, as Commander Third Fleet."

Before I left Tokyo, I had requested retirement as soon as I was relieved of command. Chester Nimitz gave my application a damn nice endorsement, and Ernie King put on one as complimentary as he ever puts on anything; but instead of being released, I was given another sugarplum—promotion to fleet admiral—and kept on active duty until April 1, 1947. Now, at long last, my story is done. I have nothing more to add except to repeat what I told the *South Dakota's* company as my flag was being hauled down for the last time:

"I am terminating a seagoing career of slightly over 45 years. This is far from a pleasure, but I deem it necessary for men of my age to step aside so that younger men can take over the greatest Navy in the world. . . .

"You have heard the nation say, 'Well done!' I say it again and again: 'Well done! Well done! Well done!' May you all have happy careers! Godspeed and God bless you!"

Index

293

294

295

299

Melville, destroyer, 27, 36
Meredith, destroyer, 101
Merrill, Rear Adm. Aaron S. ("Tip"),
  158, 159, 177, 180, 181, 183, 184
Messina, disaster at, 13
Mexico, 20, 52
Miami, light cruiser, 225
Midway, 72, 73, 77, 83, 84, 101, 105, 131,
  179
  Battle of, 107
"Mighty Mo" *(see Missouri)*
Mikasa, Jap battleship, 12, 13
  flag of, 280
Mili, 89
  (See also Marshall Islands)
Miller, destroyer, 225
Miller, Lt. Hugh Barr, Jr., 164, 167
Mindanao, 198–200, 230, 242
  (See also Philippines)
Mindora Island, 211, 225, 246
  invasion of, 234, 236
Mine layers, 159
Mine sweepers, 179, 259
Minneapolis, heavy cruiser, 134
Minnesota, battleship, 19
Mississippi, battleship, 46
Missouri, battleship, first, 9, 166
  second, 1, 9, 197, 239, 250, 259, 262,
    270, 272, 277, 286, 290
    signing of surrender on, 274, 275,
      281, 283
Mitchell, Maj. Gen. Ralph J., 186
Mitscher, Capt. (later Vice Adm.) Marc
  A. ("Pete"), 40, 101, 102, 158, 197,
  198, 202, 208, 211, 215, 217, 221,
  233, 247, 251, 285, 286
"Mizzy" *(see Missouri)*
Monaghan, destroyer, 240
Monsoons, 245
Monssen, destroyer, 101, 126, 127
Montchamps, Governor, 137
Monterey, light carrier, 238
Montgomery, Gen., 143
Montgomery, Rear Adm. Alfred E., 183
Montpelier, light cruiser, 177, 180
Montrose, Colo., 290
Moore, "Country," 63
Moosbrugger, Comdr. Frederick, 171, 185
Morris, destroyer, 120
Morris, Frank, 168
Moulton, Lt. (later Capt.) H. Douglas,
  77, 81, 139, 181, 184, 186, 189, 215,
  235, 270
Mueller, Maj. Gen. Paul J., 201
Mulcahy, Maj. Gen. Francis Patrick, 251

Munda, 140, 141, 147, 153, 154, 157, 159,
  160, 163, 170, 179
  capture of, 164, 165
  (See also New Georgia)
Muroran, 250, 261
  (See also Hokkaido)
Murray, Capt. (later Rear Adm.) George
  D., 75, 94, 120
Murray, Capt. Stuart S., 251, 281
Musashi, Jap battleship, 214
Mussolini, 206
Mustin, destroyer, 120
Myako Jima, 205

N

Nagasaki, 266
Nagato, Jap battleship, 262–264, 280
Nagoya, 264, 266
Naha, 205
  (See also Okinawa)
Nandi, 105, 106, 134
  (See also Fiji Islands)
Nansei Shoto chain, 204, 235
Nashville, light cruiser, 101–103
Naval Academy, 2–9, 24, 50, 280
Naval War College, 54, 128
Navy, 84, 101, 112, 113, 117, 133, 144n.,
  158, 171, 189, 204, 235, 251, 274,
  281, 292
  alphabet of, 148
  expansion of, in 1940, 68
    under Theodore Roosevelt, 8, 10
  at Guadalcanal, 120–123
  in Japan, 277–290
  at Leyte Gulf, 217–227
  at Mindoro, 236
  at Pearl Harbor, 72, 73, 75–84
  plans of, for Pacific defense, 73
  reduction in appropriations for, 44
  strength of, after Guadalcanal, 134
    in 1939, 66
  weakness of, in 1940, 71, 72
    in 1942, 97
    in 1943, 115
    after World War I, 70
  (See also Halsey, Adm.; Navy Dept.;
    Task Forces)
Navy Cross, 37n., 134, 149, 164, 167
Navy Day, 1945, 286
Navy Dept., 84, 134, 139, 140, 289, 291
  Bureau of Aeronautics, 54
  Bureau of Navigation, 52
  Bureau of Personnel, 111, 146

303

308

309

Y

Yamamoto, Adm. Isoruku, 155, 157
Yamashita, Gen., 242
Yap, 194, 195, 197, 198, 200
   (*See also* Palau Islands)
Yarnall, destroyer, 37–40, 42, 62
Yarnell, Adm. Harry E., 70
Yokohoma, 12, 14, 285, 287
Yokosuka, 258, 264, 268
   airbase at, 279
Yokosuka Naval Base, 13, 262, 263, 268,
   275, 276, 279, 280
Yontan, 205

Yorktown, carrier, 65, 66, 69, 85, 105, 112,
   277
Young, Comdr. Howard L. ("Cy"), 81
Yu-Shan, 103, 105
   (*See also* Doolittle, Lt. Gen.)

Z

Zanana, 160
Zeilen, destroyer, 47
"Zekes," Jap fighter planes, 141, 157,
   224, 273
Zero Day, 120
"Zeros" (*see* "Zekes")